MATHS AND STATISTICS
FOR BUSINESS

J A

Essential Maths for Students

Series editors: Anthony Croft and Robert Davison,
Department of Mathematical Sciences,
De Montfort University, Leicester.

Also available

Foundation Maths
Croft and Davison

Forthcoming

Maths for Computing and Information Technology
Giannasi and Low

Maths and Statistics for the Built Environment
Bacon

Essential Maths for Students

MATHS AND STATISTICS FOR BUSINESS

Michelle Lawson
Stephanie Hubbard
Paul Pugh

Department of Mathematical Sciences
De Montfort University, Leicester

Longman
Scientific &
Technical

Longman Scientific & Technical
Longman Group UK Limited
Longman House, Burnt Mill, Harlow
Essex CM20 2JE, England
and Associated Companies throughout the world

First published 1995

British Library Cataloguing in Publication Data
A catalogue entry for this title is available from the British Library.

ISBN 0-582-23187-6

Set by 16 in 10/12pt Times

Produced by Longman Singapore Publishers (Pte) Ltd.
Printed in Singapore

Contents

Preface

Careful decision making lies at the core of managing any successful business. Decisions are often based on the analysis of data. Mathematical and statistical techniques can be used to present clearly and analyse this data. Thus mathematical and statistical techniques underpin the decision making process.

The purpose of this book

The purpose of *Maths and Statistics for Business* is to cover in a single text the statistics and business mathematics required in foundation and first year business-related courses. Such courses include degrees and Higher National Diplomas in Business and Finance, Accounting, Economics, Management and Management Science.

The key areas of data presentation and statistical analysis are covered in Chapters 1 to 11. In addition the important mathematical topics of index numbers, linear programming and financial mathematics are explained in Chapters 12, 13 and 14 respectively. We have included topics which we think are particularly important in business-related courses and which have the widest applicability.

Throughout the book, we have adopted an informal and readable style with the emphasis being placed on real and relevant applications. Thus you, the student, do not become frustrated with theoretical and abstract aspects of the statistical and mathematical methods. The text and worked examples have been written clearly so that you should be able to work through the material with the minimum assistance from a tutor. It is also suitable for self-study. Key results and formulae are highlighted in the text, so that it will be valuable as a revision aid.

A basic level of numeracy and algebra has been assumed but previous statistical knowledge is not required.

Using this book

Each chapter begins with a set of objectives. This is a list of statements explaining what you should be able to do after reading the chapter and completing the exercises.

The best strategy for using the book would be to read through each section, carefully studying all the worked examples and solutions. It is often a good idea to then cover the solution and try working through the example again for yourself. It is only by doing the calculation for yourself that the techniques will be mastered.

After each topic within a chapter, there are self-assessment questions for you to complete. These are quick and easy ways for you to test your understanding and recall the main points of each topic. It will be advantageous for you to produce written answers to these questions. The answers to them all can be found in the text, and so if you cannot answer one of them after you have read the text, you should return to the appropriate section and revise it.

Practising the statistical and mathematical methods for yourself is essential if you are to understand fully the techniques described in this book. After each topic there are exercises which allow you to do this using relevant business-related examples. The outline solutions to these exercises can be found at the end of the book.

Finally, at the end of each chapter there are test exercises. These are provided so that your tutor can set assignments or tests to assess your understanding of all the topics in a chapter.

We hope that you find *Maths and Statistics for Business* a useful and enjoyable book.

Michelle Lawson
Stephanie Hubbard
Paul Pugh

1 Introduction

Objectives

At the end of this chapter you should be able to

- understand the terms **data set**, **raw data**, **variable** and **value**

- decide whether data are qualitative, discrete quantitative or continuous quantitative

- appreciate how data are collected

- understand the terms **population** and **sample**

- understand why a sample needs to be taken at **random** from a population

Business decisions are often made on the basis of numeric facts, e.g. rising share prices, falling inflation rates, unemployment figures, expected level of demand, interest rates. These numeric facts are known as data. Mathematics and statistics involve the collection, presentation, analysis and interpretation of such data. This book considers how this information is obtained and how it can be effectively used to aid the decision process.

The notation used to represent data, the types of data which can be collected and the methods of collection are considered in this chapter.

1.1   Definitions and notation

The following is a list of general terms used when referring to data. Worked Example 1.1 is used to illustrate these terms.

Data set   A list of any data collected in a given study.
Raw data   A list of the data in the form in which it is collected.
Variable   A characteristic of interest.
Values   Data collected for a variable.

The following notation is used to represent the values of items for a variable X:

x_1 represents the value of the first item of X
x_2 represents the value of the second item of X

and so on. If there are n items of data collected for the variable, the last item is represented by x_n. In general, the ith item is represented by x_i, where $i = 1, 2, \ldots, n$.

Worked example

1.1 The following data was recorded for the 15 applicants who were short listed for a job. Define the data set, the raw data, the variables and the values.

Age (years)	Gender[a]	Aptitude test result (%)	Communication skills rating[b]	Number of previous jobs
18	M	70.3	1	1
23	M	62.6	3	3
25	F	72.0	1	2
19	M	60.1	2	1
22	F	52.4	2	2
25	F	81.6	2	2
21	F	40.8	1	1
18	M	59.2	2	1
26	M	64.9	2	2
31	F	64.5	3	4
22	M	69.7	1	2
29	M	75.7	1	3
17	M	38.3	2	0
19	F	63.8	2	1
24	M	61.0	3	2

Notes: [a] M, male; F, female. [b] 1, good; 2, average; 3, poor.

Solution The data set refers to all the information recorded on the 15 applicants. The raw data is the list of numbers and letters as they were collected. There are five variables recorded in this data set:

Variable 1   Age (years)
Variable 2   Gender
Variable 3   Aptitude test result (%)
Variable 4   Communication skills rating
Variable 5   Number of previous jobs

The values are the data collected for each variable. For example, consider the age variable; applicant 1 (generally referred to as item 1) is aged 18 so the value of the first item of the age variable is 18, i.e. $x_1 = 18$.

Self-assessment questions 1.1

1. Define the following terms: (a) data set, (b) raw data, (c) variable, (d) value.

2. What notation would be used to represent the first, fifth and tenth values of a variable?

Exercise 1.1

The following data are recorded for ten manufacturers of household electrical appliances.

A	B	C	D	E	F
1	26	1523	3	NE	3
2	18	1057	4	SW	3
3	7	680	2	NE	3
4	30	1871	6	SE	1
5	19	1111	4	NW	2
6	12	926	5	NE	3
7	24	1495	3	Mid	1
8	11	894	5	SE	2
9	9	750	4	NE	3
10	21	1232	3	Mid	2

Notes: A, company; B, turnover (£100 000); C, number of employees; D, number of different appliances made; E, location in the country; F, change in profit from the previous year (1, increase; 2, stable; 3, decrease)

(a) How many variables are recorded in this data set?
(b) How many items are recorded for each variable?
(c) What is the value of the seventh item of variable C?

1.2   Types of data

The two types of data discussed in this book are called **qualitative data** and **quantitative data**.

Qualitative data

In qualitative data the values of items represent categories. These categories can be recorded using either numbers or letters. For example, in Worked Example 1.1, gender is a qualitative variable where the categories, male and female, are represented using the letters M and F respectively. The communication skills rating is also a qualitative variable but the categories are represented by numbers: 1, good; 2, average; 3, poor. These numbers are used as labels for categories, and are meaningless as quantities.

Quantitative data

In quantitative data, the values of the items are always numeric and represent a measurement. There are two types of quantitative data; **discrete quantitative** and **continuous quantitative.** Items of a discrete quantitative variable can take only certain values. Usually discrete quantitative variables have integer values. For example, in Worked Example 1.1, the number of previous jobs held by an applicant is a discrete quantitative variable since the number can only be represented using an integer – it is not possible to have 1.5 previous jobs. However, it is possible for discrete quantitative variables to have non-integer values. For example, ladies shoe sizes can be 3, $3\frac{1}{2}$, 4, $4\frac{1}{2}$ etc. Shoe sizes such as 3.16 are not possible, so the variable is discrete. Items of a continuous quantitative variable can take any value over a range or interval. In Worked Example 1.1, the aptitude test result is a continuous quantitative variable. The results are measured as a percentage and can take any value over the range 0–100. However, for the purposes of recording the results, the percentages have been rounded to one decimal place. Age is also a continuous quantitative variable since it is measured over time. However, it has been rounded down to the nearest year.

Self-assessment questions 1.2

1. Define what is meant by a 'qualitative variable'.
2. Define what is meant by a 'quantitative variable'.
3. Discuss the difference between discrete and continuous quantitative variables.

Exercises 1.2

1. State whether the following variables are qualitative, discrete quantitative or continuous quantitative:

    (a) salary,
    (b) marital status,
    (c) number of defective items in a production process,
    (d) lifetime of an electrical component,
    (e) number of televisions sold in one year,
    (f) make of car owned.

2. Refer to Exercise 1.1.

    (a) Which of the variables are qualitative and which are quantitative?
    (b) For the quantitative variables, which are discrete and which are continuous?

1.3   Collection of data

Data can be collected from many sources. Companies keep records on sales, profits, employees etc. and routinely collect information for publications such as annual reports. Other data is readily available from public and government sources. For example, the Central Statistical Office produces monthly and annual data on important variables such as unemployment figures, balance of payments and the Retail Price Index. If data is not readily available, it can be collected using either an **experiment** or a **survey**.

An **experiment** is performed under controlled conditions. One or more of the variables are controlled and the effects on the other variables are measured. For example, suppose a company is interested in how the amount spent on advertising affects the number of sales. They decide to fix the amount spent on advertising at a different level in each of 12 consecutive months. In each month the number of sales is recorded. This method of collecting data is called an experiment since the amount spent on advertising is controlled and the resulting effect on sales is observed.

A **survey** is performed when the variables cannot be controlled. For example, if a company wants to predict the future level of demand for its product, it is not possible to control the factors which will influence future demand. Instead, the company can market test the product in selected stores and from this estimate the total demand. Questionnaires are often used to collect data from surveys.

Self-assessment questions 1.3

1. Define what is meant by an 'experiment'.
2. Define what is meant by a 'survey'.
3. What methods are normally used to collect data in a survey?

1.4   Populations and samples

A **population** is the set of all possible items, usually relating to a group of people or objects, which is of interest in a particular study. A **sample** is a selection of items taken from a population which is used for investigation. It is often very time consuming and expensive to gather information on all items in the population in order to make decisions. For example, if a company wants to investigate the future demand for a new product, it is usually impossible to ask all potential consumers (the population) whether or not they will purchase the product. In this case, a sample of potential consumers would be used to establish the demand. This sample will not provide the exact value of the future demand, but it can be used to provide an **estimate**. The accuracy of any decisions made using a sample will depend on how **representative** the sample is of the population as a whole and on the number of items included in the sample. In order for a sample to be representative, the items contained in the sample must be selected at **random**, so that every item in the population has an equal chance of being included in the sample. This concept is discussed in more detail in Chapter 7. The accuracy of decisions can also be improved by increasing the size of the sample. Chapters 8 and 9 illustrate how decisions about populations can be made using samples.

Self-assessment questions 1.4

1. Define what is meant by a 'population'.
2. Define what is meant by a 'sample'.
3. Why is a sample rather than a population usually investigated in detail?
4. A sample must be representative of the population. Explain the meaning of this statement.
5. State two ways in which the accuracy of decisions made using a sample can be increased.

2 Descriptive statistics: tables and graphs

<table>
<tr><td>

Objectives

</td><td>

When you have read this chapter you should be able to

- represent qualitative data using frequency distributions, relative frequency distributions, bar charts and pie charts

- represent continuous quantitative data using grouped frequency distributions, grouped relative frequency distributions and histograms

- represent discrete quantitative data

</td></tr>
</table>

Raw data is often difficult to understand and interpret. We are often interested in describing and summarizing the whole set of data rather than the individual items. Thus data needs to be summarized using tables and graphs. For example, trends in sales figures are difficult to see when you look at the sales figures themselves. However, increasing or decreasing sales trends are easy to spot when the data has been summarized in a graph.

This chapter discusses the most frequently used methods of summarizing data using tables and graphs.

2.1 Summarizing qualitative data

Qualitative data is defined in Section 1.2

Frequency distributions

A **frequency distribution** is a table showing the frequency (or number) of items in each category.

Worked example

2.1 A computer company employs 27 females and 33 males. Represent this data in a frequency distribution.

Solution The frequency distribution is given in Table 2.1. This table shows the number of males and females employed by the company.

Table 2.1. Frequency distribution showing the gender of employees of a computer company

Gender of employees	Number of employees
Male	33
Female	27
	Total 60

Relative frequency distribution

The **relative frequency of a category** is the proportion of items in the category. If there are *n* items in a set of data, then the relative frequency of a category is defined as follows.

KEY POINT

$$\text{Relative frequency of a category} = \frac{\text{frequency of category}}{n} \qquad [2.1]$$

The relative frequency can also be expressed as a percentage as follows.

KEY POINT

$$\text{Percentage of items in a category} = \text{relative frequency} \times 100 \qquad [2.2]$$

The **relative frequency distribution** is a table showing the relative frequency of the items in each category. It can be used to show the proportion or percentage of items in each category.

Worked examples

2.2 For the computer company employees data given in Worked Example 2.1, find the relative frequency of the female category and the percentage of females.

Solution Frequency of females = 27, total number of employees = 60.
Using [2.1], the relative frequency of females is

$$\frac{27}{60} = 0.45$$

Using [2.2], the percentage of females is

$$0.45 \times 100 = 45\%$$

2.3 Represent the computer company employees data given in Worked Example 2.1 in a relative frequency distribution.

Solution The relative frequency distribution is given in Table 2.2.

Gender of employees	Proportion of employees
Male	0.55
Female	0.45
Total	1.00

Table 2.2. Relative frequency distribution showing the gender of employees of a computer company

Bar charts

A **bar chart** is a graph showing the frequency or relative frequency distribution of a set of data. The horizontal axis specifies the labels used for the categories. The vertical axis shows the scale representing the frequencies or relative frequencies.

Worked examples

2.4 Draw a bar chart to graphically present the frequency distribution of the computer company employees data given in Worked Example 2.1.

Solution

The frequency distribution is given in Table 2.1

A bar chart showing the frequency distribution of the computer company employees data is given in Figure 2.1.

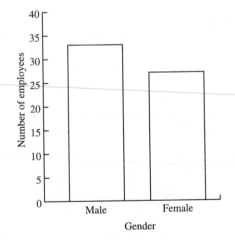

Figure 2.1. Bar chart showing the number of employees of each gender in a computer company

2.5 Draw a bar chart to graphically present the relative frequency distribution of the computer company employees data given in Worked Example 2.1. Use percentages to represent the relative frequencies.

The relative frequency distribution is given in Table 2.2

Solution

A bar chart showing the percentage of male and female employees of the computer company data is given in Figure 2.2.

Figure 2.2. Bar chart showing the percentage of employees of each gender in a computer company

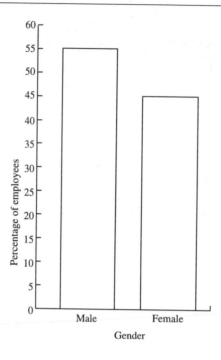

Pie charts

A **pie chart** is a diagram showing the frequency or relative frequency distribution of a set of data. The slices of the pie usually represent the percentage of items in each category. If there are too many categories a pie chart will contain too much information to be of any use. To avoid this, pie charts should only be used when there are six or fewer categories.

To draw a pie chart, first draw a circle (this represents the pie). Then divide the pie into slices which correspond to the frequency, relative frequency or percentage of items in each category. The size of each slice is calculated using the following formula.

KEY POINT

> Number of degrees for a category
> = Relative frequency of a category × 360   [2.3]

Worked examples

2.6   For the computer company employees data given in Worked Example 2.1, how many degrees would there be in the slice of the pie which represents the males?

Solution   Using [2.1] the relative frequency of males = 33/60 = 0.55. Using [2.3],

Number of degrees for male category $= 0.55 \times 360$ degrees

$= 198$ degrees

2.7   For the computer company employees data given in Worked Example 2.1, draw a pie chart to show the percentage of males and females.

Solution

The relative frequency distribution is given in Table 2.2

Figure 2.3. Pie chart showing the percentage of employees of each gender in a computer company

Figure 2.3 shows the percentage of male and female employees in a computer company in a pie chart.

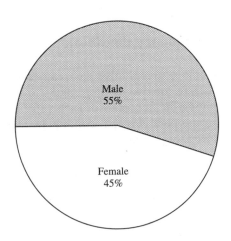

Male
55%

Female
45%

Self-assessment questions 2.1

1. Why do we need to summarize data?
2. What is a frequency distribution?
3. What is a relative frequency distribution?
4. What does a bar chart represent and how is it constructed?
5. What does a pie chart represent and how is it constructed?

Exercise 2.1

A double glazing company conducted a survey of 200 owner occupied houses to investigate the number of households which had full double glazing (all windows and doors), partial double glazing (some windows and doors) and no double glazing. Of the 200 houses surveyed, 30 had full double glazing, 68 had partial double glazing and 102 had no double glazing.

(a) Summarize the data using a frequency distribution.
(b) Summarize the data using a relative frequency distribution.
(c) Draw a bar chart to represent the frequency distribution.
(d) Draw a bar chart to represent the percentage of households with each level of double glazing.
(e) Draw a pie chart to represent the relative frequency distribution.

2.2   Summarizing quantitative data

Quantitative data is defined in Section 1.2

There are two types of quantitative data; discrete and continuous. The tables and graphs which are appropriate to summarize quantitative data depend on the type of data. The following three sections describe the methods appropriate for summarizing continuous quantitative data whilst the fourth section describes methods which are appropriate for summarizing discrete quantitative data.

Grouped frequency distribution

Since continuous quantitative data can take any value over a specified range, it is rare for two or more items to have exactly the same value. Thus, counting the frequency of each value is not an appropriate way to summarize the data. Instead, continuous quantitative data are **grouped** into non-overlapping **classes**.

The **grouped frequency distribution** is a table showing the frequency (or number) of items in each of the classes.

To construct the grouped frequency distribution for a set of data, the number, width and limits of each of the classes must be determined.

Step 1:   Number of classes

If there are too few classes, the frequency distribution will not provide an accurate summary of the variation in the data. If there are too many classes there will only be a few items in each class.

As a general guideline, there should be between 5 and 20 classes, depending on the number of items in the set of data. A frequency distribution for a data set containing a small number of items should have a smaller number of classes than a data set containing many items.

Step 2:   Width of classes

The **width** of a class is the range of values covered by the class. We will focus on the most common case where all of the classes have the same width.

The width of the classes will depend on the number of classes chosen in Step 1. For a given set of data, a small number of classes must result in a larger class width and vice versa. An **approximate class width** can be calculated as follows:

KEY POINT

$$\text{Approximate class width} = \frac{\text{largest value} - \text{smallest value}}{\text{number of classes}} \qquad [2.4]$$

If necessary, the approximate class widths calculated using [2.4] can be adjusted. For example, if a class width of 2.14 is suggested, this could be adjusted to a class width of 2 or 2.5. This adjustment may result in a slightly greater or smaller number of classes.

The person constructing the table must judge the best number and width of the classes. This is usually done by trial and error.

Step 3:   Class limits

The **lower class limit** defines the smallest value assigned to a class. The **upper class limit** defines the largest value assigned to a class. The limits must be defined so that no classes overlap i.e. the value of an item must fall in one and only one class. There should also be no gaps between the classes into which values can fall. The first class should contain the value of the smallest item and the last class should contain the value of the largest item.

Step 4:   Constructing the table

Count the number of items that fall into each class. Present the frequency of each class in a table.

Worked example

2.8   The manager of a delicatessen conducted a survey of the value of the sales in his shop on one day. The data given below shows the values (£) of 32 sales made on one day. Construct a table showing the frequency distribution.

6.49	8.90	22.95	13.39
18.63	4.44	24.99	4.44
34.98	8.12	8.99	6.99
21.25	24.99	1.26	9.97
9.98	3.99	4.35	12.49
2.19	7.75	11.99	1.69
4.65	4.50	9.85	13.89
10.45	7.49	29.97	2.77

Solution

Step 1:   Number of classes

There are 32 sales values in the survey. This is a relatively small sample so only a few classes, say five, should be used.

Step 2:   Width of classes

First determine the smallest and largest value in the data set.

Largest value = £34.98
Smallest value = £1.26
Number of classes = 5

The approximate class width is calculated using [2.4]:

$$\text{Approximate class width} = \frac{34.98 - 1.26}{5} = 6.744$$

This approximate class width could be adjusted to £7.

Step 3:   Class limits

The smallest value is £1.26. This value would be included in the lowest class if the lower limit was £1.00. Step 2 suggested that the class width should be £7. Thus the upper limit of the first class should be £8.00. However, if we start the next class at £8.00, then the first and second intervals will overlap. Thus, we set the upper limit of the first class at £7.99 (this is the highest possible value which would not fall into the second class). The second class would be £8.00 to £14.99. The last class would be £29.00 to £35.99. Thus the last class includes the largest value. Note that the upper class limits are chosen so that the intervals do not overlap.

Step 4:   Constructing the table

Count the number of items falling into each of the classes. The grouped frequency distribution is given in Table 2.3.

Table 2.3. Grouped frequency distribution showing the value of sales at a delicatessen

Sales value (£)	Number of sales
1.00– 7.99	14
8.00–14.99	11
15.00–21.99	2
22.00–28.99	3
29.00–35.99	2
Total	32

Grouped relative frequency distribution

The **grouped relative frequency distribution** is a table showing the proportion (or percentage) of items in each of the grouped classes. If there are n items in the data set, the relative frequency is calculated as:

KEY POINT

$$\text{Relative frequency of a class} = \frac{\text{frequency of class}}{n} \qquad [2.5]$$

The percentage of items in each class can be calculated as:

KEY POINT

$$\text{Percentage of items in a class} = \text{relative frequency of class} \times 100 \qquad [2.6]$$

Worked example

2.9 Construct a grouped relative frequency table to represent the percentages for the sales data given in Worked Example 2.8.

Solution Table 2.4 shows a grouped relative frequency table for the sales data.

Table 2.4. Grouped relative frequency distribution showing the value of sales at a delicatessen

Sales value (£)	Percentage of sales
1.00– 7.99	43.750
8.00–14.99	34.375
15.00–21.99	6.250
22.00–28.99	9.375
29.00–35.99	6.250
Total	100

The grouped frequency distribution is given in Table 2.3

Histogram

A **histogram** is a graph showing the grouped frequency or grouped relative frequency distribution of a set of data. The horizontal axis represents the variable of interest. If all the classes are of the same width then the vertical axis represents the frequency or relative frequency. The vertical axis should begin at zero so that the height of the bars represents the frequency or relative frequency. The bars of the histogram are not separated since they represent continuous data.

Worked example

2.10 For the sales data given in Worked Example 2.8, draw a histogram to represent the grouped relative frequency distribution.

Solution A histogram of the sales data is given in Figure 2.4.

Figure 2.4. Histogram showing the grouped relative frequency distribution of sales at a delicatessen

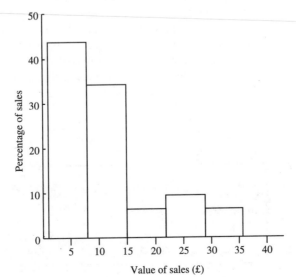

The grouped relative frequency distribution is given in Table 2.4

Summarizing discrete quantitative data

If the data is discrete and there are only a few (five or less) different values in the data set, then the data can be summarized using the tables and graphs described in Section 2.1 for qualitative data.

If the data is discrete and many (six or more) different values have occurred, then the methods for describing qualitative data are not appropriate since there are too many different values. In this case, the data can be summarized using the tables and graphs described in this section for continuous quantitative data. Note that if a histogram is used to represent discrete data, the bars should be separated by a space to indicate the discrete nature of the data.

Worked examples

2.11 An automatic cash dispenser is situated outside a bank. A survey of the usage of the dispenser was performed. The numbers of customers using the dispenser during 30 consecutive ten minute periods are given below.

2	1	3	3	0	2	4	2	3	3
3	3	2	2	3	1	3	4	3	1
4	3	0	1	2	4	2	3	4	3

(a) Which methods would be appropriate to summarize this data?
(b) Summarize the data using an appropriate table and graph.

Solution (a) 0, 1, 2, 3 and 4 customers used the automatic cash dispenser in the ten minute periods, so only five of the many possible values have occurred in this particular survey. In this case the methods appropriate for summarizing qualitative data can be used, i.e. frequency distribution, relative frequency distribution, bar chart and pie chart.
(b) Table 2.5 shows the frequency distribution for the data. Figure 2.5 shows the bar chart representing the frequency distribution.

Table 2.5. Frequency distribution showing the number of customers using an automatic cash dispenser during 30 consecutive ten minute periods

Number of customers in a ten minute period	Frequency
0	2
1	4
2	7
3	12
4	5
Total	30

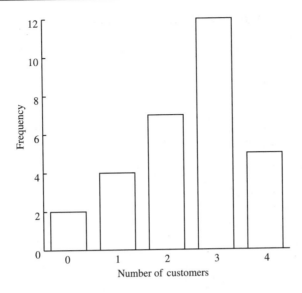

Figure 2.5. Bar chart showing the number of customers using an automatic cash dispenser during 30 consecutive ten minute periods

2.12   A lock manufacturer employs 200 people. The Personnel Officer has conducted a survey of 40 employees to investigate the number of days absent from work due to illness during one year. The data are given below.

10	15	2	27	4	2	15	1	3	1
16	1	1	31	2	17	25	7	4	15
3	12	13	18	10	1	5	42	4	26
24	3	25	22	7	6	11	24	3	4

(a) What methods would be appropriate to summarize this data?
(b) Summarize the data using an appropriate table and graph.

Solution   (a) Many different numbers of days absent were recorded. Thus the methods appropriate for summarizing continuous quantitative data can be used, e.g. grouped frequency distribution, grouped relative frequency distribution and histogram.

(b) Table 2.6 shows the grouped frequency distribution for the data. Figure 2.6 shows a histogram representing the grouped frequency distribution.

Table 2.6. Frequency distribution showing the number of days absent from work for a sample of 40 employees at a lock manufacturing company

Number of days absent	Frequency
1– 7	20
8–14	5
15–21	6
22–28	7
29–35	1
36–42	1
Total	40

Figure 2.6. Histogram showing the number of days absent from work for a sample of 40 employees at a lock manufacturing company

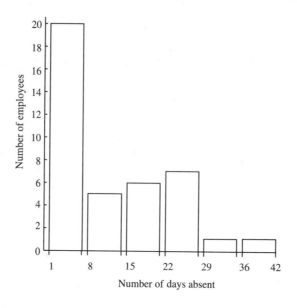

Self-assessment questions 2.2

1. How would you construct a grouped frequency distribution for continuous quantitative data?
2. What is the difference between a histogram used to represent continuous quantitative data and a histogram used to represent discrete quantitative data?
3. If a data set contains values 1, 2 and 3, what methods are most appropriate to summarize this data?
4. You are presented with a discrete quantitative set of data which contains many different values. What methods are most appropriate to summarize this data?

Exercises 2.2

1. A large computer software company conducted a survey of the hours worked by their part-time staff. The part-time staff work 18, 20 or 24 hours per week. A sample of the weekly working hours of 35 part-time employees is given below.

18	20	20	24	20	18	20	20	20
20	24	18	20	18	20	18	20	18
24	18	24	24	20	20	24	24	20
18	20	18	20	24	18	20	20	

(a) Represent the data as a frequency distribution and a relative frequency distribution.
(b) Draw a bar chart to represent the relative frequency distribution.

2. The 1993 monthly sales figures (£000s) of ABC Ltd are given below.

Month	Sales (£000s)	Month	Sales (£000s)
January	18.39	July	19.98
February	21.62	August	26.11
March	23.49	September	29.64
April	30.00	October	21.73
May	29.22	November	20.05
June	26.53	December	9.64

(a) Summarize the monthly sales figures using a bar chart.

(b) The Managing Director wants to investigate the quarterly sales figures, i.e. she wants to look at the total sales in each quarter (first quarter is January, February and March, second quarter is April, May and June etc.).
  (i) Construct a table to show the quarterly sales figures.
  (ii) Present the frequency distribution of the quarterly sales figures using a bar chart.

(c) Comment on the trends in the monthly and quarterly sales figures.

3. The breaking strength of a fibre is tested in a laboratory. Forty samples of the fibre are tested and the breaking strengths (in grams) are given below.

2.143	2.143	2.148	2.158	2.137	2.137	2.147	2.140
2.124	2.133	2.134	2.164	2.165	2.145	2.142	2.169
2.168	2.170	2.162	2.130	2.133	2.162	2.137	2.156
2.168	2.145	2.125	2.137	2.151	2.149	2.134	2.151
2.150	2.146	2.122	2.149	2.156	2.161	2.168	2.131

(a) Represent the data in a grouped frequency distribution and a grouped relative frequency distribution.

(b) Draw a histogram to represent the grouped relative frequency distribution.

(c) The fibre is supposed to have a breaking strength of at least 2.125 g. Comment on this in the light of the samples of fibre tested in this experiment.

4. The following data represent the number of telephone calls made weekly to the switchboard of a company over a one year period.

425	540	315	614	329	510	328	642	523	442	679
647	414	517	518	625	485	401	663	546	556	357
362	576	539	427	308	529	644	472	637	457	
513	489	309	583	466	567	758	565	650	588	
528	699	316	737	526	598	524	424	763	338	

> (a) Which methods are appropriate to summarize this data?
> (b) Use an appropriate table to summarize the frequency distribution of the weekly number of telephone calls.
> (c) Use an appropriate graph to illustrate the frequency distribution found in (b).

Test exercises

1. A high street ladies' clothes retailer returns all faulty goods to the manufacturer. The data given below show the number of each type of garment returned to the manufacturer in a one month period.

Type of garment	Number returned to the manufacturer
Dress	12
Jumper	0
Cardigan	47
Blouse	23
Skirt	36
Total	188

(a) Draw a bar chart to represent the frequency distribution.
(b) Construct a relative frequency distribution to show the percentage of each type of garment which is returned to the manufacturer.
(c) Illustrate the relative frequency distribution in (b) using a pie chart.
(d) Comment on the distribution of the faulty garments.

2. A supermarket is considering introducing a training programme to reduce the number of errors made by their cashiers. A limited amount of money is available, and there is only enough money to be able to concentrate on one type of error. They have collected data on the number of errors made by the cashiers at one branch over a one month period. This data is given below.

Type of error	Number of errors made
Incorrect entering of items	31
Giving wrong change	16
Errors with cheques	24
Errors with credit cards	9
Errors with coupons	8
Total	88

(a) Draw a bar chart to represent the frequency distribution.

(b) Construct a relative frequency distribution to show the percentage of each type of error.

(c) Illustrate the relative frequency distribution in (b) using a pie chart.

(d) Advise the management of the supermarket on where the training money would be most effectively spent.

3. A dentist conducted an experiment to monitor the effectiveness of a new toothpaste for children. The following data show the number of cavities sustained by children using this toothpaste over a six month period.

0	1	0	1	1	2	0	3	0	0	2	1	1
1	2	1	1	0	1	1	1	1	2	0	0	0
4	0	1	0	2	1	0	0	1	0	3	1	2
2	0	0	3	2	0	3	1	0	1	1	0	1

(a) Construct a frequency distribution for this data.

(b) Draw a bar chart to represent the frequency distribution found in (a).

(c) What conclusions can be drawn about the effectiveness of this toothpaste. What other information would you require in order to be able to advise children to use this toothpaste instead of their usual brand?

4. A dairy have conducted a survey of the number of bottles of milk ordered daily by people on a housing estate. The numbers of bottles ordered by people on the estate on a Monday are given below.

3	2	1	0	1	2	1	1	1	1
1	1	2	1	2	1	1	0	1	2
2	1	1	3	1	1	2	2	1	1

(a) Construct a frequency distribution for this data.

(b) Draw a bar chart to represent the frequency distribution in (a).

(c) Comment on the distribution of the numbers of bottles of milk ordered on a Monday on this housing estate.

5. A mail order company guarantee that their goods will be dispatched within five working days, and that, wherever possible, goods will be dispatched within three working days. The data given below show the number of days taken to dispatch goods for a random sample of 1000 orders.

Number of working days to dispatch	Number of orders
1	31
2	662
3	157
4	93
5	57
Total	1000

(a) Draw a bar chart to represent the frequency distribution.
(b) Construct a relative frequency distribution to show the percentage of orders dispatched for each number of days.
(c) Illustrate the relative frequency distribution in (b) using a pie chart.
(d) Using this sample of data, are the company meeting their guarantee that all goods are dispatched within five working days? Are they also justified in saying that, wherever possible, the goods are dispatched within three working days? Justify your answers.

6. The numbers of units produced by 180 workers in an engineering factory in one working week are given below.

Number of units	Number of workers
500–509	8
510–519	18
520–529	23
530–539	37
540–549	47
550–559	26
560–569	16
570–579	5
Total	180

(a) The number of units produced is a discrete quantitative variable but a grouped frequency distribution has been used to represent the data. Explain why using continuous quantitative methods is justifiable in this case.
(b) Draw a histogram to represent the frequency distribution of the number of units produced by these 180 workers.
(c) Comment on the distribution of the number of units produced by these workers.

7. Forty companies took part in a survey to investigate their annual expenditure on marketing their product. The data (£000s) are given below.

22	28	31	35	43	48	52	56	58	63
60	52	30	51	27	46	44	46	34	39
48	38	43	40	41	55	35	21	64	45
45	47	25	53	72	32	58	48	31	54

(a) Construct a grouped frequency distribution for the annual expenditure on marketing.
(b) Illustrate the grouped frequency distribution given in (a) using a histogram.
(c) Briefly describe the amount spent on marketing each year by these 40 companies.

8. The frequency distribution of the lifetime (hours) of 300 steam irons produced by one factory is given below.

Lifetime	Number of steam irons
300–399.99	12
400–499.99	59
500–599.99	84
600–699.99	72
700–799.99	41
800–899.99	26
900–999.99	6
Total	300

(a) Construct a grouped relative frequency distribution to show the percentage of irons in each class of lifetimes.

(b) Draw a histogram to show the percentage of irons in each class.

(c) The manufacturers are considering the length of time they should guarantee the irons for. Advise the manufacturers on a reasonable guarantee period for the product. Give reasons for your answer.

9. The Personnel Manager of a large electronics company has constructed a grouped frequency distribution of the income of male and female employees in the company. This distribution is given below.

Income (£)	Number of males	Number of females
5000 to <10000	3	12
10000 to <15000	46	55
15000 to <20000	82	37
20000 to <25000	20	13
25000 to <30000	8	4
30000 to <35000	3	1
35000 to <40000	1	0

(a) Illustrate the frequency distribution of the income of males and females on one histogram.

(b) Compare the distribution of the income of males and females. Does this company appear to operate an equal pay scale for males and females?

3 Descriptive statistics: numerical measures

<table>
<tr><td>**Objectives**</td><td>When you have read this chapter you should be able to

• calculate the mean, median and mode of a set of data

• calculate the range, variance and standard deviation of a set of data</td></tr>
</table>

Chapter 2 discussed how data can be summarized using tables and graphs. This chapter will look at how a set of data can be summarized numerically.

There are two types of numerical measure: **measures of central location** and **measures of variation.**

3.1   Measures of central location

Measures of central location provide information on the typical, or average, value of a set of data, e.g. the typical annual salary of a managing director. There are many measures of central location. This book considers the three most common measures: the mean, the median and the mode. The weighted mean, which will be used in Chapter 12, will also be discussed.

The mean

The mean, commonly known as the average, of a set of data is calculated by adding the values of all the items together and dividing by the number of items.

The mean can be calculated for a population and a sample using either the raw data or a frequency distribution.

Your scientific calculator may be able to calculate the mean using the raw data

Using the raw data

<table>
<tr><td>**KEY POINT**</td></tr>
<tr><td>Examples of the Σ notation are given in Appendix B</td></tr>
</table>

Population mean	$\mu = \dfrac{\Sigma x_i}{N}$	$i = 1, 2, \ldots, N$	[3.1]
Sample mean	$\bar{x} = \dfrac{\Sigma x_i}{n}$	$i = 1, 2, \ldots, n$	[3.2]

where x_i represents the value of the ith item in the population or sample, N represents the number of items in the population, n represents the number of items in the sample, μ represents the population mean and $\bar{x}$ represents the sample mean.

Using a frequency distribution

KEY POINT

$$\text{Sample mean} \quad \bar{x} = \frac{\Sigma x_i f_i}{n} \quad i = 1, 2, \ldots, k \qquad [3.3]$$

where x_i represents the value of the ith category or the midpoint of the ith class, f_i represents the frequency of the ith category or class, k represents the number of categories or classes and n represents the number of items in the sample.

The midpoint of a class can be calculated using the following formula:

KEY POINT

$$\text{Midpoint of class} = \frac{\text{lower class limit} + \text{upper class limit}}{2} \qquad [3.4]$$

Note that if the mean is calculated from a grouped frequency distribution, the values of items in a class are replaced by the midpoint of the class. Thus, the mean calculated using [3.3] will be an approximation to the sample mean.

Properties of the mean

For numeric data, the mean can always be calculated and for a given sample of data it is unique. The mean takes account of all the values in a sample. This is a good property if there are no unusual items, i.e. if there are no extremely small or extremely large values. However, if some of the items are unusual, the sample mean may not be an accurate reflection of a typical value. For example, consider the following numbers:

~ AFFECTED BY
EXTREEMES

112	106	108	114	29

The mean of these five numbers is 93.8. If the unusually small value of 29 is removed, then the mean of the remaining four numbers is 110. Thus, the unusually small value has reduced the value of the sample mean.

Worked examples

3.1 Calculate the mean of the following samples of data:

(a) 3.6   4.3   7.1   2.4   5.9   6.0   7.3   4.8   3.1

(b) 2319   6237   3422   5601   7390   8125   5133   8218   6634   7340
1278   3195   7321   8830

Solution   (a) $\Sigma x_i = 3.6 + 4.3 + 7.1 + \cdots + 3.1 = 44.5$
$n = 9$
Using [3.2], sample mean $\bar{x} = 44.5/9 = 4.9444$.
(b) $\Sigma x_i = 2319 + 6237 + 3422 + \cdots + 7321 + 8830 = 81043$
$n = 14$
Using [3.2], sample mean $\bar{x} = 81043/14 = 5788.7857$.

3.2   (a) Find the mean of the following data using
(i) the raw data
(ii) a frequency distribution.

| 2 | 0 | 4 | 2 | 1 | 3 | 1 | 0 | 3 | 1 | 0 | 3 |
| 3 | 2 | 3 | 1 | 0 | 3 | 2 | 1 | 1 | 4 | 2 | 1 |

(b) Comment on the answers to (i) and (ii).

Solution   (a) (i) Using the raw data
$\Sigma x_i = 2 + 0 + 4 + 2 + \cdots + 2 + 1 = 43$
$n = 24$
Using [3.2], sample mean $\bar{x} = 43/24 = 1.7917$.
(ii) A frequency distribution and values of $x_i f_i$ are given in Table 3.1.
Now $n = \Sigma f_i = 24$ and $\Sigma x_i f_i = 43$. Using [3.3], sample mean
$\bar{x} = 43/24 = 1.7917$.
(b) The answers to (i) and (ii) are exactly the same. This is always true for
an ungrouped frequency distribution.

Table 3.1. Frequency distribution and values of $x_i f_i$

Value of category x_i	Frequency f_i	$x_i f_i$
0	4	0
1	7	7
2	5	10
3	6	18
4	2	8
Total	24	43

3.3   (a) Find the mean of the following data using

(i) the raw data   (ii) a grouped frequency distribution.

27.8	33.2	16.3	31.4	9.9	21.1	40.5
35.7	32.5	34.4	46.7	21.8	34.5	13.7
57.9	16.6	45.9	6.1	42.3	18.2	38.2
20.7	45.6	12.3	61.6	24.4	53.8	23.1
37.0	32.1	59.3	27.3	39.5	24.2	33.2

(b) Comment on the answers to (i) and (ii).

Table 3.2. Frequency distribution and values of $x_i f_i$ for Worked Example 3.3

Class	Midpoint x_i	Frequency f_i	$x_i f_i$
0.0– 9.9	4.95	2	9.90
10.0–19.9	14.95	5	74.75
20.0–29.9	24.95	8	199.60
30.0–39.9	34.95	11	384.45
40.0–49.9	44.95	5	224.75
50.0–59.9	54.95	3	164.85
60.0–69.9	64.95	1	64.95
		Total 35	1123.25

Solution   (a) (i)   Using the raw data
$$\Sigma x_i = 27.8 + 33.2 + 16.3 + \cdots + 24.2 + 33.2 = 1118.8$$
$$n = 35$$
Using [3.2], sample mean $\bar{x} = 1118.8/35 = 31.9657$.

(ii) A frequency distribution and values of $x_i f_i$ are given in Table 3.2. Now $n = \Sigma f_i = 35$ and $\Sigma x_i f_i = 1123.25$. Using [3.3], sample mean $\bar{x} = 1123.25/35 = 32.0929$.

(b) The answers to (i) and (ii) are not the same. This is because the actual values have been replaced by the midpoint of the class in the calculation. Thus, the mean calculated in (ii) is an estimate of the sample mean.

3.4

The frequency distribution was constructed in Worked Example 2.11

An automatic cash dispenser is situated outside a bank. The manager conducted a survey to investigate the number of customers using the dispenser. The following data shows the number of customers using the machine in 30 consecutive ten minute periods. The frequency distribution is given in Table 3.3.

2	1	3	3	0	2	4	2	3	3
3	3	2	2	3	1	3	4	3	1
4	3	0	1	2	4	2	3	4	3

Calculate the sample mean number of customers using the cash machine in a ten minute period using

(a) the raw data
(b) the frequency distribution.

Table 3.3. Frequency distribution showing the number of customers using an automatic cash dispenser during 30 consecutive ten minute periods

Number of customers in a ten minute period x_i	Frequency f_i
0	2
1	4
2	7
3	12
4	5
Total	30

Solution   (a) $\Sigma x_i = 2 + 1 + 3 + 3 + \cdots + 2 + 3 + 4 + 3 = 74$
$n = 30$
Using [3.2], sample mean $\bar{x} = 74/30 = 2.4667$.
(b) $\Sigma x_i f_i = (0 \times 2) + (1 \times 4) + (2 \times 7) + (3 \times 12) + (4 \times 5) = 74$
Using [3.3], sample mean $\bar{x} = 74/30 = 2.4667$.

Table 3.4. Grouped frequency distribution showing the value of sales at a delicatessen

Sales value (£)	Number of sales f_i
1.00– 7.99	14
8.00–14.99	11
15.00–21.99	2
22.00–28.99	3
29.00–35.99	2
Total	32

The frequency distribution was constructed in Worked Example 2.8

3.5   The manager of a delicatessen conducted a survey of the value of the sales in his shop on one day. The data given below shows the values (£) of a sample of 32 sales made on one day. Table 3.4 shows the grouped frequency distribution.

6.49	8.90	22.95	13.39
18.63	4.44	24.99	4.44
34.98	8.12	8.99	6.99
21.25	24.99	1.26	9.97
9.98	3.99	4.35	12.49
2.19	7.75	11.99	1.69
4.65	4.50	9.85	13.89
10.45	7.49	29.97	2.77

Calculate the sample mean value of the sales in the delicatessen using

(a) the raw data
(b) the grouped frequency distribution.
(c) Comment on any differences between the answers to (a) and (b).

Solution   (a) $n = 32$ $\Sigma x_i = 6.49 + 8.90 + \cdots + 29.97 + 2.77 = 358.78$
Using [3.2], sample mean $\bar{x} = 358.78/32 = £11.21$.
(b) In order to calculate the sample mean using the grouped frequency table, the midpoint of each of the classes must first be determined. Using [3.4], the midpoint of the first class is

$$\frac{1.00 + 7.99}{2} = 4.495$$

The midpoints of all of the classes are given in Table 3.5. The sample mean is calculated using [3.3],
$\Sigma x_i f_i = (4.495 \times 14) + (11.495 \times 11) + \cdots + (32.495 \times 2) = £367.84$
Sample mean $\bar{x} = 367.84/32 = £11.50$.

Table 3.5. Grouped
frequency distribution and
midpoints of the sales data

Sales value (£)	Midpoint x_i	Number of sales f_i
1.00– 7.99	4.495	14
8.00–14.99	11.495	11
15.00–21.99	18.495	2
22.00–28.99	25.495	3
29.00–35.99	32.495	2
Total		32

(c) The values of the mean calculated in (a) and (b) are different. This is because the raw data have been replaced by the midpoint of the classes in (b). The two answers will only ever be the same if the raw data are exactly equal to the midpoints of the classes.

The median

The **median** is the value of the middle item when the data are placed in order from smallest to largest. If there are an odd number of items then there will be a middle value which is the median. If there are an even number of items then there will not be a middle value. In this case the median is the mean of the two middle values when the data are placed in order from smallest to largest.

Placing the items in order from smallest to largest is known as **ranking the data**. The item with the smallest value has rank 1, the second smallest has rank 2 and so on. Thus the median is the value of the item which has half of the ranked data below it and half above it. This concept can be extended to **quartiles**. The **lower quartile** is the value of the item which has a quarter (25%) of the ranked data below it and three-quarters (75%) above it. Similarly the **upper quartile** is the value of the item which has three-quarters (75%) of the ranked data below it and a quarter (25%) above it.

Properties of the median

The median can be calculated for any set of data and for a given set of data the median is unique. The median only considers the values of the middle items, and thus it is not affected by the values of unusually small or large items.

Worked examples

3.6 Calculate the median of the data given in Worked Example 3.1.

Solution   (a) First rank the data from smallest to largest:

Rank	1	2	3	4	5	6	7	8	9
Value	2.4	3.1	3.6	4.3	4.8	5.9	6.0	7.1	7.3

The middle value is the fifth ranked item. Thus the median is 4.8.

(b) First rank the data in order from smallest to largest:

Rank	1	2	3	4	5	6	7
Value	1278	2319	3195	3422	5133	5601	6237

Rank	8	9	10	11	12	13	14
Value	6634	7321	7340	7390	8125	8218	8830

The median is the mean of the seventh and eighth values, i.e.

$$\text{median} = \frac{6237 + 6634}{2} = 6435.5$$

3.7 Find the median of the data given in Worked Example 3.2 using
(a) the raw data
(b) a frequency distribution.

Solution   (a) First rank the data from smallest to largest:

Rank	1	2	3	4	5	6	7	8	9	10	11	12
Value	0	0	0	0	1	1	1	1	1	1	1	2

Rank	13	14	15	16	17	18	19	20	21	22	23	24
Value	2	2	2	2	3	3	3	3	3	3	4	4

The median is the mean of the two middle values, i.e. the mean of the twelfth and thirteenth values:

$$\text{median} = \frac{2 + 2}{2} = 2$$

(b) A frequency distribution and item numbers are given in Table 3.6. From Table 3.6 we can see that the twelfth and thirteenth ranked items are contained in the category with value 2. Thus the median is 2.

Table 3.6. Distribution of the items listed by category for Worked Example 3.2

Value of category	Frequency	Item numbers
0	4	1–4
1	7	5–11
2	5	12–16
3	6	17–22
4	2	23–24

3.8 Find the median of the data given in Worked Example 3.3 using

(a) the raw data
(b) a grouped frequency distribution.

Table 3.7. Distribution of the items listed by category for worked Example 3.3

Value of category	Frequency	Item numbers
0.0– 9.9	2	1–2
10.0–19.9	5	3–7
20.0–29.9	8	8–15
30.0–39.9	11	16–26
40.0–49.9	5	27–31
50.0–59.9	3	32–34
60.0–69.9	1	35

Solution   (a) First rank the data in order from smallest to largest:

Rank	1	2	3	4	5	6	7	8
Value	6.1	9.9	12.3	13.7	16.3	16.6	18.2	20.7

Rank	9	10	11	12	13	14	15	16
Value	21.1	21.8	23.1	24.2	24.4	27.3	27.8	31.4

Rank	17	18	19	20	21	22	23	24
Value	32.1	32.5	33.2	33.2	34.4	34.5	35.7	37.0

Rank	25	26	27	28	29	30	31	32
Value	38.2	39.5	40.5	42.3	45.6	45.9	46.7	53.8

Rank	33	34	35
Value	57.9	59.3	61.6

The median is the middle value, i.e. the eighteenth value:

median = 32.5

(b) The frequency distribution and item numbers are given in Table 3.7. From this table we can see that the eighteenth value falls in the interval 30–39.9. Thus we only need to rank the observations in this interval (see (a)). The eighteenth value is 32.5, i.e. the median is 32.5. Note: the work involved in calculating the median is reduced if the frequency distribution is used.

3.9   Calculate the median of the sales data given in Worked Example 3.5.

Solution   There are 32 items in this sample. Thus the median will be the mean value of the two middle items, i.e. the mean value of the sixteenth and seventeenth ranked items. From the frequency distribution given in Table 3.5, we can see that the second class (8.00–14.99) contains the fifteenth to the twenty-fifth ranked items. Thus, we only have to arrange the values belonging to this class in order from smallest to largest in order to find the median.

Table 3.8 shows the ranks of the values in the class 8.00–14.99. The median is the mean of the sixteenth and seventeenth ranked

Rank	15	16	17	18	19	20	21	22	23	24	25
Value	8.12	8.90	8.99	9.85	9.97	9.98	10.45	11.99	12.49	13.39	13.89

Table 3.8. Sales data in class 8.00–14.99 ranked in order from smallest to largest

items:

$$\text{sample median} = \frac{8.90 + 8.99}{2} = 8.945$$

The mode

The **mode** is the value, category or class that occurs with the highest frequency.

Properties of the mode

The mode is very easy to find and is thus used as a guide to the typical value in a sample. The mode has the advantage that it can be found for qualitative data as well as quantitative data. The main problems with the mode are that it may not exist (no two values, categories or classes are exactly the same) or it may not be unique (there may be two or more values, categories or classes which occur with the highest frequency).

Worked examples

3.10   Find the mode for the data given in Worked Example 3.1.

Solution   (a) None of the values occurs more than once. Therefore the mode does not exist.
(b) None of the values occurs more than once. Therefore the mode does not exist.

3.11   Find the mode for the data given in Worked Example 3.2.

Solution   The category 1 occurs with the highest frequency (7). Therefore the mode is 1.

3.12   Find the mode for the data given in Worked Example 3.3.

Solution   The class which occurs with the greatest frequency is 30–39.9 (11). This is the modal class.

3.13   The following data represent the grades given to job applicants in an aptitude test.

A B D A D A D D D B B B A D C B C B D D

Table 3.9. Frequency distribution of the grades awarded in an aptitude test

Category	Frequency
A	4
B	6
C	2
D	8

Find the modal grade.

Solution   The frequency distribution is given in Table 3.9. D is the modal grade since it occurs with the highest frequency (8).

3.14   For the automatic cash dispenser data given in Worked Example 3.4, calculate the modal number of customers using the dispenser in a ten minute period.

Solution   The frequency distribution for this data is given in Table 3.3. From the frequency distribution, the modal number of customers is three since this occurs with the highest frequency (12).

3.15   For the delicatessen sales data in Worked Example 3.5, calculate the modal class of the sales.

Solution   The frequency distribution for this data is given in Table 3.4. From the frequency distribution, the modal class of sales is £1.00–7.99 since this occurs with the highest frequency (14).

The weighted mean

The mean discussed at the beginning of the chapter assumes that each item is of equal importance. We say that the **weight** of each item is the same. In some situations, e.g. in the calculation of the Retail Price Index (Chapter 12), some items are more important than others. In this case, more important items are given a higher weight than less important items. A **weighted mean** can be calculated which takes account of the relative importance (weight) of each item. The weighted mean is calculated as follows.

KEY POINT

Your scientific calculator may be able to calculate a weighted mean

$$\text{Weighted mean} \quad \bar{x}_w = \frac{\Sigma w_i x_i}{\Sigma w_i} \qquad [3.5]$$

where w_i represents the weight (relative importance) of the ith item and x_i represents the value of the ith item.

Worked example

3.16 In the data given below, larger values are given a greater importance and thus a higher weight than smaller values. Calculate the weighted mean.

x_i	8.2	5.6	7.3	9.8	7.1	6.2	9.0
w_i	16	4	11	30	9	6	24

Solution
$$\Sigma w_i x_i = (16 \times 8.2) + (4 \times 5.6) + (11 \times 7.3) + (30 \times 9.8) + (9 \times 7.1)$$
$$+ (6 \times 6.2) + (24 \times 9.0)$$
$$= 845$$
$$\Sigma w_i = 16 + 4 + 11 + 30 + 9 + 6 + 24 = 100$$

Using [3.5], the weighted mean is

$$\bar{x}_w = \frac{845}{100} = 8.45$$

Self-assessment questions 3.1

1. State how the sample mean is calculated using

   (a) the raw data
   (b) a frequency distribution
   (c) a grouped frequency distribution.

2. How is the sample median calculated when there are

   (a) an odd number of items in the sample
   (b) an even number of items in the sample.

3. State the advantages and disadvantages of

   (a) the mean— no accuracy
   (b) the median
   (c) the mode.

4. When is the weighted mean $\bar{x}_w$ used in preference to the sample mean $\bar{x}$?

Exercises 3.1

The frequency distribution may have been calculated in Exercise 2.1

1. A double glazing company conducted a survey of 200 owner occupied houses to investigate the number of households which had full double glazing (all external windows and doors), partial double glazing (some external windows and doors) and no double glazing. Of the 200 houses surveyed, 30 had full double glazing, 68 had partial double glazing and 102 had no double glazing.

   (a) Calculate the mode.
   (b) Is it possible to calculate the mean and median for this data? Explain your answer.

The frequency distribution may have been calculated in Exercises 2.2, Question 1

2. A large computer software company conducted a survey of the hours worked by their part-time staff. The part-time staff work 18, 20 or 24 hours per week. A sample of the weekly working hours of 35 part-time employees is given below.

18	20	20	24	20	18	20
20	24	18	20	18	20	18
24	18	24	24	20	20	24
18	20	18	20	24	18	20
20	20	20	18	24	20	20

(a) Calculate the mean.
(b) Calculate the median.
(c) Calculate the mode.

3. The 1993 monthly sales figures (£000s) of ABC Ltd are given below.

Month	Sales (£000s)	Month	Sales (£000s)
January	18.39	July	19.98
February	21.62	August	26.11
March	23.49	September	29.64
April	30.00	October	21.73
May	29.22	November	20.05
June	26.53	December	9.64

(a) Calculate the average monthly sales figure.
(b) The Managing Director wants to investigate the quarterly sales figures, i.e she wants to look at the total sales in each quarter (first quarter is January, February and March, the second quarter is April, May and June etc.). Calculate the average quarterly sales figure.

4. The breaking strength of a fibre is tested in a laboratory. Forty samples of the fibre are tested and the breaking strengths (in grams) are given below.

2.143	2.143	2.148	2.158	2.137	2.137	2.147	2.140
2.124	2.133	2.134	2.164	2.165	2.145	2.142	2.169
2.168	2.170	2.162	2.130	2.133	2.162	2.137	2.156
2.168	2.145	2.125	2.137	2.151	2.149	2.134	2.151
2.150	2.146	2.122	2.149	2.156	2.161	2.168	2.131

(a) Use the raw data to

    (i) calculate the mean   (ii) calculate the median
    (iii) calculate the mode.

(b) Use the grouped frequency distribution found in Exercises 2.2, Question 3, to
    (i) calculate the mean   (ii) calculate the median
    (iii) calculate the modal class.

3.2   Measures of variation

Measures of variation provide information about the variability or spread of a set of data, for example the variability of the salary of managing directors. When summarizing a set of data, a measure of central location alone does not provide enough information. A measure of variation must also be used since two sets of data may have the same mean but very different variability. For example, a manufacturing process should produce steel sheets between 6 mm and 12 mm thick. Two machines are used to manufacture the steel sheets. The thicknesses of a sample of sheets taken from the two machines are as follows.

Machine	Thickness (mm)				
A	7	8	9	10	11
B	15	4	5	20	1

The mean thickness for each machine is 9 mm but the variability is much greater for machine B than for machine A. All of the steel sheets produced by machine A meet the required specifications but none of the sheets produced by machine B do so.

There are many measures of variation. We will focus on the three most commonly used measures: the range, the variance and the standard deviation.

The range

The **range** is simply the difference between the largest and smallest values in the set of data:

Range = largest value − smallest value   [3.6]

Properties of the range

The range is very quick and simple to calculate and is thus used as a general indication of the variability of a set of data. For numeric data, the range can always be calculated and for a given sample of data it is unique. The range only considers the smallest and largest values in a set of data. If one or both of these values are very unusual the range will give a misleading impression of the variability of the data.

Worked examples

3.17 Calculate the range for the data given in Worked Example 3.1.

Solution (a) The largest value is 7.3 and the smallest value is 2.4. Using [3.6], range = 7.3 − 2.4 = 4.9.
(b) The largest value is 8830 and the smallest value is 1278. Using [3.6], range = 8830 − 1278 = 7552.

3.18 Calculate the range for the data given in Worked Example 3.2 using the raw data.

Solution The largest value is 4 and the smallest value is 0. Using [3.6], range = 4 − 0 = 4.

3.19 Calculate the range for the data given in Worked Example 3.3 using the raw data.

Solution The largest value is 61.6 and the smallest value is 6.1. Using [3.6], range = 61.6 − 6.1 = 55.5.

3.20 Calculate the range of the cash dispenser data given in Worked Example 3.4.

Solution The largest value is 4 and the smallest value is 0. Using [3.6], range = 4 − 0 = 4.

3.21 Calculate the range of sales values given in Worked Example 3.5.

Solution The largest sales value is £34.98 and the smallest sales value is £1.26. Using [3.6], range = 34.98 − 1.26 = £33.72.

The variance

The variance is based on the difference between each value and the mean of the data. The **variance** is defined as the average squared deviation from the mean. The variance of a population is defined as follows.

Population variance $\sigma^2 = \dfrac{\Sigma(x_i - \mu)^2}{N}$ $i = 1, 2, \ldots, N$ [3.7]

where x_i represents the value of the ith item in the population, N represents the number of items in the population and μ represents the mean of the population. The variance of a population can be estimated from a sample of data and such an estimate is called the **sample variance**. However, when using the sample to estimate the population variance, we cannot simply replace the population size, N, with the sample size, n. It can be shown that if you do divide by n then this will result in an underestimate of the population variance. If you divide by $n - 1$ when a sample is used to estimate a population variance, then a more accurate estimate will be obtained. An estimate of the population variance using a sample can be calculated using either the raw data or a frequency distribution.

Using the raw data

Sample variance $s^2 = \dfrac{\Sigma(x_i - \bar{x})^2}{n - 1}$ $i = 1, 2, \ldots, n$ [3.8]

where x_i represents the value of the ith item in the sample, n represents the number of items in the sample and $\bar{x}$ represents the sample mean. In practice, [3.8] is not used to calculate the sample variance. It is easier to use the following equivalent equation.

Sample variance $s^2 = \dfrac{(\Sigma x_i^2) - n\bar{x}^2}{n - 1}$ $i = 1, 2, \ldots, n$ [3.9]

where x_i^2 represents the square of the value of the ith item in the sample, n represents the number of items in the sample and $\bar{x}$ represents the sample mean.

Using a frequency distribution

Sample variance $s^2 = \dfrac{(\Sigma x_i^2 f_i) - n\bar{x}^2}{n - 1}$ $i = 1, 2, \ldots, k$ [3.10]

where x_i^2 represents the square of the value of the ith category or the midpoint of the ith class ([3.4]), f_i represents the frequency of the ith category or class, k represents the number of categories or classes, n

represents the number of items in the sample and $\bar{x}$ represents the sample mean.

Note that if the sample variance is calculated from a grouped frequency distribution then the values of items in a class are replaced by the midpoint of the class. Thus the variance obtained using [3.10] will be an approximation to the sample variance.

Properties of the variance

For numeric data, the sample variance can always be calculated, and it is unique. The variance takes account of all values in a set of data. If there are any unusually small or large values, the sample variance may not be an accurate reflection of the variability. The variance is measured in squared units. For example, if the raw data are measured in £, the variance will be measured in £^{2}.

Worked examples

3.22   Calculate the sample variance for the data given in Worked Example 3.1.

Solution   (a) First calculate a data summary:
$$n = 9 \quad \Sigma x_i = 44.5 \quad \Sigma x_i^2 = 244.37$$
Using [3.2], the sample mean $\bar{x} = 44.5/9 = 4.9444$. Using [3.9], the sample variance

$$s^2 = \frac{244.37 - (9 \times 4.9444^2)}{8}$$

$$= 3.0433$$

(b) First calculate a data summary:
$$n = 14 \quad \Sigma x_i = 81\,043 \quad \Sigma x_i^2 = 543\,162\,959$$
Using [3.2], the sample mean $\bar{x} = 81043/14 = 5788.7857$. Using [3.9], the sample variance

$$s^2 = \frac{543\,162\,959 - (14 \times 5788.7857^2)}{13}$$

$$= 5\,694\,030.821$$

3.23   (a) Calculate the sample variance for the data given in Worked Example 3.2 using

(i) the raw data   (ii) a frequency distribution.

(b) Comment on the answers to (i) and (ii).

Solution   (a) (i) First calculate a data summary:
$$n = 24 \quad \Sigma x_i = 43 \quad \Sigma x_i^2 = 113$$
Using [3.2], the sample mean $\bar{x} = 43/24 = 1.7917$. Using [3.9], the

Table 3.10. Frequency distribution and values of $x_i^2 f_i$

Value of category x_i	Frequency f_i	$x_i^2 f_i$
0	4	0
1	7	7
2	5	20
3	6	54
4	2	32
Total	24	113

sample variance

$$s^2 = \frac{113 - (24 \times 1.7917^2)}{23}$$

$$= 1.5633$$

(ii) Table 3.10 shows the frequency distribution and values of $x_i^2 f_i$. First calculate a data summary:

$n = \Sigma f_i = 24 \qquad \Sigma x_i = 43 \qquad \Sigma x_i^2 f_i = 113$

Using [3.3], the sample mean $\bar{x} = 43/24 = 1.7917$. Using [3.10], the sample variance

$$s^2 = \frac{113 - (24 \times 1.7917^2)}{23} = 1.5633$$

(b) The answers to (i) and (ii) are exactly the same. This is always true for an ungrouped frequency distribution.

3.24 (a) Calculate the sample variance for the data given in Worked Example 3.3 using

(i) the raw data, (ii) a frequency distribution.

(b) Comment on the answers to (i) and (ii).

Solution (a) (i) First calculate a data summary:

$n = 35 \qquad \Sigma x_i = 1118.8 \qquad \Sigma x_i^2 = 42\,596.56$

Using [3.2], the sample mean $\bar{x} = 1118.8/35 = 31.9657$. Using [3.9], the sample variance

$$s^2 = \frac{42\,596.56 - (35 \times 31.9657^2)}{34} = 200.9809$$

(ii) Table 3.11 shows the frequency distribution and values of $x_i^2 f_i$. First calculate a data summary:

$n = \Sigma f_i = 35 \qquad \Sigma x_i f_i = 1123.25 \qquad \Sigma x_i^2 f_i = 42\,962.5875$

Using [3.3], the sample mean $\bar{x} = 1123.25/35 = 32.0929$. Using [3.10], the sample variance

$\Sigma x_i f_i$ was found in Worked Example 3.3

$$s^2 = \frac{42\,962.5875 - (35 \times 32.0929^2)}{34} = 203.3585$$

Table 3.11. Frequency distribution and values of $x_i^2 f_i$

Value of category	Midpoint x_i	Frequency f_i	$x_i^2 f_i$
0.0– 9.9	4.95	2	49.0050
10.0–19.9	14.95	5	1117.5125
20.0–29.9	24.95	8	4980.0200
30.0–39.9	34.95	11	13 436.5275
40.0–49.9	44.95	5	10 102.5125
50.0–59.9	54.95	3	9058.5075
60.0–69.9	64.95	1	4218.5025
		Total 35	42 962.5875

(b) The answers to (i) and (ii) are not the same. This is because the actual values have been replaced by the midpoint of the class in the calculation. Thus, the variance calculated in (ii) is an estimate of the sample variance.

3.25 Calculate the sample variance of the sales data given in Worked Example 3.5 using

The grouped frequency distribution is given in Table 3.4

(a) the raw data,   (b) a grouped frequency distribution.

Solution (a) The sample mean for the sales data was calculated as £11.21 in Worked Example 3.5(a). First calculate a data summary:

$n = 32$ $\Sigma x_i^2 = 6339.5164$

Using [3.9], the sample variance

$$s^2 = \frac{6339.5164 - (32 \times 11.21^2)}{31} = £^2 74.78$$

Note: exactly the same value would be obtained using [3.8].

(b) The sample mean using a grouped frequency table was calculated as £11.50 in Worked Example 3.5(b). If x_i represents the midpoint of class i, then $n = 32$ and $\Sigma x_i^2 f_i = 6482.32$. Using [3.10], the sample variance

$$s^2 = \frac{6482.32 - (32 \times 11.50^2)}{31} = £^2 72.59$$

As with the calculation of the mean, this is an approximate sample variance since the raw data values have been replaced by the midpoint of the class to which the value belongs.

The standard deviation

The **standard deviation** is the square root of the variance. The standard deviation can be calculated for a population and a sample using either the raw data or a frequency distribution.

Using the raw data

Population standard deviation

$$\sigma = \sqrt{\frac{\Sigma(x_i - \mu)^2}{N}} \quad i = 1, 2, \ldots, N \quad [3.11]$$

Sample standard deviation

$$s = \sqrt{\frac{\Sigma(x_i - \bar{x})^2}{n - 1}} \quad i = 1, 2, \ldots, n \quad [3.12]$$

where x_i represents the value of the ith item in the population or sample, N represents the number of items in the population, μ represents the mean of the population, n represents the number of items in the sample and $\bar{x}$ represents the sample mean. In practice, [3.12] is not used to calculate the sample standard deviation. It is easier to use the following equivalent equation:

Sample standard deviation $$s = \sqrt{\frac{(\Sigma x_i^2) - n\bar{x}^2}{n - 1}} \quad i = 1, 2, \ldots, n$$

$$[3.13]$$

where x_i^2 represents the square of the value of the ith item in the sample, n represents the number of items in the sample and $\bar{x}$ represents the sample mean.

Using a frequency distribution

Sample standard deviation $$s = \sqrt{\frac{(\Sigma x_i^2 f_i) - n\bar{x}^2}{n - 1}} \quad i = 1, 2, \ldots, k$$

$$[3.14]$$

where x_i^2 represents the square of the value of the ith category or the midpoint of the ith class ([3.4]), f_i represents the frequency of the ith category or class, k represents the number of categories or classes, n represents the number of items in the sample and $\bar{x}$ represents the sample mean. Note: if the sample standard deviation is calculated from a grouped frequency distribution then the values of items in a class are replaced by the midpoint of the class. Thus the standard deviation calculated using [3.14] is an approximation to the sample standard deviation.

Properties of the standard deviation

The standard deviation has the same properties as the variance except that it has an extra advantage; the standard deviation is measured in the same units as the raw data (i.e. not squared units).

Worked examples

3.26 Calculate the sample standard deviation for the data given in Worked Example 3.1.

Solution (a) From Worked Example 3.22, the sample variance $s^2 = 3.0433$. Using [3.13], the sample standard deviation $s = \sqrt{3.0433} = 1.7445$.

(b) From Worked Example 3.22, the sample variance $s^2 = 5694030.821$. Using [3.13], the sample standard deviation
$$s = \sqrt{5694030.821} = 2386.2168$$

3.27 (a) Calculate the sample standard deviation for the data given in Worked Example 3.2 using

(i) the raw data,   (ii) a frequency distribution.

(b) Comment on the answers to (i) and (ii).

Solution (a) (i) From Worked Example 3.23, the sample variance $s^2 = 1.5633$. Using [3.13], the sample standard deviation $s = \sqrt{1.5633} = 1.2503$

(ii) From Worked Example 3.23, the sample variance $s^2 = 1.5633$. Using [3.14], the sample standard deviation $s = \sqrt{1.5633} = 1.2503$

(b) The answers to (i) and (ii) are exactly the same. This is always true for an ungrouped frequency distribution.

3.28 (a) Calculate the sample standard deviation for the data given in Worked Example 3.3 using

(i) the raw data,   (ii) a frequency distribution.

(b) Comment on the answers to (i) and (ii).

Solution (a) (i) From Worked Example 3.24, the sample variance $s^2 = 200.9809$. Using [3.13], the sample standard deviation $s = \sqrt{200.9809} = 14.1768$

(ii) From Worked Example 3.24, the sample variance $s^2 = 203.3585$. Using [3.14], the sample standard deviation $s = \sqrt{203.3585} = 14.2604$

(b) The answers to (i) and (ii) are not the same. This is because the actual values have been replaced by the midpoint of the class in the calculation. Thus, the standard deviation calculated in (ii) is an estimate of the sample standard deviation.

3.29 Calculate the sample standard deviation of the sales data given in Worked Example 3.5 using

(a) the raw data,   (b) the grouped frequency distribution.

Solution (a) From Worked Example 3.25, the sample variance $s^2 = £^2 74.78$. Using [3.13], the sample standard deviation $s = \sqrt{74.78} = £8.65$

(b) From Worked Example 3.25, the sample variance $s^2 = £^2 72.59$. Using [3.14], the sample standard deviation $s = \sqrt{72.59} = £8.52$

Self-assessment questions 3.2

1. How is the range of a sample of data calculated?
2. State how the sample variance is calculated using

   (a) the raw data
   (b) a frequency distribution
   (c) a grouped frequency distribution.

3. How is the sample standard deviation calculated from the sample variance?

4. State the advantages and disadvantages of

   (a) the range
   (b) the sample variance
   (c) the sample standard deviation

5. What adjustment must be made to the equation for the population variance in order to calculate a sample variance?

Exercises 3.2

1. Refer to the computer company data given in Exercises 3.1 Question 2.

   (a) Calculate the range.
   (b) Calculate the sample variance.
   (c) Calculate the sample standard deviation.

2. Refer to the monthly sales data of ABC Ltd given in Exercises 3.1 Question 3.

   (a) For the monthly sales data calculate
       (i)   the range
       (ii) the sample variance
       (iii) the sample standard deviation.

   (b) For the quarterly sales data, calculate
       (i)   the range
       (ii) the sample variance
       (iii) the sample standard deviation.

3. Refer to the breaking strength of a fibre data given in Exercises 3.1 Question 4.
   (a) Use the raw data to
       (i)   calculate the range

> (ii) calculate the sample variance
> (iii) calculate the sample standard deviation.
>
> (b) Use the grouped frequency distribution found in Exercises 2.2 Question 3 to
>
>   (i) calculate the sample variance
>   (ii) calculate the sample standard deviation.

Test exercises

1. A high street ladies clothes retailer returns all faulty goods to the manufacturer. The data below show the number of each type of garment returned to the manufacturer in a one month period.

Type of garment	Number returned to the manufacturer
Dress	12
Jumper	70
Cardigan	47
Blouse	23
Skirt	36
Total	188

   (a) Which type of garment is returned most often?
   (b) Is it possible to calculate the mean, median, sample variance and sample standard deviation for this data? Explain your answer.

2. A dentist conducted an experiment to monitor the effectiveness of a new toothpaste for children. The following data show the number of cavities sustained by children using this toothpaste over a six month period.

You may have found the frequency distribution in Chapter 2 Test Exercises, Question 3

```
0  1  0  1  1  2  0  3  0  0  2  1  1
1  2  1  1  0  1  1  1  1  2  0  0  0
4  0  1  0  2  1  0  0  1  0  3  1  2
2  0  0  3  2  0  3  1  0  1  1  0  1
```

   (a) Use the frequency distribution to calculate
       (i)   the mean number of cavities
       (ii) the median number of cavities
       (iii) the modal number of cavities
       (iv) the range of the number of cavities
       (v)   the sample variance of the number of cavities
       (vi) the sample standard deviation of the number of cavities.

(b) Which measure of central location is most appropriate to use for this data? Which measure of variation is most appropriate to use for this data? Explain your answers.

(c) If the raw data was used instead of the frequency distribution, would the answers to (a) change? Explain your answer.

3. A dairy have conducted a survey of the number of bottles of milk ordered daily by people on a housing estate. The number of bottles ordered by people on the estate on a Monday are given below.

You may have found the frequency distribution in Chapter 2 Test Exercises, Question 4

3	2	1	0	1	2	1	1	1	1
1	1	2	1	2	1	1	0	1	2
2	1	1	3	1	1	2	2	1	1

(a) Use the frequency distribution to calculate
   (i)   the mean number of bottles
   (ii) the median number of bottles
   (iii) the modal number of bottles
   (iv) the range of the number of bottles
   (v)   the sample variance of the number of bottles
   (vi) the sample standard deviation of the number of bottles.

(b) On a second housing estate 56 people have milk delivered. Assuming that this estate has the same distribution of the number of bottles ordered, how many bottles should the milkman have on the milk float in order to cope with the demand?

4. A mail order company guarantee that their goods will be dispatched within five working days, and that, wherever possible, goods will be dispatched within three working days. The data given below show the number of days taken to dispatch goods for a random sample of 1000 orders.

You may have found the frequency distribution in Chapter 2 Test Exercises, Question 5

Number of working days to dispatch	Number of orders
1	31
2	662
3	157
4	93
5	57
Total	1000

(a) Use the frequency distribution to calculate
   (i)   the mean number of working days
   (ii) the sample variance of the number of working days
   (iii) the sample standard deviation of the number of working days.

(b) Using this sample of data, are the company meeting their guarantee that all goods are dispatched within five working days? Are they also justified in saying that, wherever possible, the goods are dispatched within three working days? Justify your answers.

5. The numbers of units produced by 180 workers in an engineering factory in one working week are given below.

You may have found the grouped frequency distribution in Chapter 2 Test Exercises, Question 6

Number of units	Number of workers
500–509	8
510–519	18
520–529	23
530–539	37
540–549	47
550–559	26
560–569	16
570–579	5
Total	180

(a) Use the grouped frequency distribution to calculate
  (i)   the mean number of units
  (ii) the median number of units
  (iii) the modal number of units
  (iv) the range of the number of units
  (v)   the sample variance of the number of units
  (vi) the sample standard deviation of the number of units.

(b) Which measure of central location is most appropriate to use for this data? Which measure of variation is most appropriate to use for this data? Explain your answers.

(c) If the raw data was used instead of the frequency distribution, would the answers to (a) change? Explain your answer.

6. Forty companies took part in a survey to investigate their annual expenditure on marketing their product. The data (£000s) are given below.

You may have found the grouped frequency distribution in Chapter 2 Test Exercises, Question 7

22	28	31	35	43	48	52	56	58	63
60	52	30	51	27	46	44	46	34	39
48	38	43	40	41	55	35	21	64	45
45	47	25	53	72	32	58	48	31	54

(a) Use the raw data to calculate
  (i)   the mean annual expenditure on marketing
  (ii) the median annual expenditure on marketing
  (iii) the modal annual expenditure on marketing
  (iv) the range of the annual expenditure on marketing
  (v)   the sample variance of the annual expenditure on marketing
  (vi) the sample standard deviation of the annual expenditure on marketing.

(b) Use the grouped frequency distribution to calculate
  (i)   the mean annual expenditure on marketing
  (ii) the median annual expenditure on marketing
  (iii) the modal annual expenditure on marketing
  (iv) the range of the annual expenditure on marketing
  (v)   the sample variance of the annual expenditure on marketing
  (vi) the sample standard deviation of the annual expenditure on marketing.

(c) Briefly describe the annual expenditure on marketing using an appropriate measure of central location and variation.

7. The frequency distribution of the lifetime (hours) of 300 steam irons produced by one factory is given below.

You may have found the grouped frequency distribution in Chapter 2 Test Exercises, Question 8

Lifetime (hours)	Number of steam irons
300–399.99	12
400–499.99	59
500–599.99	84
600–699.99	72
700–799.99	41
800–899.99	26
900–999.99	6
Total	300

(a) Use the grouped frequency distribution to calculate
  (i)   the mean lifetime
  (ii) the median lifetime
  (iii) the modal lifetime
  (iv) the range of the lifetimes
  (v)   the sample variance of the lifetimes
  (vi) the sample standard deviation of the lifetimes.

(b) Which measure of central location is most appropriate for this data? Which measure of variation is most appropriate for this data? Give reasons for your answers.

(c) The manufacturers are considering the length of time they should guarantee the irons for. Advise the manufacturers on a reasonable guarantee period for the product. Give reasons for your answer.

8. The personnel manager of a large electronics company has constructed a grouped frequency distribution of the income of male and female employees in the company. This distribution is given below.

You may have found the grouped frequency distribution in Chapter 2 Test Exercises, Question 9

Income (£)	Number of males	Number of females
5000 to <10000	3	12
10000 to <15000	46	55
15000 to <20000	82	37
20000 to <25000	20	13
25000 to <30000	8	4
30000 to <35000	3	1
35000 to <40000	1	0

(a) Use the grouped frequency distribution to calculate
  (i)   the mean income of males and females
  (ii) the median income of males and females
  (iii) the modal income of males and females
  (iv) the range of the income of males and females
  (v)   the sample variance of the income of males and females
  (vi) the sample standard deviation of the income of males and females.

(b) Which measure of central location is most appropriate for this data? Which measure of variation is most appropriate for this data? Give reasons for your answers.

(c) Compare the distribution of the income of males and females. Does this company appear to operate an equal pay scale for males and females?

4 Introduction to probability theory

<table>
<tr><td>Objectives</td><td>

When you have read this chapter you should be able to

- explain the terms **experiment**, **sample space** and **event**
- state the basic rules of probability
- interpret a probability
- calculate probabilities using the classical and relative frequency methods
- draw and interpret a contingency table
- explain and calculate relationships between probabilities
- understand the terms **conditional probability** and **independence**

</td></tr>
</table>

Probabilities are associated with situations involving doubt or uncertainty about the outcome. For example, which horse to bet on in a race, whether to buy shares in a company, how many orders a firm will get in a week, all involve decision making in situations with uncertainty.

Probability theory attempts to attach some measure of certainty to the outcome.

4.1 Experiments, sample space and counting

Experiments and sample space

In probability terms an **experiment** is defined as a process which generates a well-defined outcome that is not predictable in advance, but where we do know all of the possible outcomes.

Example

4.1 For the following experiments all the possible outcomes have been listed.

Experiment	Possible outcomes
Rolling a die	1, 2, 3, 4, 5, 6
Selecting a component off a production line for inspection	D, defective; N, non-defective
A bid for a contract	S, success; F, failure
Examination result	A, B, C, F (= fail)
Demand for a new product	0, 1, 2, 3, . . . , ∞

When we can write down all the possible outcomes of our experiment we have defined what is called the **sample space**. The sample space is usually denoted by the letter S and the possible outcomes in S are listed in curly brackets, { }. For Example 4.1 the sample spaces, S, have been defined in Example 4.2.

Example

4.2

Experiment	Sample space
Rolling a die	$S = \{1, 2, 3, 4, 5, 6\}$
Selecting a component from a production line for inspection	$S = \{D, N\}$
A bid for a contract	$S = \{S, F\}$
Examination result	$S = \{A, B, C, F\}$
Demand for a new product	$S = \{0, 1, 2, \ldots, \infty\}$

This notation is not restricted to simple experiments with just one outcome, since in many experiments the outcomes represent the combination of the outcomes of several stages.

Example

4.3 If we select two components from a production line for inspection, then the outcome of the experiment could be two defective, two non-defective or one defective and one non-defective component. The sample space in this case will be written as follows:

$$S = \{(D,\ D),\ (N,\ N),\ (D, N),\ (N, D)\}$$

where the round brackets contain the possible outcomes, with the first value representing the first component selected and the second value representing the second selected. The outcomes (D, N) and (N, D) are different in terms of probability.

We can represent the outcomes of this type of experiment on a **tree diagram** as shown in Figure 4.1.

We do not always need to write down all of the possible outcomes in the sample space but it is useful to be able to determine how many outcomes there are altogether. The following basic rule of counting can often be used to determine the total number of outcomes.

Figure 4.1. Tree diagram to represent the outcomes of selecting two components from a production line for inspection

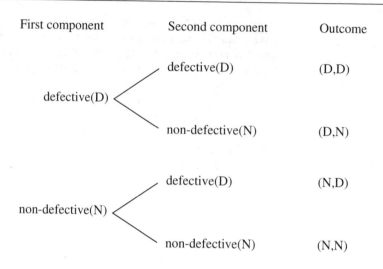

First component	Second component	Outcome
defective(D)	defective(D)	(D,D)
	non-defective(N)	(D,N)
non-defective(N)	defective(D)	(N,D)
	non-defective(N)	(N,N)

Basic rule of counting

If an experiment consists of several steps, the first having n_1 outcomes, the second having n_2 outcomes and so on, then the total number of possible experimental outcomes will be

$$n_1 \times n_2 \times \ldots$$ [4.1]

Example

4.4   Consider selecting two components for inspection from a production line as in Example 4.3. There are two steps to this experiment (selecting the first component and then selecting the second component). Each step has two possible outcomes – the component being defective (D) or non-defective (N) – therefore $n_1 = 2$ and $n_2 = 2$. Thus altogether there are $n_1 \times n_2 = 2 \times 2 = 4$ possible outcomes.

Events

We are usually interested in determining the probability of one or more of the experimental outcomes. The collection of outcomes that we are interested in is called an **event** and is denoted by a capital letter. Events are defined in the same way as the sample space.

An event is said to **occur** when one of the outcomes in the event is obtained when the experiment is carried out.

Examples

4.5

Experiment	Possible events
Rolling a die	Event A = rolling a six = {6} Event B = rolling an even number = {2, 4, 6}
Selecting two components off a production line for inspection	Event C = at least one defective = {(D,D), (D,N), (N,D)}
Examination result	Event D = a pass = {A, B, C}
Demand for a new product	Event E = demand is for >10 = {11, 12, 13, . . . , ∞}

4.6   If we roll a die and it lands on a 4 then event A in Example 4.5 has not occurred but event B has occurred.

Self-assessment questions 4.1

1. What is the sample space of an experiment?
2. When is an event said to occur?

Exercises 4.1

1. For the following experiments list the sample space, S.

   (a) Surveying a consumer on his use of two products A and B.
   (b) The number of orders made in a week for a particular component.
   (c) A team's result in a game of football.
   (d) Tossing two coins.

2. If a die is rolled and a coin is tossed, draw a tree diagram to represent all the possible outcomes of the experiment.
3. A production process has three stages, the first stage can be completed on three different machines, A, B or C, the second on two machines, D and E, and the third on two machines, F and G. Draw a tree diagram to represent the different combinations of machines that can be used to complete the three stages of the process. Use the basic rule of counting to confirm that you have listed all of the possible outcomes.
4. For the experiments in Question 1, list the outcomes in the following events.

   (a) The consumer uses at least one of the two products A and B.
   (b) At most four orders are made.
   (c) The team does not gain a point from the game.
   (d) Exactly one tail occurs.

4.2   Probability

A **probability** is a numerical measure of the chance that an event occurs. If our event is denoted by A then we denote the probability of event A occurring by $P(A)$.

$P(A)$ = probability of event A occurring

Basic rules of probability

1. Probabilities always lie in the range 0 to 1, so for event A

KEY POINT

$$0 \leq P(A) \leq 1$$

2. If the probabilities of all the possible outcomes of the experiment are calculated their sum will be equal to 1, hence

KEY POINT

$$P(S) = 1 \qquad \text{where } S \text{ is the sample space}$$

Interpretation of probability

If A is the event of interest then the following interpretations can be used:

1. if $P(A)$ is close to 1 then event A is very likely to occur;
2. if $P(A)$ is close to 0 then event A is unlikely to occur;
3. if $P(A) = 1$ then event A is certain to occur;
4. if $P(A) = 0$ then event A is certain not to occur;
5. other values of $P(A)$ indicate on an increasing scale how likely event A is to occur.

Assigning probabilities

There are three general methods for assigning probabilities to events:

1. the classical method
2. the relative frequency method
3. the subjective method.

These are now discussed in more detail.

The classical method

If the sample space, S, for an experiment consists of n outcomes which are all equally likely to occur, and the event of interest, A, consists of k of these outcomes, then this method defines the probability that event A will occur as

KEY POINT

$$P(A) = \frac{k}{n} \qquad\qquad [4.2]$$

Worked example

4.7   If we roll a die any of the six sides are equally likely to appear. If the events of interest are

> Event A = rolling a six
> Event B = rolling an even number

Find the probabilities $P(A)$ and $P(B)$.

Solution   Using the classical method for equally likely outcomes [4.2] there are six possible outcomes in the sample space (1, 2, 3, 4, 5 or 6) so $n = 6$. Event A has only one outcome, {6}, so $k = 1$ and hence

$$P(A) = \frac{1}{6} = 0.1667$$

Event B has three outcomes, {2, 4, 6}, so $k = 3$ and hence

$$P(B) = \frac{3}{6} = 0.5$$

The relative frequency method

When the exact probability cannot be calculated using the classical method then an experiment or survey can be used to find an estimate of the probability. If the experiment or survey is repeated under exactly the same conditions n times and event A is observed to occur k times, then the probability of event A occurring is estimated to be

KEY POINT

$$P(A) = \frac{k}{n} \qquad\qquad [4.3]$$

Worked example

4.8   Fifty components are selected at random from a production line, and six are observed to be below standard. Estimate the probability that a component taken off this production line will be below standard.

Solution   The experiment has been repeated 50 times, 50 components were taken off the production line, so the relative frequency method can be used with $n = 50$. Let A be the event that a component is below standard, six of the components were below standard so $k = 6$, and hence

$$P(A) = \frac{6}{50} = 0.12$$

The subjective method

In many situations it is not possible to use the above methods so probabilities have to be based on a person's belief that the event will occur. The degree of belief will be based on the scale 0 to 1, where a probability of 1 means that the person believes that the event is certain to occur. If the person is an expert in the given situation then they can give good estimates of the probabilities. This method can also be used in conjunction with the two previous methods if a person believes that other circumstances should be taken into account. Probabilities found using this method may not be the same for any two experts.

Example

4.9   The following situations require the subjective method of assigning probabilities: the probability of a horse winning a race will be based on expert (bookmaker) opinion of the past and present form, type of race, going etc.; a financial expert should be able to assign probabilities to the price of shares rising and falling.

Self-assessment questions 4.2

1. What range of values can a probability take on?
2. How would you interpret a probability of an event occurring being close to 1?
3. What is the sum of the probabilities of all of the outcomes in the sample space?
4. What requirement do the experimental outcomes need to satisfy so that the classical method of assigning probabilities can be used?
5. When do we use the relative frequency method of assigning probabilities?
6. What problems may arise when using the subjective method of assigning probabilities?

Exercises 4.2

1. Which of the following values cannot be probabilities?

   (a) 0.995   (b) 0   (c) 0.001   (d) 10/9   (e) 52/79   (f) −0.8

2. A card is drawn at random from a pack of 52 playing cards.

    (a) Which method of assigning probabilities would you use for this experiment?
    (b) For the card drawn find the probability of the following events:
      (i) A, it is a red card   (iii) C, it is an ace
      (ii) B, it is a spade   (iv) D, it is the jack of hearts

3. A survey of 350 households gave the following data on the number of children under 16 living in each household.

Number of children under 16	Frequency
0	185
1	51
2	90
3 or more	24
Total	350

    (a) Which method of assigning probabilities would you use for this data?
    (b) Find the probability of the following events
      (i)   A, a household selected has no children,
      (ii) B, a household selected has three or more children,
      (iii) C, a household selected has at least one child.

4. A firm is assessing how many orders are placed for a particular product in a week. The weekly number of orders placed over the past year have been recorded and are given below.

Number of orders placed	Frequency
less than 250	3
250–499	11
500–749	28
750–999	9
1000 or more	1
Total	52

    Find the probability that in a week there are

    (a) less than 250 orders placed,
    (b) 750–999 orders placed,
    (c) 1000 or more orders placed,
    (d) less than 1000 orders placed.

Relationships between events in probability   **4.3**

Complement of an event

The **complement** of an event A is the event that A does not occur. It is denoted by $\bar{A}$ and contains all of the experimental outcomes in the sample space that are not contained in event A. Either A or $\bar{A}$ is certain to occur when the experiment is carried out as both events together contain all the outcomes in the sample space, hence in probability terms

KEY POINT

$$P(A) + P(\bar{A}) = 1 \qquad\qquad [4.4]$$

and so

KEY POINT

$$P(\bar{A}) = 1 - P(A) \qquad\qquad [4.5]$$

Worked example

4.10   Worked example 4.7 considered rolling a die, with event A being rolling a 6. List the outcomes in event $\bar{A}$ and find $P(\bar{A})$.

Solution   Sample space $S = \{1, 2, 3, 4, 5, 6\}$, event $A = \{6\}$. $\bar{A}$ will contain all outcomes in S not occurring in event A, hence

$$\bar{A} = \{1, 2, 3, 4, 5\}$$

and, using [4.5],

$$P(\bar{A}) = 1 - P(A)$$
$$= 1 - 0.1667 = 0.8333$$

Probability of two events, A and B, both occurring

We are often interested in the probability that two events will both occur when the experiment is carried out. To find the probability of both events occurring we are finding the probability of all of the outcomes that events A and B have in common, hence this is often referred to as the **intersection** or **joint probability**. In probability terms it is denoted as

$$P(A \text{ and } B)$$

or

$$P(A \cap B)$$

$P(A \text{ and } B)$ will be used in this book.

Worked example

4.11   Worked Example 4.7 considered two events, A and B, for the rolling of a die. Find the probability of both events occurring, i.e. P(A and B).

Solution   Event A = rolling a six = {6}
Event B = rolling an even number = {2, 4, 6}

Event (A and B) will contain any outcomes that A and B have in common, hence event (A and B) = {6}.

There are six possible outcomes for the experiment, so using the classical method of assigning probabilities,

$$P(\text{A and B}) = \tfrac{1}{6} = 0.1667$$

Probability of either event A, event B or both occurring

To determine the probability of either or both of two events, A and B, occurring we are determining the probability of just event A occurring, just event B occurring or both A and B occurring. In probability terms it is denoted as:

P(A or B)

or

$P(\text{A} \cup \text{B})$

P(A or B) will be used in this book.

The following **addition law of probability** is used to determine the above probability.

Addition law of probability

KEY POINT

$$P(\text{A or B}) = P(\text{A}) + P(\text{B}) - P(\text{A and B}) \qquad [4.6]$$

When we add the individual terms P(A) and P(B), the probabilities of the outcomes that A and B have in common are included in both terms. Subtracting the term P(A and B) ensures that the outcomes in common are only included once.

Worked examples

4.12   Worked Example 4.7 considered two events, A and B, for the rolling of a die. Find the probability of either A or B or both events occurring.

Solution   Event A = rolling a six = {6} $P(A) = 0.1667$
Event B = rolling an even number = {2, 4, 6} $P(B) = 0.5$
Event (A and B) = rolling a six = {6} $P(A \text{ and } B) = 0.1667$

Event (A or B) will contain any outcomes that are in A or B or both. Using the addition law, [4.6],

$$P(A \text{ or } B) = P(A) + P(B) - P(A \text{ and } B)$$

$$= 0.1667 + 0.5 - 0.1667 = 0.5$$

The outcome 'rolling a six' occurs in both events and therefore has to be subtracted.

4.13   A survey of 200 of the employees of a large company showed that 130 were males, 160 owned a car and of the car owners 112 were males. Let A be the event that an employee selected is male and B be the event that an employee selected owns a car. Find the probability that an employee selected is

1. (a) male, (b) a car owner;
2. (a) female, (b) not a car owner;
3. a male car owner;
4. either a male or a car owner or both.

Solution   1. Using the relative frequency method:

(a) there are 130 males out of a total of 200 employees surveyed, hence

$$P(A) = \tfrac{130}{200} = 0.65$$

(b) there are 160 car owners out of a total of 200 employees surveyed, hence

$$P(B) = \tfrac{160}{200} = 0.80$$

2. We need to find the probabilities of the complements of events A and B:

(a) $\bar{A}$, employee selected is female,

$$P(\bar{A}) = 1 - P(A) = 1 - 0.65 = 0.35$$

(b) $\bar{B}$, employee does not own a car,

$$P(\bar{B}) = 1 - P(B) = 1 - 0.80 = 0.20$$

3. The probability that an employee is a male car owner $P(A \text{ and } B)$. 112 of the car owners were male, hence

$$P(A \text{ and } B) = \tfrac{112}{200} = 0.56$$

4. The probability of an employee being either a male or a car owner or both is $P(A \text{ or } B)$. Using the addition law, [4.6],

$$P(A \text{ or } B) = P(A) + P(B) - P(A \text{ and } B)$$

$$= 0.65 + 0.80 - 0.56 = 0.89$$

Mutually exclusive events

When two events, A and B, have no experimental outcomes in common we say that they are **mutually exclusive**. In this case

KEY POINT

$$P(\text{A and B}) = 0$$

and hence the addition law, [4.6], can be simplified to [4.7]

Addition law for mutually exclusive events

KEY POINT

$$P(\text{A or B}) = P(\text{A}) + P(\text{B}) \qquad [4.7]$$

Worked example

4.14   A fair die is rolled, let event A be that an odd number is rolled and event B be that an even number is rolled. Are events A and B mutually exclusive?

Solution   Event A = odd number = {1, 3, 5}
Event B = even number = {2, 4, 6}

The two events have no outcomes in common, hence they are mutually exclusive.

4.15   In Worked Example 4.13 we found that the probability that an employee was a male car owner was $P(\text{A and B}) = 0.56$, hence these two events A and B are not mutually exclusive.

Contingency tables

Relative frequency data for two events, A and B, is often presented in a table called a **contingency table**, and from this table probabilities can easily be determined. A contingency table will be illustrated using the data for Worked Example 4.13.

The information given in Worked Example 4.13 has been summarized in Table 4.1. The other values in the table can easily be determined because the columns should add down to the totals at the bottom and the rows add across to the totals at the side. The completed information is given in Table 4.2.

We can find probabilities using the contingency table by dividing all of the values in the table by the overall total, 200. These probabilities are given in Table 4.3. The probabilities in Table 4.3 are the values of the probabilities shown in Table 4.4, hence the questions in Worked Example 4.13 could be answered using Table 4.3.

Table 4.1. Table containing the given information for two events
Note: A, employee is male; B, employee owns a car

	Male A	Ā	Total
Car B	112		160
B̄			
Total	130		200

Table 4.2. Contingency table containing the completed information for two events
Note: A, employee is male; B, employee owns a car

	A	Ā	Total
B	112	$160 - 112 = 48$	160
B̄	$130 - 112 = 18$	$70 - 48 = 22$	$200 - 160 = 40$
Total	130	$200 - 130 = 70$	200

Table 4.3. Table containing the probabilities for two events
Note: A, employee is male; B, employee owns a car

	A	Ā	Total
B	$112/200 = 0.56$	$48/200 = 0.24$	$160/200 = 0.8$
B̄	$18/200 = 0.09$	$22/200 = 0.11$	$40/200 = 0.2$
Total	$130/200 = 0.65$	$70/200 = 0.35$	$200/200 = 1$

Table 4.4. Probabilities represented in a table

	A	Ā	Total
B	P (A and B)	P (Ā and B)	P(B)
B̄	P (A and B̄)	P (Ā and B̄)	P(B̄)
Total	P(A)	P(Ā)	1

Self-assessment questions 4.3

1. Describe, in words, the following events: A, A and B, A or B.
2. State the addition law for two events E and F.
3. When are two events said to be mutually exclusive?

Exercises 4.3

1. If $P(A) = 0.26$, $P(B) = 0.46$ and $P(A \text{ and } B) = 0.12$ find

   (a) $P(\bar{A})$ (b) $P(\bar{B})$ (c) $P(A \text{ or } B)$

2. A card is drawn at random from a pack of 52 playing cards.

   (a) Write down the following events in terms of the events A, B, C and D in Exercises 4.2, Question 2:
   (i) a black card is drawn
   (ii) the ace of spades is drawn

(iii) an ace or a red card is drawn

(iv) a red card or a spade is drawn.

(b) Find the probabilities of events (i)–(iv) in (a).

(c) Which of the following pairs of events are mutually exclusive

(i) A, B   (ii) A, C   (iii) A, D   (iv) B, C   (v) B, D   (vi) C, D

3. An estate agent has collected data on 250 house buyers: 123 purchased houses under £40,000 and 90 were first time buyers of whom 73 purchased houses under £40,000. Let A be the event that a buyer is a first time buyer and B be the event that a buyer purchases a house under £40,000. Write down the events below in terms of events A and B and determine the probabilities:

(a) (i) buyer is a first time buyer

(ii) buyer purchasing a house under £40,000

(b) (i) buyer is not a first time buyer

(ii) buyer purchasing a house for £40,000 or more

(c) buyer is a first time buyer purchasing a house under £40,000

(d) buyer is a first time buyer or is purchasing a house under £40,000.

4. Complete the following contingency table and determine $P(A)$, $P(B)$, $P(\bar{A})$, $P(\bar{B})$, $P(A \text{ and } B)$, $P(\bar{A} \text{ and } B)$, $P(A \text{ or } B)$ and $P(\bar{A} \text{ or } B)$.

	A	$\bar{A}$	Total
B	42		90
$\bar{B}$			
Total	70		150

5. For the estate agent's data in Question 3 draw up a contingency table using the information given. Use the table to draw another table containing the probabilities and answer parts (a)–(d) in Question 3 from the table.

6. Eighty applicants for a job were assessed as either good or poor for their oral and written communication skills. The resulting assessments are given in the contingency table below.

		Written		
		Good	Poor	Total
Oral	Good	17	21	38
	Poor	12	30	42
Total		29	51	80

From the contingency table find the probability that a given applicant has

(a) poor oral communication
(b) good written communication
(c) good oral and written communication
(d) poor oral but good written communication
(e) good oral or written communication.

4.4   Conditional probability

In many circumstances the probability of an event A occurring may be influenced by the information that another event B has already occurred. For example, the probability of rain today may be influenced by the fact that it rained yesterday, and interest rates may be influenced by a change in inflation rates. Thus when we find the probability of event A we need to take into account the probability of event B occurring.

This type of probability is called **conditional probability** and is denoted by

$$P(A \mid B)$$

The vertical bar indicates that we have been given the information that event B has occurred, and the probability is interpreted as the probability of event A given event B.

Worked example

4.16   Consider the data for Worked Example 4.13 in Table 4.2. If we know that an employee selected owns a car find the probability that the employee is male.

Solution   We need to find the probability that the employee selected is male given that we know they own a car, i.e. $P(A \mid B)$. We know the employee owns a car so this reduces the total number of employees we are interested in from

200 to 160. We also know that 112 of the car owners were male so, using the relative frequency method,

$$P(A \mid B) = \frac{112}{160} = 0.7$$

It can be shown that this probability can be determined as follows using the equivalent probabilities in Table 4.3,

$$P(A \mid B) = \frac{0.56}{0.80} = 0.7$$

Conditional probability can also be determined using the following equations.

KEY POINT

$$P(A \mid B) = \frac{P(A \text{ and } B)}{P(B)} \qquad [4.8]$$

$$P(B \mid A) = \frac{P(A \text{ and } B)}{P(A)} \qquad [4.9]$$

Worked example

4.17   In Worked Example 4.16 we found $P(A \mid B)$ using the relative frequency method. Use [4.8] to find the same probability.

Solution   From Table 4.3

$$P(A \text{ and } B) = 0.56, \quad P(B) = 0.80$$

Hence, using [4.8],

$$P(A \mid B) = \frac{0.56}{0.80} = 0.7$$

Multiplication law for probability

The **multiplication rule** is based on the definition of conditional probability and is used to find $P(A \text{ and } B)$. Rearranging equations [4.8] and [4.9] gives the following multiplication rule.

Multiplication rule

$$P(A \text{ and } B) = P(B) \times P(A \mid B) \qquad [4.10]$$

or

$$P(A \text{ and } B) = P(A) \times P(B \mid A) \qquad [4.11]$$

Worked example

4.18 An order of 200 items contains 12 that are defective. If two items are selected at random find the probability that both are defective.

Solution   Let

Event A = first item selected is defective
Event B = second item selected is defective

then, $P(A) = \frac{12}{200} = \frac{3}{50}$. When the second item is selected, there are only 199 items left and only 11 are defective, hence we are determining the conditional probability of B given that A has occurred.

$$P(B \mid A) = \frac{11}{199}$$

and, using [4.11],

$$P(A \text{ and } B) = P(A)P(B \mid A) = \frac{3}{50} \times \frac{11}{199} = \frac{33}{9,950}$$

This example assumes that the first item is not replaced before the second is selected, a process called **sampling without replacement.**

Independent events

Two events, A and B, are said to be **independent** if and only if

KEY POINT

$$P(A \mid B) = P(A) \tag{4.12}$$

or

KEY POINT

$$P(B \mid A) = P(B) \tag{4.13}$$

The events in Worked Example 4.16 are not independent as $P(A \mid B) = 0.7$ and $P(A) = 0.65$, hence $P(A \mid B) \neq P(A)$. These events are said to be **dependent.**

If the events A and B are independent the multiplication rule, equations [4.10] and [4.11], can be reduced to the following.

Multiplication rule for independent events

KEY POINT

$$P(A \text{ and } B) = P(A) \times P(B) \tag{4.14}$$

The multiplication rule can be used to show that two events are independent.

Worked example

4.19   A fair coin is tossed twice, let

> Event A = tail on the first toss
> Event B = head on the second toss

Show that events A and B are independent.

Solution   To show that A and B are independent we need to show that $P(A \text{ and } B) = P(A) \times P(B)$. The sample space $S = \{(H, H), (H, T), (T, H), (T, T)\}$, hence

> Event A = {(T, H), (T, T)}
> Event B = {(H, H), (T, H)}
> Event (A and B) = {(T, H)}

Therefore,

> $P(A) = 2/4 = 1/2$
> $P(B) = 2/4 = 1/2$
> $P(A \text{ and } B) = 1/4$

and

> $P(A) \times P(B) = (1/2) \times (1/2) = 1/4 = P(A \text{ and } B)$

Hence, events A and B are independent.

Self-assessment questions 4.4

1. State, in words, what is meant by conditional probability.
2. State the formula we can use to find $P(C \mid D)$.
3. When are two events P and Q said to be independent?
4. State the multiplication rule for two independent events, E and F.

Exercises 4.4

1. For parts (a) and (b) below calculate $P(A \mid B)$ and $P(B \mid A)$ and determine whether A and B are independent.

    (a) $P(A) = 0.45$, $P(B) = 0.32$, $P(A \text{ and } B) = 0.17$.
    (b) $P(A) = 0.8$, $P(B) = 0.3$, $P(A \text{ and } B) = 0.24$.

2. (a) If $P(A) = 0.2$, $P(B) = 0.4$ and $P(A \mid B) = 0.375$, find $P(A \text{ and } B)$.

(b) If $P(A) = 0.7$, $P(B) = 0.5$, and $P(B \mid A) = 0.5$, find $P(A$ and $B)$.

3. For the estate agent's data in Exercises 4.3, Question 3, find the following probabilities:

   (a) the buyer is a first time buyer given that he or she is purchasing a house under £40,000;
   (b) the buyer is purchasing a house £40,000 or more given that he or she is not a first time buyer.

4. For the applicant communication skills assessment given in Exercises 4.3, Question 6, find the probabilities that a given applicant has

   (a) good oral skills given that they have good written skills,
   (b) poor written skills given that they have good oral skills.

5. A bag contains four red and three black balls. If a ball is selected at random find the probability that it is a red ball. If a second ball is then drawn find the probability that both balls are red if

   (a) the first ball is replaced before drawing the second,
   (b) the first ball is not replaced before drawing the second.

6. A company has 60 people from a certain area on its mailing list, of which 25 are over 60 years old. What is the probability that if two people are selected at random from the list they are both over 60 years old.

7. Consider drawing two cards from a pack of 52 playing cards. Let

   Event A = the first card is a heart
   Event B = the second card is a red card

   Calculate $P(A$ and $B)$.

Test exercises

1. Describe when two events, A and B, are

   (a) mutually exclusive
   (b) independent.

2. A transport firm has to make a delivery to two towns, I then II. There are two routes, A and B, which the van driver can take from the factory to town I, three possible routes, C, D and E, from town I to town II and three routes, F, G and H, from town II back to the factory. Draw a tree diagram to show all the possible combinations of routes the van driver can take to make the deliveries and get back to the factory. Use the rule of counting to confirm the total number of

combinations. If the van driver is equally likely to pick any of the routes on each stage of the journey, find the probability that he chooses

(a) route A between the factory and town I
(b) route D between towns I and II
(c) routes F or H between town II and back to the factory
(d) routes B, D and F for the whole journey.

3. An insurance company divides its clients applying for car insurance into two age groups, 'under 27' and '27 and over'. In a particular year 84 of the 316 clients were under 27. After one year, 113 of the clients had made a claim on their insurance, of which 39 were under 27. Using the relative frequency method of assigning probabilities, find the probability that a randomly selected client

(a) is under 27
(b) has made a claim
(c) is under 27 and has made a claim
(d) is under 27 and has not made a claim
(e) is 27 or over or has not made a claim
(f) is under 27 given that they did not make a claim
(g) has made a claim given that they are 27 or over.

Are these events independent?

4. In a survey of 200 companies conducted over several years, 12 were no longer trading in 1993. 56 of the companies had made redundancies in 1991, of whom eight were no longer trading in 1993. Draw a contingency table of the information given. Use the table to draw a table of probabilities and find the probability that a given company:

(a) did not make redundancies in 1991
(b) is still trading in 1993
(c) is no longer trading given that they made redundancies in 1991
(d) is still trading given that they made redundancies in 1991.

5. A firm produces six reports, A, B, C, D, E and F, each year, of which one is selected for presentation. If all of the reports are equally likely to be selected each year, find the probability that

(a) report A will be selected
(b) report C will be selected in two successive years.

6. A company with 192 employees wants to survey employees on their views of the working conditions. If 22 of the employees have been working with the company for less than six months, find the probability that if two employees are selected at random for the survey,

(a) one has been working with the company for less than six months
(b) both have been working with the company for less than six months.

5 Discrete probability distributions

Objectives	When you have read this chapter you should be able to

- understand the basic ideas of discrete random variables and probability distributions
- recognize binomial and Poisson random variables
- find probabilities associated with binomial and Poisson random variables
- use a Poisson approximation to the binomial distribution

5.1 Random variables and probability distributions

In many situations it is important to be able to assign probabilities to all the possible outcomes of an experiment. For example, a double glazing company may want to calculate the probabilities that a salesman makes 0, 1, 2 or more sales in a single day.

Random variables

An experiment is usually represented by a capital letter, such as X, and the outcomes of the experiment by a lower case letter, x. X is called a **random variable** because the value it takes in a given experiment is a chance or random outcome. For example, in the above example the random variable, X, would be the number of sales in a single day for the salesman and it could take the values $x = 0, 1, 2, \ldots$.

There are two types of random variable:

1. When the outcomes of the experiment or the values of the random variable can only be a countable number of values, i.e. discrete outcomes, the random variable is called a **discrete random variable**.
2. When the random variable can take any value over a range of values it is called a **continuous random variable**. Continuous random variables are discussed in Chapter 6.

Worked example

5.1 The following are discrete random variables, identify the values the random variables can take:

1. the number of customers entering a shop during a day;
2. the shoe sizes of a sample of 100 females;
3. the number of positive answers to a survey question answered by 20 people;
4. the number of telephone calls to a company in a given hour.

Solution 1. There could be 0, 1, 2, 3, . . . customers entering the shop.
2. The shoe sizes could be 3, $3\frac{1}{2}$, 4, $4\frac{1}{2}$, . . .
3. The number of positive answers could be 0, 1, 2, . . . 19, 20.
4. The number of telephone calls could be 0, 1, 2, 3, . . .

Probability distributions

The **probability distribution** of a discrete random variable, X, gives the probabilities associated with all of the outcomes, x, of the random variable. These probabilities are written as $P(X = x)$ or just $P(x)$ and can be represented in a table, a bar chart or by a formula.

Example

5.2 Let X represent the number of sales per day for a double glazing salesman over 30 working days. The frequency distribution and corresponding probability distribution, calculated using the relative frequency method, is shown in Table 5.1. The probability distribution is represented in a bar chart in Figure 5.1.

Properties of a discrete random variable

There are three important properties associated with a discrete random variable X:

1. the probabilities associated with all the possible values of X lie between 0 and 1;
2. the sum of the probabilities, $P(x)$, equals 1;
3. to find the probability of several outcomes of X we add the probabilities, so the probability that X equals either 0 or 1 is $P(0) + P(1)$. For instance, in the salesman example given in Table 5.1,

Table 5.1. The frequency distribution and probability distribution for the number of sales for a double glazing salesman

Number of sales (x)	Frequency	Probability P(x)
0	12	0.400
1	15	0.500
2	2	0.067
3	1	0.033
Total	30	1.000

Figure 5.1. Bar chart representing the probability distribution for the number of sales for a double glazing salesman

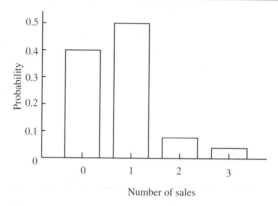

the probability that the salesman makes fewer than three sales is

$$P(X < 3) = P(0) + P(1) + P(2) = 0.4 + 0.5 + 0.067 = 0.967$$

There are several important types of discrete random variables but we will only discuss two of them; the binomial and Poisson random variables.

The mean and variance can be calculated for discrete random variables, but we will only consider the cases of the binomial and Poisson random variables. For random variables the mean is usually called the **expected value** of the random variable as it provides an indication of the outcome we would most likely expect to occur. It is not always calculated to be exactly one of the outcomes, but should be rounded to the nearest outcome. This is illustrated in Worked Example 5.6. The variance provides a measure of how the outcome that occurs may vary about the mean.

Self-assessment questions 5.1

1. Describe the two different types of random variable.
2. How can we represent the probability distribution of a discrete random variable?
3. What are the three properties associated with a discrete random variable?
4. What is another name for the mean of a random variable?

Exercises 5.1

1. Below are listed a series of experiments and associated random variables. State whether or not the random variable is discrete and identify the values that the discrete random variables can take.

Experiment	Random variable (X)
(a) Observing a production line	Number of defective items produced
(b) Health study of overweight employees	Number of kilograms of weight loss after a diet
(c) Telephone survey on television viewing ratings	Number of viewers of a Channel 4 programme
(d) Observing employees at work	Number of hours to complete a given task
(e) Planting 20 seeds	Number of seeds that germinate

2. Which of the following tables cannot represent probability distributions?

(a) x	$P(x)$	(b) x	$P(x)$	(c) x	$P(x)$
0	0.5	−10	1/3	5	0.6
1	0.2	0	1/3	6	0.3
2	0.3	10	1/3	7	−0.2
3	0.1			8	0.3

3. For the given probability distribution find the following probabilities.

   (a) $P(X = 22)$ (b) $P(X = 21 \text{ or } 22)$ (c) $P(X > 21)$

x	$P(x)$
20	0.16
21	0.28
22	0.34
23	0.19
24	0.03

5.2   The binomial distribution

Many types of experiment have only two outcomes, termed 'success' and 'failure', where success refers to the outcome of interest and failure refers to the other outcome. For example, in an investigation of the number of female applicants for a job, success is an applicant being female and failure is an applicant being male.

Other types of experiment can be categorized into only two outcomes, the outcomes of interest (success) and any other outcomes (failure). For example, if we are interested in a die landing with an even number face up, then the outcomes 2, 4 and 6 represent success and the outcomes 1, 3 and 5 represent failure.

These types of experiment can be classed as **binomial experiments** but they must possess the following properties:

1. there must be a fixed number, n, of identical repetitions of the experiment, called **trials**;
2. the trials must be independent, i.e. the outcome of one trial does not influence the outcome of another trial;
3. each trial can have only two outcomes, which will be called 'success' (S) and 'failure' (F);
4. the probability of success, $P(S)$, usually just written as p, is the same for each trial, thus the probability of failure is $P(F) = 1 - p$;
5. the experimenter is interested in the number of successes, represented by the random variable X, out of n trials.

Worked example

5.3   Based on past experience, the manager of an electrical superstore estimates that of the total number of customers making a purchase, 40% spend £200 or more. He is interested in determining the probability that two of the next four customers will spend £200 or more. Show that this experiment satisfies the properties of a binomial experiment.

Solution   1. The experiment considers the next four customers purchasing from the superstore, each customer can be considered to be a trial.
2. The purchase of each customer can be assumed to be independent.
3. Two outcomes are possible for each customer, they spend £200 or more (success) or they spend less than £200 (failure).
4. The probability that a customer spends £200 or more is the same for each customer.
5. The manager is interested in two of the next four customers spending £200 or more.

Hence, this experiment satisfies all the properties of a binomial experiment.

Calculating probabilities for binomial random variables

The number of successes, X, arising from a binomial experiment is called a **binomial random variable** and with the associated probabilities, $P(x)$, is called a **binomial distribution**. The probabilities for x successes in n trials of a binomial experiment can be computed using the following formula for the binomial distribution.

The binomial distribution

$$P(x) = \frac{n!}{x!(n-x)!}p^x(1-p)^{n-x} \qquad \text{for } x = 0, 1, 2, \ldots, n \qquad [5.1]$$

where p represents the probability of success, $1-p$ represents the probability of failure, n is the number of trials, x is the number of successes in n trials and $n! = n \times (n-1) \times (n-2) \times \cdots \times 3 \times 2 \times 1$.

Worked examples

5.4 For the electrical superstore problem, Worked Example 5.3, the manager is interested in determining the probability that two of the next four customers will spend £200 or more. Find this probability.

Solution The number of trials is the number of customers so $n = 4$, success is that the customer spends £200 or more, the probability of success $p = 0.40$ (40% spend over £200) and the random variable X is the number of customers spending £200 or more out of the next four customers. The manager is interested in two of the next four customers spending £200 or more, so applying [5.1] gives

$$P(X = 2) = P(2) = \frac{4!}{2!(4-2)!}0.40^2(1-0.40)^{4-2}$$

$$= (6)(0.16)(0.36)$$

$$= 0.3456$$

Hence, the probability of two of the next four customers spending £200 or more is 0.3456.

5.5 For the electrical superstore problem, Worked Examples 5.3 and 5.4, find the probability that

(a) two or more of the next four customers will spend £200 or more,
(b) less than two of the next four customers will spend £200 or more.

Solution (a) $P(X \geq 2) = P(2) + P(3) + P(4)$
and, using [5.1] and the solution to Worked Example 5.4,

$$P(X \geq 2) = 0.3456 + \frac{4!}{3!1!}0.40^3 0.60^1 + \frac{4!}{4!0!}0.40^4 0.60^0$$

$$= 0.3456 + 0.1536 + 0.0256$$

$$= 0.5248$$

Hence, the probability of two or more of the next four customers spending £200 or more is 0.5248.

(b) $P(X < 2) = P(0) + P(1)$

$$= \frac{4!}{0!4!}0.40^0 0.60^4 + \frac{4!}{1!3!}0.40^1 0.60^3$$

$$= 0.1296 + 0.3456$$

$$= 0.4752$$

or, because we know that the probabilities sum to 1 and using (a),

$$P(X < 2) = 1 - P(X \geq 2) = 1 - 0.5248 = 0.4752$$

$0! = 1$, $0.60^0 = 1$ and $0.40^0 = 1$ (Appendix A)

Hence, the probability that less than two of the next four customers spend £200 or more is 0.4752.

The mean and variance of a binomial random variable

The mean and variance of a binomial random variable can be calculated using the following equations. The mean of a binomial random variable X is given by

KEY POINT

$$\mu = np \qquad [5.2]$$

The variance of a binomial random variable X is given by

$$\sigma^2 = np(1 - p) \qquad [5.3]$$

where n is the number of trials and p is the probability of success. The mean is interpreted as the expected number of successes in n trials.

Worked example

5.6 For the electrical superstore problem, Worked Example 5.3, find the expected number (mean) of the next four customers who will spend £200 or more. Also find the variance.

Solution $n = 4$ and $p = 0.40$
Using [5.2],
mean $\mu = np = 4 \times 0.40 = 1.6$
It is expected that 1.6 of the next four customers will spend £200 or more. In practice, we would interpret this as two of the next four customers.
Using [5.3],
variance $\sigma^2 = 4 \times 0.4 \times 0.60 = 0.96$

Self-assessment questions 5.2

1. What properties must an experiment possess to be classed as a binomial experiment?
2. What do the probabilities represent for a binomial random variable?
3. State the formula used to calculate binomial probabilities?
4. Which formulae should be used to find the mean and variance of a binomial random variable?

Exercises 5.2

1. Eight per cent of items produced on a machine in the past have been defective. If ten of the items produced during a day are selected at random describe the conditions under which this could be taken as a binomial experiment.
2. For a binomial experiment with $n = 5$ and $p = 0.7$, find the probabilities of (a) three successes, (b) five successes, (c) no successes, (d) more than two successes, and (e) three or fewer successes.
3. For a binomial random variable X with $n = 50$ and $p = 0.03$, find the following probabilities:

   (a) $P(X = 0)$ (b) $P(X = 1)$ (c) $P(X < 2)$ (d) $P(X \geq 2)$

4. In Question 1, 8% of items produced on a machine in the past have been defective. If ten of the items produced during a day are selected at random find the probability that

   (a) none of the items are defective
   (b) exactly one of the items is defective
   (c) less than three of the items are defective
   (d) three or more of the items are defective.

   Calculate the expected number and variance of the items that will be defective.

5. For binomial distributions with the following n and p, calculate the mean and variance.

   (a) $n = 5$, $p = 0.7$ (b) $n = 50$, $p = 0.03$ (c) $n = 50$, $p = 0.97$

6. A company has discovered that in the past the probability that their graduate employees stay with the company for more than one year is 0.78. Find the probability that out of the next 15 new graduate employees at least 12 will stay with the company for more than one year.

5.3	The Poisson distribution

The **Poisson distribution** is useful when dealing with the number of occurrences of a particular event over a specified interval, where the interval can be time or space. A random variable must have the following properties to be classed as a Poisson random variable:

1. the probability of an occurrence of the event in any interval is the same as for any other interval of equal length;
2. the occurrence of the event in any interval is independent of the occurrence in any other interval.

The following random variables can possess these properties:

> The number of telephone calls arriving at a switchboard in a one hour period
> The number of faults in a length of plastic tubing
> The number of customers arriving at a cash desk in a shop
> The number of cars breaking down daily in a ten mile stretch of motorway

Calculating probabilities for Poisson random variables

The probabilities for a Poisson random variable, i.e. the probabilities of x occurrences of an event in a specified interval, can be calculated using the following formula for a Poisson distribution.

The Poisson distribution

KEY POINT

$$P(x) = \frac{\lambda^x \, e^{-\lambda}}{x!} \qquad \text{for } x = 0, 1, 2, \ldots, \infty \qquad [5.4]$$

e and $x!$ can be found on many calculators

where λ represents the average or expected number of occurrences of the event in the specified interval, e $= 2.71828$, x represents the number of occurrences of the event of interest and $x! = x(x-1) \times (x-2) \times \cdots \times 3 \times 2 \times 1$.

Note: the Poisson random variable has no limit on the number of occurrences.

Worked examples

5.7 On average, five phone calls arrive over a ten minute period to the switchboard of a factory. Find the probability that over a given ten minute period

(a) exactly five phone calls will arrive,
(b) between four and six phone calls will arrive.

Solution X is the number of phone calls arriving at the switchboard over a ten minute period. Assuming that the properties of a Poisson random variable are satisfied with λ equal to five phone calls over a ten minute period,

(a) $P(5) = \dfrac{5^5 \, e^{-5}}{5!} = 0.1755$

Hence, the probability of exactly five phone calls is 0.1755.

(b) $P(4 \leq X \leq 6) = P(4) + P(5) + P(6)$

$$= \frac{5^4 \, e^{-5}}{4!} + 0.1755 + \frac{5^6 \, e^{-5}}{6!}$$

$$= 0.1755 + 0.1755 + 0.1462$$

$$= 0.4972$$

Hence, the probability of between four and six phone calls arriving is 0.4972.

5.8   A company that prints fabrics has discovered that on average there is a flaw in the fabric every 20 m. The company buys the fabric in 60 m lengths and wants to find the probability that a 60 m length will have more than two flaws.

Solution X is the number of flaws in a 60 m length of fabric. Assuming that the properties of a Poisson random variable are satisfied, then if there is on average one flaw every 20 m, then on average there will be three flaws every 60 m, so λ is equal to three flaws in a 60 m length of fabric. Hence, the probability of more than two flaws in a 60 m length is

$$P(X \geq 2) = P(3) + P(4) + P(5) + P(6) + \cdots$$

$$= 1 - \{P(0) + P(1) + P(2)\}$$

$$= 1 - \left(\frac{3^0 \, e^{-3}}{0!} + \frac{3^1 \, e^{-3}}{1!} + \frac{3^2 \, e^{-3}}{2!} \right)$$

$$= 1 - (0.0498 + 0.1494 + 0.2240) = 0.5768$$

The mean and variance of a Poisson random variable

The mean and variance of a Poisson random variable can be calculated using the following formulae. The mean of a Poisson random variable X is given by

KEY POINT

$$\mu = \lambda = \text{the expected number of occurrences} \qquad [5.5]$$

The variance of a Poisson random variable X is given by

KEY POINT

$$\sigma^2 = \lambda \qquad\qquad\qquad\qquad [5.6]$$

Worked example

5.9   For the fabric printing company problem, Worked Example 5.8, find the expected number (mean) and variance of the number of flaws in a 60 m length of fabric.

Solution   On average there is one flaw every 20 m, so it is expected that there are three flaws every 60 m, hence μ is equal to three flaws every 60 m, with a variance, σ^2, of three flaws.

Self-assessment questions 5.3

1. What properties must a random variable possess to be classed as a Poisson random variable?
2. State the formula used to calculate Poisson probabilities.
3. Interpret the mean μ for a Poisson random variable.

Exercises 5.3

1. For a Poisson random variable X, with $\lambda = 7$, find the following probabilities

   (a) $P(X = 7)$ (b) $P(X = 6)$ (c) $P(5 < X < 9)$
   (d) $P(5 \leq X < 8)$ (e) $P(X < 5)$ (f) $P(X \geq 5)$

2. Customers arrive, on average, at a post office two every five minutes. Find the probability that during a given five minutes

   (a) no customers will arrive
   (b) exactly one customer will arrive
   (c) less than three customers will arrive
   (d) between one and three customers will arrive
   (e) more than three customers will arrive.

3. The number of admissions at a casualty department of a hospital during the night shift can be assumed to be a Poisson random variable with $\lambda = 20$. Find the probability that there will be between 18 and 21 admissions during a given night shift.
4. A large company estimates that on average one mistake is made each month in paying the salaries of their employees. Determine the probability that in a given month at least one mistake is made.

5.4   The Poisson approximation to the binomial distribution

In many situations it is difficult and tedious to calculate the binomial distribution because n, the number of trials, is large. The Poisson distribution can be used as an approximation to the binomial distribution if p, the probability of success, is small when n is large. The approximation will be accurate if $p \leq 0.05$ and $n \geq 20$.

To use this approximation, take the Poisson mean to be the binomial mean, i.e. $\lambda = np$, and work out probabilities using the Poisson distribution as before.

Worked example

5.10 A large consignment of a component contains 1% that are defective. Use the Poisson approximation to the binomial distribution to find the probability that among 300 components selected at random from the consignment fewer than three will be defective.

Solution Binomial: $n = 300$, $p = 0.01$, $np = 3$.
The Poisson approximation will be accurate as $p \leq 0.05$ and $n \geq 20$. X is the number of defective components among the 300 selected at random.
Using $\lambda = \mu = np = 3$

$$P(X < 3) = P(0) + P(1) + P(2)$$

$$= \frac{3^0\, e^{-3}}{0!} + \frac{3^1\, e^{-3}}{1!} + \frac{3^2\, e^{-3}}{2!}$$

$$= 0.0498 + 0.1494 + 0.2240$$

$$= 0.4232$$

Hence, the probability that there are fewer than three defective components in a consignment of 300 is 0.4232.

Self-assessment questions 5.4

1. Under what circumstances does the Poisson distribution give an accurate approximation to the binomial distribution?
2. What do we take the Poisson mean, μ, to be when approximating a binomial distribution?

Exercises 5.4

1. For a binomial random variable, X, with $n = 50$ and $p = 0.01$, use both the binomial distribution and the Poisson approximation to find $P(X < 2)$.

2. For a binomial random variable, X, with $n = 100$ and $p = 0.03$, use the Poisson approximation to determine the following probabilities:

(a) $P(X = 2)$ (b) $P(X = 0)$ (c) $P(X < 4)$ (d) $P(X \geq 2)$
(e) $P(2 \leq X \leq 4)$

3. It has been shown from records that the probability that a car breaks down on a certain stretch of motorway is 0.00024. Using the Poisson approximation to the binomial distribution find the probability that among the next 3000 cars using this stretch of motorway

(a) none will break down
(b) more than one will break down.

4. A coach operator estimates that 0.7% of its customers make a complaint. Find the probability that out of the next 500 customers there will be more than three complaints.

Test exercises

1. For a binomial random variable, X, with $n = 10$ and $p = 0.8$, find the following probabilities:

(a) $P(X = 8)$ (b) $P(X \geq 8)$ (c) $P(X < 7)$ (d) $P(7 < X < 10)$

Calculate the mean and variance.

2. A factory has eight machines all of which are equally likely to break down. It has been worked out that the probability that a machine will break down during a day is 0.1. Find the probability that none of the machines will break down on a given day. The factory cannot produce enough components if more than two of the machines break down in a given day, find the probability of this occurring.

3. For a Poisson random variable, X, with $\lambda = 5$, find the following probabilities:

(a) $P(X = 4)$ (b) $P(4 \leq X \leq 6)$ (c) $P(X < 7)$ (d) $P(X \geq 3)$

4. A typist makes, on average, two mistakes on a page. Find the probability that on a given page there are no more than three mistakes.

5. A bank operates a single queuing system for its three tills. From past experience, on average five customers join the queue every ten minutes during the lunchtime, 12:30 to 13:30. How many customers, on average, will join the queue during a given lunchtime? Find the probability that between 30 and 33 customers join the queue during a given lunchtime.

6. For a binomial random variable, X, with $n = 300$ and $p = 0.025$, use the Poisson approximation to the binomial distribution to find the probability that $X < 7$.

7. A firm is considering distributing leaflets advertising its products. It is estimated that 0.5% of leaflets will result in a sale. Find the probability that, out of 10000 leaflets distributed, between 48 and 50 sales result.

6 Continuous probability distributions

Objectives

When you have read this chapter you should be able to

• understand the basic ideas of continuous random variables

• recognize a normal distribution curve

• find probabilities associated with normal random variables

• use a normal approximation to the binomial distribution

6.1 Introduction to continuous random variables

A continuous random variable can take on any value over a range or interval of values, for example the time taken to complete a journey or the heights of a group of females.

We do not calculate probabilities for the random variable taking on specific values, instead we calculate probabilities for continuous random variables lying within a given range of values.

As for discrete random variables, probabilities associated with continuous random variables can often be represented by a formula; this is called a **probability density function** (p.d.f.) for a continuous random variable and is denoted by $f(x)$. This function can be plotted on a graph, where the probability density function $f(x)$ represents the height of the function for particular values of x. It does not, however, directly provide probabilities; the probability that the continuous random variable takes on values over a given interval is represented by the area under the graph of $f(x)$ over the given interval (Figure 6.1).

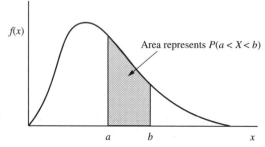

Figure 6.1. Probability for a continuous random variable

Examples of probability statements for continuous random variables are as follows. If X is a continuous random variable, then $P(20 < X < 30) =$ the probability that X lies between 20 and 30, $P(X < 10.5) =$ the probability that X is less than 10.5 and $P(X > 0.67) =$ the probability that X is greater than 0.67. $P(X = 26)$ is not a valid probability statement for a continuous random variable, but $P(25.5 < X < 26.5)$ could be used as an approximation. Thus, we do not use the $\geq$ and $\leq$ signs for continuous random variables.

Properties of a continuous random variable

The probability density function curve covers the entire range of probability and hence the area under the curve is equal to 1.

Self-assessment questions 6.1

1. Define a continuous random variable.
2. What is a probability density function?
3. How do we find probabilities for continuous random variables?
4. What is the total area under the probability density function curve?

6.2

The normal distribution

The most important continuous probability distribution is the **normal probability distribution**, and it can be applied to a wide variety of random variables such as the heights and weights of males of a similar age, the time to complete a task or the accuracy of a set of measurements.

In order to use the normal distribution the random variable should be continuous, but in certain situations it can be used as an approximation for a discrete random variable (see Section 6.5).

The probability density function that defines the normal distribution is given as follows and displays a symmetric bell-shaped curve when plotted (Figure 6.2):

KEY POINT

π and e can be found on most calculators, but this formula is rarely used in practice

$$ f(x) = \frac{1}{\sigma\sqrt{2\pi}} e^{-(x-\mu)^2/2\sigma^2} \qquad \text{for } -\infty < x < \infty \qquad [6.1] $$

where μ represents the mean, σ represents the standard deviation, $\pi = 3.14159$ and e $= 2.71828$.

Figure 6.2. Probability
density function for a
normal random variable

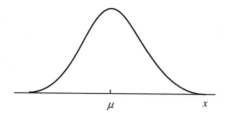

Properties of a normal random variable and its probability density function

There are several important properties of a normal random variable, X, and its probability density function.

1. The total area under the normal probability density function curve is equal to 1 (this is true for any continuous random variable).
2. The curve approaches the horizontal axis as the random variable, X, increases and decreases, but never actually touches it.
3. The highest point on the curve occurs at the mean, μ, which is also the median and mode.
4. The curve is symmetrical about the mean, μ, i.e. the area to the right of the mean is the same as the area to the left of the mean. This means that $P(X < \mu) = P(X > \mu) = 0.5$.
5. The position of the curve depends on the value of the mean, μ (Figure 6.3).
6. The shape of the curve depends on the value of the standard deviation, σ (Figure 6.4). A larger standard deviation results in a flatter, wider spread distribution.
7. Ninety per cent of the area under the normal curve lies between -1.64σ and 1.64σ; 95% of the area under the normal curve lies between -1.96σ and 1.96σ; 99% of the area under the normal curve lies between -2.58σ and 2.58σ.
8. Probabilities for normal random variables are given by areas under the normal curve (Figure 6.5). To find the area under a normal curve we use a special type of normal distribution called a **standard normal distribution** which is described in Section 6.3.

Figure 6.3. The position of
the normal curve

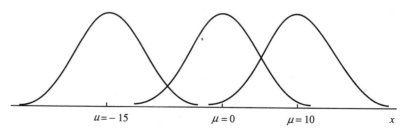

Figure 6.4. The shape of
the normal curve

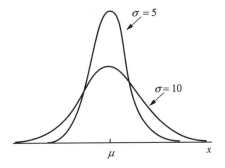

Figure 6.5. Probabilities
for a normal random
variable

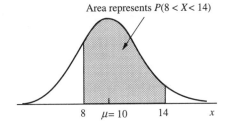

Self-assessment questions 6.2

1. What is the shape of the normal curve?
2. What determines the position and shape of a normal curve?
3. How do we find probabilities for a normal random variable?

Exercise 6.2

1. For each of the diagrams (i) and (ii) in Figure 6.6, which of the normal curves, A or B, has

   (a) the highest mean
   (b) the highest standard deviation.

Figure 6.6. Normal curves
for Exercise 6.2

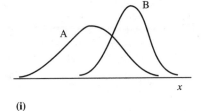

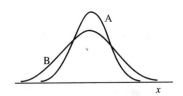

(i)   (ii)

6.3　The standard normal distribution

The **standard normal distribution** is a special case of a normal distribution, having a mean $\mu = 0$ and standard deviation $\sigma = 1$ (Figure 6.7). A standard normal random variable is usually denoted by Z as opposed to X for other normal random variables.

Figure 6.7. The standard normal curve

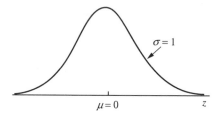

Finding probabilities associated with a standard normal random variable

As for any normal distribution, the area under the standard normal curve represents the probability. Because of its importance, tables of the areas under the standard normal curve have been constructed. An example of such a table has been presented in Appendix C.

Using the standard normal table for $P(Z < z)$

A portion of the standard normal table has been reproduced in Table 6.1. The four/five decimal place numbers in the table represent the area under the standard normal curve to the left of a value z. This is the probability that Z is less than the value z, $P(Z < z)$, shown by the shaded area in Figure 6.8. The value z must be a positive number rounded to two decimal places, where the first decimal place is given in the left-hand column and the second decimal place in the top row.

Table 6.1. Sample of the standard normal table giving areas under the standard normal curve

z	0.00	0.01	0.02	0.03	0.04	...
.						
.						
.						
1.3	0.9032	0.9049	0.9066	0.9082		
1.4	0.9192	0.9207	0.9222	0.9236		
1.5	0.9332	0.9345	0.9357	0.9370		
1.6	0.9452	0.9463	0.9474	0.9484		
.						
.						

Figure 6.8. Area given in the standard normal table

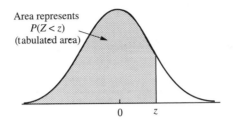

Area represents
$P(Z < z)$
(tabulated area)

Worked examples

6.1   Find $P(Z < 1.43)$ using the standard normal table.

Solution   Go down the left-hand column in Table 6.1 to the value 1.4, and across the top to the value 0.03. The number in the table, 0.9236, is the area under the standard normal curve to the left of 1.43, i.e. $P(Z < 1.43) = 0.9236$, as illustrated in Figure 6.9.

Figure 6.9. Area under a standard normal curve for $P(Z < 1.43)$

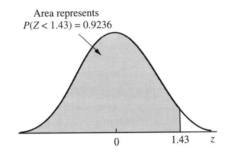

Area represents
$P(Z < 1.43) = 0.9236$

6.2   Find $P(Z < 0.387)$ using the standard normal table.

Solution   Rounding 0.387 to two decimal places gives 0.39. Using the table in Appendix C, $P(Z < 0.39) = 0.6517$.

The main table gives areas for values of z up to 2.99, for values up to 3.9 use the smaller table below the main table. For values greater than 3.9 the area to the left will be 1 to four decimal places, although it never exactly reaches 1.

Worked example

6.3   Find $P(Z < 3.4)$ using the standard normal table.

Solution   From the smaller table in Appendix C, $P(Z < 3.4) = 0.99966$.

Using the standard normal table for other probabilities

The tables can also be used to find other probabilities, or areas under the curve, such as $P(Z > z)$, $P(Z < -z)$ and $P(z_1 < Z < z_2)$.

$P(Z > z)$

For positive values of z, we can find greater than probabilities by considering the areas shown in Figure 6.10. The figure shows us that the following equation can be used,

KEY POINT

$$P(Z > z) = 1 - P(Z < z) \qquad [6.2]$$

where $P(Z < z)$ can be found from the standard normal table.

Worked example

6.4   Find $P(Z > 0.387)$.

Solution   Using [6.2],

$$P(Z > 0.387) = 1 - P(Z < 0.387) = 1 - P(Z < 0.39) = 1 - 0.6517$$
$$= 0.3483$$

$P(Z > -z)$ **and** $P(Z < -z)$

For values of z less than 0, we need to firstly convert them to positive values. To find $P(Z > -z)$ consider the areas shown in Figure 6.11. The figure shows us that the areas $P(Z > -z)$ and $P(Z < z)$ are the same, hence we can use

KEY POINT

$$P(Z > -z) = P(Z < z) \qquad [6.3]$$

and $P(Z < z)$ can be found from the standard normal table. To find $P(Z < -z)$ consider the areas shown in Figure 6.12. The figure shows us that the areas $P(Z < -z)$ and $P(Z > z)$ are the same, hence we can use

KEY POINT

$$P(Z < -z) = P(Z > z) = 1 - P(Z < z) \qquad [6.4]$$

and $P(Z < z)$ can be found from the standard normal table.

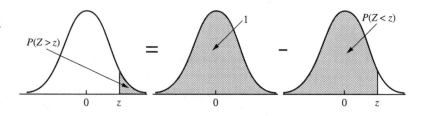

Figure 6.10. Area under a standard normal curve for $P(Z > z)$

Figure 6.11. Area under a standard normal curve for $P(Z > -z)$

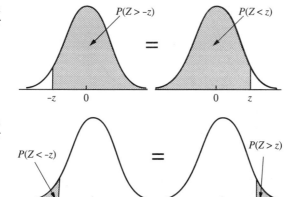

Figure 6.12. Area under a standard normal curve for $P(Z < -z)$

Worked example

6.5 Find the following probabilities:
(a) $P(Z > -1.63)$,
(b) $P(Z < -2.09)$.

Solution (a) Using [6.3] and Figure 6.13,
$P(Z > -1.63) = P(Z < 1.63) = 0.9484$ from the standard normal table.

(b) Using [6.4],
$P(Z < -2.09) = P(Z > 2.09) = 1 - P(Z < 2.09)$
$= 1 - 0.9817$ from the standard normal table
$= 0.0183$

$P(z_1 < Z < z_2)$

To find the probability that Z lies between two values z_1 and z_2, consider the areas in Figure 6.14. The figure shows us that the area between z_1 and z_2 is the same as the difference between the areas $Z < z_2$ and $Z < z_1$,

Figure 6.13. Area under a standard normal curve, see Worked Example 6.5(a)

Figure 6.14. Area under a standard normal curve for $P(z_1 < Z < z_2)$

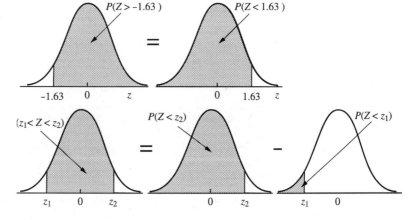

Figure 6.15. Area under a standard normal curve, see Worked Example 6.5(a)

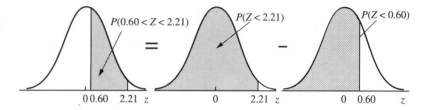

hence

$$P(z_1 < Z < z_2) = P(Z < z_2) - P(Z < z_1) \qquad [6.5]$$

and the probabilities on the right-hand side of this equation can be found as before.

Worked example

6.6   Find the following probabilities:

(a) $P(0.60 < Z < 2.21)$,
(b) $P(-1.44 < Z < 0.96)$.

Solution   (a) Using [6.5] and Figure 6.15,

$$P(0.60 < Z < 2.21) = P(Z < 2.21) - P(Z < 0.60)$$
$$= 0.9864 - 0.7257$$
$$= 0.2607$$

(b) Using [6.5],

$$P(-1.44 < Z < 0.96) = P(Z < 0.96) - P(Z < -1.44)$$
$$= P(Z < 0.96) - P(Z > 1.44) \qquad \text{using [6.4]}$$
$$= P(Z < 0.96) - \{1 - P(Z < 1.44)\}$$
$$= 0.8315 - (1 - 0.9251)$$
$$= 0.8315 - 0.0749$$
$$= 0.7566$$

Self-assessment questions 6.3

1. What are the mean and standard deviation for a standard normal random variable?
2. What letter is used to denote a standard normal random variable?
3. What probability can we look up directly from the standard normal tables?

Exercises 6.3

1. Find the following probabilities, using the standard normal table, and sketch the corresponding area.

   (a) $P(Z < 2.52)$ (b) $P(Z < 1.80)$ (c) $P(Z < 0.923)$ (d) $P(Z < 0)$
   (e) $P(Z < 2.99)$ (f) $P(Z < 3.7)$ (g) $P(Z < 3.1)$

2. Find the following probabilities and sketch the corresponding areas.

   (a) $P(Z > 1.88)$ (b) $P(Z > 0.846)$ (c) $P(Z > 3.1)$
   (d) $P(Z > 2.06)$ (e) $P(Z > 0)$

3. Find the following probabilities and sketch the corresponding areas.

   (a) $P(Z > -0.88)$ (b) $P(Z < -1.54)$ (c) $P(Z > -2.92)$
   (d) $P(Z < -0.07)$

4. Find the following probabilities and sketch the corresponding areas.

   (a) $P(1.16 < Z < 1.89)$ (b) $P(-2.00 < Z < 2.00)$
   (c) $P(-1.99 < Z < -0.06)$

5. Find the following probabilities.

   (a) $P(Z > 2.24)$ (b) $P(-0.9 < Z < 0.9)$ (c) $P(Z < -1.99)$
   (d) $P(Z > -3)$ (e) $P(0 < Z < 1)$

6.4   Determining probabilities for any normal distribution

We can find probabilities for any normal distribution that has a mean μ and standard deviation σ by converting the distribution to a standard normal distribution.

If X is a normal random variable with mean μ and standard deviation σ, and Z is a standard normal random variable with mean 0 and standard deviation 1, then the following equation can be used to convert X to Z, i.e. we subtract the mean from X and divide by the standard deviation.

KEY POINT

$$Z = \frac{X - \mu}{\sigma} \qquad [6.6]$$

Hence, if we wish to find $P(X < x)$ we use the following equation [6.7]. This is illustrated in Figure 6.16.

Figure 6.16. Converting to a standard normal distribution

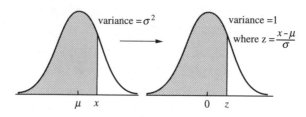

$$P(X < x) = P\left(\frac{X - \mu}{\sigma} < \frac{x - \mu}{\sigma}\right) = P\left(Z < \frac{x - \mu}{\sigma}\right) \qquad [6.7]$$

KEY POINT

The standard normal tables can then be used to find $P(Z < (x - \mu)/\sigma)$.

Worked examples

6.7   If X is a normal random variable with mean 25 and standard deviation 10, find the following probabilities: (a) $P(X < 40)$, (b) $P(X > 20)$, (c) $P(15 < X < 35)$.

Solution   Using [6.7] with $\mu = 25$ and $\sigma = 10$:

(a) $P(X < 40) = P\left(Z < \dfrac{40 - 25}{10}\right) = P(Z < 1.5) = 0.9332$

(b) $P(X > 20) = P\left(Z > \dfrac{20 - 25}{10}\right) = P(Z > -0.5) = P(Z < 0.5)$

$\qquad = 0.6915$

(c) $P(15 < X < 35) = P\left(\dfrac{15 - 25}{10} < Z < \dfrac{35 - 25}{10}\right) = P(-1 < Z < 1)$

$\qquad = P(Z < 1) - P(Z < -1)$

$\qquad = P(Z < 1) - \{1 - P(Z < 1)\}$

$\qquad = 0.8413 - (1 - 0.8413) = 0.6826$

6.8   A company that manufactures a component for a machine claims that the lifetime of the component is normally distributed with an average lifetime of 30 hours and a standard deviation of four hours. Find the probability that any component selected will last

(a) less than 40 hours
(b) less than 25 hours
(c) more than 37 hours
(d) between 26 and 32 hours.

The company guarantees to replace any components that do not last more than 20 hours. Find the probability that a component will have to be replaced under guarantee.

Solution Let X, a normal random variable, represent the lifetimes of the components, with mean $\mu = 30$ hours and standard deviation $\sigma = 4$ hours.

(a) $P(X < 40) = P\left(Z < \dfrac{40 - 30}{4}\right) = P(Z < 2.5) = 0.99379$

(b) $P(X < 25) = P\left(Z < \dfrac{25 - 30}{4}\right) = P(Z < -1.25) = P(Z > 1.25)$

$$= 1 - P(Z < 1.25) = 1 - 0.8944 = 0.1056$$

(c) $P(X > 37) = P\left(Z > \dfrac{37 - 30}{4}\right) = P(Z > 1.75) = 1 - P(Z < 1.75)$

$$= 1 - 0.9599 = 0.0401$$

(d) $P(26 < X < 32) = P\left(\dfrac{26 - 30}{4} < Z < \dfrac{32 - 30}{4}\right)$

$$= P(-1 < Z < 0.5)$$
$$= P(Z < 0.5) - P(Z < -1)$$
$$= P(Z < 0.5) - \{1 - P(Z < 1)\}$$
$$= 0.6915 - (1 - 0.8413) = 0.6915 - 0.1587$$
$$= 0.5328$$

Guarantee period is up to 20 hours, therefore we need to find $P(X < 20)$:

$$P(X < 20) = P\left(Z < \dfrac{20 - 30}{4}\right) = P(Z < -2.5) = 1 - P(Z < 2.5)$$

$$= 1 - 0.99379 = 0.00621$$

Self-assessment question 6.4

What is the relationship between Z, a standard normal random variable, and X, a normal random variable with mean μ and standard deviation σ?

Exercises 6.4

1. If X is a normal random variable with mean $\mu = 70$ and standard deviation $\sigma = 8$, find the following probabilities.

(a) $P(X < 75)$ (b) $P(X < 95)$ (c) $P(X > 95)$ (d) $P(X < 60)$
(e) $P(X > 50)$ (f) $P(60 < X < 80)$ (g) $P(55 < X < 65)$

2. An office manager has observed that the time it takes her staff to complete a particular task is normally distributed, with an

average time of 50 minutes and a standard deviation of seven minutes. What is the probability that a member of staff will take

(a) longer than one hour
(b) less than 30 minutes
(c) between 50 and 60 minutes?

3. A garage offers a guarantee period of one year on a car part. The lifetime of the part is normally distributed with an average of 2.2 years and standard deviation of six months. What is the probability that a part will fail in the guarantee period?

6.5   The normal approximation to the binomial distribution

As discussed previously in Section 5.4, the binomial distribution is difficult to calculate for large values of n. In that section we used the Poisson approximation for small values of p when n is large. The normal approximation can be used for values of p close to 0.5 when n is large. The approximation works well when both $np > 5$ and $n(1 - p) > 5$. To use this approximation, take the normal mean μ to be the binomial mean, np, and the normal variance σ^2 to be the binomial variance, $np(1 - p)$. We are approximating a discrete distribution with a continuous distribution so we need to make an adjustment called a **continuity correction**. To find the binomial probability $P(X = x)$, we use the normal probability $P(x - 0.5 < X < x + 0.5)$, hence the continuity correction is -0.5 and 0.5.

Worked example

6.9   If X is a binomial random variable with $n = 20$ and $p = 0.47$, find the following probabilities:

(a) $P(X < 9)$
(b) $P(X \geq 12)$.

Solution   A normal approximation would be appropriate (p is close to 0.5, $np = 9.4$ and $n(1 - p) = 10.6$, both greater than 5)

$$\mu = np = 9.4 \qquad \sigma^2 = np(1 - p) = 4.982 \qquad \sigma = 2.232$$

(a) Using the binomial distribution we would need to calculate

$$P(X < 9) = P(X \leq 8) = P(X = 0) + P(X = 1) + P(X = 2) + \cdots + P(X = 8)$$

With the continuity correction we need to find
$P(X < (8 + 0.5)) = P(X < 8.5)$ for the normal approximation.

$$P(X < 8.5) = P\left(Z < \frac{8.5 - 9.4}{2.232}\right) = P(Z < -0.403) = 1 - P(Z < 0.403)$$

$$= 0.3446$$

(b) Using the binomial distribution we would need to calculate

$$P(X \geq 12) = P(X = 12) + P(X = 13) + P(X = 14) +$$

$$\cdots + P(X = 20)$$

With the continuity correction we need to find $P(X > 12 - 0.5) = P(X > 11.5)$ for the normal approximation.

$$P(X > 11.5) = P\left(Z > \frac{11.5 - 9.4}{2.232}\right) = P(Z > 0.941)$$

$$= 1 - P(Z < 0.941) = 0.1736$$

Self-assessment question 6.5

When is it appropriate to use a normal approximation to the binomial distribution?

Exercises 6.5

1. If X is a binomial random variable with $p = 0.30$, would a normal approximation be appropriate if (a) $n = 15$, (b) $n = 25$?
2. If X is a binomial random variable with $n = 30$ and $p = 0.52$, find, using a normal approximation, (a) $P(X \leq 16)$, (b) $P(X > 22)$ and (c) $P(10 \leq X \leq 20)$.
3. A particular brand of a product has 45% of the total sales of the product. If 200 people are surveyed about the brand they use, what is the probability that less than half of them use this particular brand.

Test exercises

1. If Z is a standard normal random variable, find the following probabilities

   (a) $P(Z > 0)$ (b) $P(Z < 1.96)$ (c) $P(Z > 0.84)$ (d) $P(Z < -2.833)$
   (e) $P(Z > -3.4)$ (f) $P(Z > 3)$ (g) $P(0.267 < Z < 2.43)$
   (h) $P(-2.1 < Z < 2.1)$ (i) $P(-0.5 < Z < 1.5)$
   (j) $P(-2.1 < Z < -0.99)$

2. If X is a normal random variable with mean $\mu = 15$ and standard deviation $\sigma = 3$, find the following probabilities.

(a) $P(X < 20)$ (b) $P(X < 10)$ (c) $P(X > 18)$ (d) $P(X > 16.5)$
(e) $P(X > 13)$ (f) $P(12 < X < 18)$ (g) $P(10 < X < 15)$
(h) $P(11 < X < 14)$

3. The research department of an automobile association has test driven used cars and has found that the number of miles per gallon for used cars of a particular make, age and engine size is approximately normally distributed with a mean of 35 and a standard deviation of 2.1. Find the probability that the number of miles per gallon for a given car will be (a) more than 40, (b) more than 33, (c) less than 35, (d) between 30 and 40.

4. Certain manufactured items are sold in boxes which are stated to contain a weight of at least 750 g. The actual weight in a box varies, being approximately normally distributed with mean 765 g and standard deviation 10 g. Calculate the probability that a box selected will have below the stated 750 g weight.

5. When is the normal distribution a good approximation to the binomial?

6. If X is a binomial random variable with $n = 30$ and $p = 0.55$, find the following probabilities using a normal approximation to the binomial.

(a) $P(X < 16)$ (b) $P(X > 20)$ (c) $P(11 < X < 23)$ (d) $P(10 < X < 15)$

7. Thirty per cent of delegates who attend courses at a computer company are female. What is the probability that out of 100 delegates on a particular course:

(a) more than 40 are female
(b) fewer than 25 are female
(c) between 22 and 35 are female.

7 Sampling and sampling distributions

Objectives

When you have read this chapter you should be able to

- select a simple random sample from a population

- calculate a point estimate of the mean and standard deviation of a population using a sample

- understand the concept of a sampling distribution

- define the sampling distribution of the sample means

There are two main ways of gathering data – by experiments and by surveys. An experiment is used when the actions of the population can be controlled, for example when recording how long a hair dryer lasts under test conditions. A survey is used when it is not possible to control the population, for example when trying to estimate the potential demand for a new product.

It is often not practical to survey all the items in a population (it is usually too expensive and time consuming to survey the whole population). Instead, a smaller group called a **sample** is used to make decisions about characteristics of the population. For example, a market research company wishes to investigate how many people would buy a new product. It is not possible for them to interview the entire population. Instead they would interview a sample. It is important that the sample is truly representative of the population. If not, then the conclusions drawn from the sample may be very misleading. For example, if the sample contained mostly males and the product is more likely to be purchased by females, then there could be a large underestimate of potential demand.

7.1 Collecting data using a simple random sample

There are many methods of collecting a sample of data. All of these methods aim to ensure that the sample is representative of the population. One of the most commonly used methods is the **simple random sample** (SRS). In a simple random sample taken from a large population, the items are selected independently such that every item in the population has an equal chance of being included in the sample. Random number tables (Appendix D) can be used to randomly select the sample. The method is illustrated in the following example.

Example

7.1 A shoe machinery manufacturer is conducting an inventory of the production costs of all items sold by the Made To Order (MTO) department over the last 20 years. During this time, hundreds of thousands of items have been made to order and sold. For the purposes of demonstrating how a simple random sample is selected, it is not practical to look at all of these items. Instead, the production costs of the 87 items sold by the MTO department over the last month will be considered. This data is given below.

1239.50	84.50	54.86	1898.43	10.49	14.70	52.36
8.42	208.64	9.33	57.52	153.67	194.23	1124.25
751.01	12.69	3.45	17.25	78.52	96.76	74.31
111.34	45.79	55.71	203.96	1982.47	450.03	678.99
78.91	236.57	659.57	22.39	457.29	22.29	25.19
2658.68	3329.28	15.98	17.62	258.31	576.34	23.27
256.29	235.46	5.46	845.65	43.21	6546.54	135.21
6.54	65.13	2654.65	35.18	798.76	54.32	1895.43
213.21	574.68	7.46	87.96	5423.13	206.57	49.87
4651.20	10.03	56.12	654.32	100.05	61.65	10.56
746.87	684.35	1210.23	41.98	7968.45	1320.54	987.46
54.13	210.00	254.66	513.20	100.21	65.87	49.51
321.21	54.94	56.32				

Choosing the arbitrary starting point can be done by closing your eyes and putting your finger on the page

Suppose the manufacturer wishes to estimate the average cost price of the items sold in the last month using a random sample of 30 production costs. The first step in selecting an SRS is to pick an arbitrary point in the random number table, e.g. the second number on the tenth row. The tenth and eleventh rows of the random number tables (Appendix D) are

56 14 80 10 76 52 38 54 84 13 99 90 22 55 41 04 72 37 89 33
29 56 62 74 12 67 09 35 89 33 04 28 44 75 01 57 87 45 52 21

These random numbers correspond to the items to be selected for the sample. If the item does not exist, the number is ignored. In the shoe manufacturers example there are 87 production costs, so any random numbers greater than 87 are ignored. If a random number is repeated it is also ignored. Reading the production costs across the rows, Table 7.1 shows the random number and the corresponding item selected in the sample.

Since the arbitrary starting point was the second number on the tenth row, the cost price relating to the first random number (56) is ignored. The next 30 numbers form the random sample (Table 7.2). The manufacturer can then use this sample to estimate the mean of all production costs of items sold in the last month.

Table 7.1. Table of items
selected in a simple
random sample of
production costs (£) in the
made to order department
of a shoe machinery
manufacturer in the last
month

Random number	Cost price (£)	Random number	Cost price (£)
14	1124.25	29	78.91
80	254.66	56	*
10	9.33	62	206.57
76	1320.54	74	41.98
52	2654.65	12	153.67
38	15.98	67	654.32
54	798.76	09	208.64
84	49.51	35	25.19
13	194.23	89	–
99	–	33	*
90	–	04	*
22	111.34	28	678.99
55	54.32	44	235.46
41	576.34	75	7968.45
04	1898.43	01	1239.50
72	684.35	57	213.21
37	3329.28	87	56.32
89	–	45	5.46
33	457.29	52	*

Notes: – random number is greater than 87; * random number is repeated.

Table 7.2. Random
sample of 30 production
costs for the shoe
machinery manufacturer
data

1124.25	254.66	9.33	1320.54	2654.65	15.98	798.76
49.51	194.23	111.34	54.32	576.34	1898.43	684.35
3329.28	457.29	78.91	206.57	41.98	153.67	654.32
208.64	25.19	678.99	235.46	7968.45	1239.50	213.21
56.32	5.46					

Self-assessment questions 7.1

1. Why are samples of data used to describe a population?
2. Describe the method by which an SRS of data is selected from a population.

Exercise 7.1

Suppose an arbitrary starting point in the random number tables (Appendix D) has been selected to be the seventh number on the third row. Using this starting point, select an SRS of 30 items from the shoe machinery manufacturer data given in Example 7.1.

7.2   Point estimates

A sample is used to estimate some characteristic of the population known as a **population parameter**. A **point estimate** is a number representing an estimate of the population parameter based on a sample. For example, the sample mean, $\bar{x}$, is a point estimate of the population mean, μ. The sample standard deviation, s, is a point estimate of the population standard deviation, σ.

Worked example

7.1 Find a point estimate of the mean, variance and standard deviation of the production costs for the shoe machinery manufacturer data using the SRS of 30 items in Example 7.1.

Solution First calculate a data summary:

$$n = 30 \qquad \Sigma x_i = 25\,299.93 \qquad \Sigma x_i^2 = 92\,655\,684.01$$

Equation [3.2] is used to calculate the point estimate of the mean

A point estimate of the mean of the production costs is

$$\bar{x} = \frac{25\,299.93}{30} = £843.33$$

A point estimate of the variance of the production costs is

Equation [3.9] is used to calculate the point estimate of the variance

$$s^2 = \frac{92\,655\,684.01 - (30 \times 843.33^2)}{29} = £^2 2\,459\,293.77$$

A point estimate of the standard deviation of the production costs is

$$s = \sqrt{2\,459\,293.77} = £1568.21$$

Self-assessment questions 7.2

1. What is a point estimate?
2. What is used as a point estimate of the population mean, μ?
3. What is used as a point estimate of the population standard deviation, σ?

Exercise 7.2

For the SRS found in Exercise 7.1 calculate
(a) a point estimate of the population mean μ
(b) a point estimate of the population variance σ^2
(c) a point estimate of the population standard deviation σ.

7.3   Introduction to the sampling distribution of the sample means $\bar{X}$

When a sample is taken from a population it can be used to find point estimates of population parameters, e.g. the population mean. If another

Figure 7.1. A histogram showing the relative frequency distribution of the sample mean production costs prices of items sold in the made to order department of a shoe machinery manufacturer

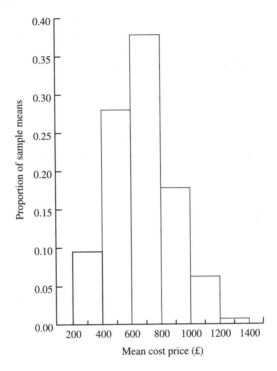

sample of the same size is taken from the population, then it too can be used to calculate a point estimate of the mean. The items selected in these samples are extremely unlikely to be exactly the same. The point estimates found in Exercise 7.2 are very unlikely to be exactly the same as the ones found in Worked Example 7.1. If many samples of the same size are taken from a population and a point estimate of the population mean is calculated for each, then we will have a set of estimates for which a frequency distribution can be determined. If we take all possible samples, the resulting frequency distribution is called the **sampling distribution of the sample means** $\bar{X}$. This concept is illustrated using Example 7.2 below.

The sampling distribution of the sample means has properties which are very useful in statistics (refer to Chapters 8 and 9). The remainder of this chapter discusses the mean, standard deviation and form of the sampling distribution of the sample means.

Example

7.2   Consider the production costs of the items sold in the MTO department of the shoe machinery manufacturer given in Example 7.1. The manufacturer wishes to investigate the average production costs of all of the items sold in the MTO department in the last 20 years. He employs a statistical consultant to take 600 SRSs, each of 30 production costs from the items sold in the last 20 years. Appendix E gives the sample means calculated for each of these 600 samples. The relative frequency distribution of the sample means is represented in a histogram (Figure 7.1). If all possible samples of the same size are taken from the items sold in the last 20 years, the frequency distribution of the sample means is known as the **sampling distribution of the sample means**.

7.4   The mean of the sampling distribution of the sample means $\bar{X}$

When we calculate the mean of all possible sample means we would expect it to be equal to the population mean, μ. Calculating the mean of several sample means will be a more accurate estimate than any one sample mean.

Worked example

7.2   Find the mean of the sample means for the 600 SRSs given in Appendix E.

Solution   The summary data is given in Appendix E. Six hundred samples were taken ($n = 600$) and the sum of the sample means $\Sigma \bar{x}_i = 400\,473$. Therefore, the mean of the sample means is $400\,473/600 = £667.45$.

7.5   The standard error of the sampling distribution of the sample means $\bar{X}$

The **standard error of the sample means**, $\sigma_{\bar{X}}$, is the standard deviation of the sampling distribution of the sample means $\bar{X}$. If the size of the samples is relatively small compared with the size of the population (less than 5% of the items in a population are selected in a sample), then the standard error of the mean is calculated using the following equation.

N.B

if 'STEM   less than 5% of the items is a popu

KEY POINT

| Standard error of the sample means | $\sigma_{\bar{X}} = \dfrac{\sigma}{\sqrt{n}}$ | [7.1] |

where σ represents the standard deviation of the population, n represents the size of the sample and $\sigma_{\bar{X}}$ represents the standard error of the sample means. If the population standard deviation is not known, the standard error of the sample means can be estimated using a point estimate of the standard deviation of the population, s.

Estimated standard error of the sample means $s_{\bar{X}} = \dfrac{s}{\sqrt{n}}$ [7.2]

where s represents the standard deviation of the sample, n represents the size of the sample and $s_{\bar{X}}$ represents the estimated standard error of the sample means. Note: as the sample size increases, the standard error of the sample means will decrease, thus providing a more accurate estimate of the population mean.

In practice only one SRS would be used to estimate the standard error of the sample means (it would be too expensive and time consuming to take many SRSs).

Worked examples

7.3   Find the estimated standard error of the sample means for the shoe machinery manufacturer data using the 600 SRSs given in Appendix E.

Solution   The standard error of the sample means is the standard deviation of the sampling distribution of the sample means. This standard error can be estimated using the standard deviation of the 600 sample means. The standard deviation of the 600 sample means is £204.52. Therefore,

$$s_{\bar{X}} = £204.52$$

7.4   Use the SRS given in Example 7.1 to estimate the standard error of the sample means.

Solution   In Worked Example 7.1 we found that a point estimate of the standard deviation of the production costs is $s = £1568.21$. This is based on a sample of 30 production costs so $n = 30$. An estimate of the standard error of the sample means using [7.2] is

$$s_{\bar{X}} = \frac{1568.21}{\sqrt{30}} = £286.31$$

7.5   A population is known to have a standard deviation of 25. A sample of ten items are taken from this population. Calculate the standard error of the sample means.

Solution   The population standard deviation $\sigma = 25$ and the sample size $n = 10$. Using [7.1], the standard error of the sample means is

$$\sigma_{\bar{X}} = \frac{25}{\sqrt{10}} = 7.91$$

7.6   A sample of size 17 is taken from a large population. The sample has a mean of 168.3 and a standard deviation of 58.9. Calculate a point estimate of the standard error of the sample means.

Solution   The point estimate of the population standard deviation $s = 58.9$ and the sample size $n = 17$. Using [7.2], the estimated standard error of the sample means is

$$s_{\bar{X}} = \frac{58.9}{\sqrt{17}} = 14.29$$

Exercises 7.5

1. A population has a standard deviation of 126.94. A sample of 25 items are taken from this population. Calculate the standard error of the sample means.
2. A sample of 40 items is taken from a population of 1 000 000 items. The sample has mean 5371.03 and standard deviation 374.64. Calculate a point estimate of the standard error of the sample means.

7.6   The t distribution

A *t* **distribution** is one of a family of distributions that look very similar to a normal distribution. All *t* distributions have the same bell shaped, symmetric appearance but the tails are slightly thicker than a corresponding normal distribution (Figure 7.2), i.e. more of a *t* distribution falls within the tails covering the very small and very large values.

The exact shape of a *t* distribution depends on a number known as the **degrees of freedom**. A *t* distribution with a low number of degrees of

Figure 7.2. Comparison of the standard normal distribution and a *t* distribution

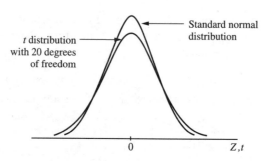

Figure 7.3. Comparison of *t* distributions for various degrees of freedom

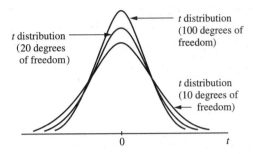

Figure 7.4. Areas in the upper tail for a *t* distribution

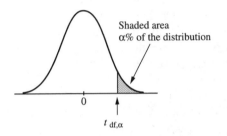

freedom has a thicker tail than a *t* distribution with a higher number of degrees of freedom (Figure 7.3). Probabilities associated with areas under the *t* distribution curve are obtained using a table (Appendix F). This table gives the value of *t* such that the area under the curve greater than *t* is a given value α (Figure 7.4). Only certain values of α are given in the table. The notation $t_{df,\alpha}$ is used for the *t* distribution where df denotes the value of the degrees of freedom and α denotes the area greater than *t*. Part of the *t* distribution table is given below.

Degrees of freedom	Area in upper tail				
	0.10	0.05	0.025	0.01	0.005
10	1.372	1.812	2.228	2.764	3.169
11	1.363	1.796	2.201	2.718	3.106
12	1.356	1.782	2.179	2.681	3.055
13	1.350	1.771	2.160	2.650	3.012
14	1.345	1.761	2.145	2.624	2.977

For example, to use the table to find the value of $t_{13,0.025}$, first find the value of the degrees of freedom in the first column, i.e. find the row corresponding to 13 degrees of freedom, and then find the column which corresponds to 0.025 in the upper tail, i.e. the fourth column in the table. $t_{13,0.025}$ is the value corresponding to the intersection of the thirteenth row and the fourth column, i.e.

$$t_{13,0.025} = 2.160,$$

i.e.

$$P(t > 2.160) = 0.025$$

Since the t distribution is symmetric around 0, the values in the lower tail are the negative of the values given in the table. For example, $P(t < -2.160) = 0.025$.

Worked examples

7.7   Find the following values: (a) $t_{4,0.1}$, (b) $t_{10,0.025}$, (c) $t_{26,0.005}$, (d) $t_{50,0.01}$.

Solution   (a) From the table given in Appendix F, $t_{4,0.1} = 1.533$.
(b) From the table given in Appendix F, $t_{10,0.025} = 2.228$.
(c) From the table given in Appendix F, $t_{26,0.005} = 2.779$.
(d) The t distribution tables do not contain the values for 50 degrees of freedom. The required value can be approximated by taking the mean of the $t_{40,0.01}$ and $t_{60,0.01}$ values:

$t_{40,0.01} = 2.423$
$t_{60,0.01} = 2.390$

Taking the mean of these two values gives

$$t_{50,0.01} = \frac{2.423 + 2.390}{2} = 2.4065$$

7.8   Find the value, x, of the t distribution with 26 degrees of freedom such that $P(t < x) = 0.025$.

Solution   From the table given in Appendix F, $t_{26,0.025} = 2.056$, i.e.

$$P(t > 2.056) = 0.025$$

Since the t distribution is symmetric around 0, $P(t < -2.056) = 0.025$, i.e. $x = -2.056$.

Exercises 7.6

1. Find the following values: (a) $t_{1,0.05}$, (b) $t_{2,0.005}$, (c) $t_{14,0.01}$, (d) $t_{22,0.10}$, (e) $t_{35,0.025}$.
2. Find the value x of the t distribution with 19 degrees of freedom such that $P(t > x) = 0.1$.
3. Find the value x of the t distribution with eight degrees of freedom such that $P(t < x) = 0.005$.

7.7   **The form of the sampling distribution of the sample means $\bar{X}$**

The form of the sampling distribution of the sample means depends on what is known about the population distribution. There are three cases to consider:

Case 1 population follows a normal probability distribution or the population standard deviation is known;

Case 2 population distribution is unknown, and the population standard deviation is estimated using a large sample (30 or more items in the sample);

Case 3 population distribution is unknown, and the population standard deviation is estimated using a small sample (less than 30 items in the sample).

Case 1:   Population follows a normal probability distribution or the population standard deviation is known

When the population is normally distributed or the population standard deviation is known, the sampling distribution of the sample means, $\bar{X}$, is normally distributed with mean μ and standard error $\sigma/\sqrt{n}$. This result does not depend upon the size of the sample.

Case 2:   Population distribution is unknown – large sample

When the population distribution is unknown, the result of the **central limit theorem** is used to find the sampling distribution of the sample means.

The central limit theorem states that when simple random samples of size n are taken from a population with mean μ and standard deviation σ, then the sampling distribution of the sample means can be approximated using a normal probability distribution with mean μ and standard error $\sigma/\sqrt{n}$, when the sample size is 30 or more.

The accuracy of using the normal distribution increases as the sample size increases above 30.

Case 3:   Population distribution is unknown – small sample

When a small sample ($n < 30$) is taken, the sampling distribution cannot be found using the central limit theorem. In this case we have to assume that the population is normally distributed. It can then be shown that the sampling distribution of the sample means $\bar{X}$ follows a t distribution with $n - 1$ degrees of freedom.

Worked examples

7.9   State, and draw, the sampling distribution of the sample means for the shoe machinery manufacturer data given in Example 7.1.

Solution   The actual population distribution of all production costs is not known. Thus we cannot automatically assume that the sampling distribution of the mean is normal. However, since the sample size is 30, the central limit theorem states that, theoretically, the sampling distribution of the sample means is approximately normally distributed, with mean £667.45 (Worked Example 7.2) and standard error £204.52 (Worked Example 7.3). Figure

7.1 shows the frequency distribution of the 600 sample means. This distribution does approximately follow a normal probability distribution. If all possible samples of 30 items are taken, then the sampling distribution of the sample means should follow a normal probability distribution.

7.10 The data given below represent a random sample of the percentage growth in sales of 11 chemists over the last 12 months. Find the sampling distribution of the sample means.

16.1   23.7   10.8   20.4   12.2   13.4   15.8   19.3   12.5   16.7   10.1

Solution First calculate a data summary:

$$n = 11 \qquad \Sigma x_i = 171 \qquad \Sigma x_i^2 = 2841.38 \qquad s = 4.2793$$

A point estimate of the mean of the sample means is

$$\bar{x} = \frac{171}{11} = 15.5454\%$$

A point estimate of the standard error of the sample means using [7.2] is

$$s_{\bar{X}} = \frac{s}{\sqrt{n}} = \frac{4.2793}{\sqrt{11}} = 1.2903\%$$

The sample is small (less than 30 numbers) so assuming that the population of percentage growth rates for all chemists is normally distributed, the sampling distribution of the sample means follows a t distribution with 10 ($n - 1$) degrees of freedom.

Self-assessment questions 7.7

1. What is a sampling distribution?
2. What is the expected value of the mean of the sample means?
3. What is the difference between a standard deviation and a standard error?
4. State the standard error of the sample means when

   (a) the population standard deviation is known
   (b) the population standard deviation is not known.

5. What distribution is used for the sampling distribution of the sample means when

   (a) the population standard deviation is known
   (b) the population standard deviation is estimated using a large sample
   (c) the population standard deviation is estimated using a small sample?

Exercises 7.7

1. A population is known to have a standard deviation of 25. A sample of ten items is taken from this population. The sample mean is 92.6.

   (a) Find a point estimate of the mean of the sample means.
   (b) Find the standard error of the sample means.
   (c) What distribution is used for the sampling distribution of the sample means?

2. A sample of size 17 is taken from a large population. The sample has a mean of 168.3 and a standard deviation of 58.9.

   (a) Find a point estimate of the mean of the sample means.
   (b) Find a point estimate of the standard error of the sample means.
   (c) What distribution is used for the sampling distribution of the sample means?

3. A sample of 65 items is taken from a very large population. The sample mean is 171.5 and the sample standard deviation is 90.

   (a) Find a point estimate of the mean of the sample means.
   (b) Find a point estimate of the standard error of the sample means.
   (c) What distribution is used for the sampling distribution of the sample means?

7.8 Practical application of the sampling distribution of the sample means $\bar{X}$

A sample is taken from a population in order to estimate the population mean. An obvious question to ask is 'how accurate is this estimate?' The sampling distribution of the sample means allows us to answer this question by stating the probability that the sample mean falls within a given distance from the true population mean. In the production costs of the shoe manufacturer example, we could ask 'what is the probability that the sample mean falls within £100 of the true mean cost price?' The nearer this probability is to 1 the more certain we are that the sample mean is within £100 of the true average cost price. The closer the probability is to 0, the less certain we are that the sample mean is within £100 of the true average cost price.

Worked example

7.11   Consider the shoe machinery manufacturer data given in Example 7.1.

(a) Find the probability that a sample mean falls within the following amounts from the mean cost price of all sales: (i) £100, (ii) £50, (iii) £10.

(b) Using the answers to (a), comment on the chances of obtaining a very accurate estimate of the population mean.

Solution   (a) From Worked Example 7.9, the sampling distribution of the sample means is normally distributed with an estimated mean of £667.45 and an estimated standard error of £204.52.

(i)   The sample mean falls within £100 of the population mean if it lies in the interval $667.45 - 100$ to $667.45 + 100$, i.e. from £567.45 to £767.45. If $\bar{X}$ represents the mean of the sample means, we want to find

$$P(567.45 < \bar{X} < 767.45)$$

The sampling distribution of $\bar{X}$ can be made to have a standard normal distribution with mean 0 and standard deviation 1 by using the relationship

$$Z = \frac{\bar{X} - \mu}{\sigma/\sqrt{n}}$$

(For further details refer to Chapter 10.) Thus we want to find

$$P\left(\frac{567.45 - 667.45}{204.52} < Z < \frac{767.45 - 667.45}{204.52}\right),$$

i.e.

$$P(-0.49 < Z < 0.49) = P(Z < 0.49) - P(Z < -0.49)$$
$$= (0.6879) - (1 - 0.6879)$$
$$= 0.3758$$

The probability of obtaining a sample mean which is within £100 of the true population mean is 0.3578.

(ii)   The sample mean falls within £50 of the population mean if it lies in the interval $667.45 - 50$ to $667.45 + 50$, i.e. from £617.45 to £717.45. If $\bar{X}$ represents the mean of the sample means, we want to find

$$P(617.45 < \bar{X} < 717.45),$$

i.e.

$$\left(\frac{617.45 - 667.45}{204.52} < Z < \frac{717.45 - 667.45}{204.52}\right),$$

i.e.

$$P(-0.25 < Z < 0.25) = P(Z < 0.25) - P(Z < -0.25)$$
$$= (0.5948) - (1 - 0.5948)$$
$$= 0.1896$$

The probability of obtaining a sample mean which is within £50 of the true population mean is 0.1896.

(iii) The sample mean falls within £10 of the population mean if it lies in the interval $667.45 - 10$ to $667.45 + 10$, i.e. from £657.45 to £677.45. If $\bar{X}$ represents the mean of the sample means, we want to find

$$P(657.45 < \bar{X} < 677.45),$$

i.e.

$$P\left(\frac{657.45 - 667.45}{204.52} < Z < \frac{677.45 - 667.45}{204.52}\right),$$

i.e.

$$P(-0.05 < Z < 0.05) = P(Z < 0.05) - P(Z < -0.05)$$
$$= (0.5199) - (1 - 0.5199)$$
$$= 0.0398$$

The probability of obtaining a sample mean which is within £10 of the true population mean is 0.0398.

(b) The probability of achieving a more accurate estimate (i.e. within a small distance from the true population mean) is smaller than the probability of achieving a less accurate estimate. In other words, the chances of obtaining a very accurate estimate from a sample are very small.

Exercise 7.8

'Fix It' is an electrical servicing company specializing in repairing computers. Over the last year they have repaired 8795 computers. A random sample of 40 of these repairs has a mean repair cost of £80.61 and a standard deviation of £31.04.

(a) Find a point estimate for the mean of the sample means.
(b) Find a point estimate of the standard error of the sample means.
(c) What distribution is used for the sampling distribution of the sample means?
(d) Find the probability that the sample mean falls within £10 of the mean of all repair costs.

Test exercises

1. (a) Find the value, x, of the t distribution with ten degrees of freedom such that $P(t < x) = 0.005$.
   (b) Find the value, x, of the t distribution with 50 degrees of freedom such that $P(t > x) = 0.10$.

2. A very large population has a standard deviation of 982.36. A sample of 100 items is taken from this population.

   (a) Find the standard error of the sample means.
   (b) What distribution is used for the sampling distribution of the sample means?

3. A sample of ten items is taken from a population of 100 000 items. The sample has a mean of 532.6 and a standard deviation of 87.2.

   (a) Find a point estimate of the population mean.
   (b) Find a point estimate of the population standard deviation.
   (c) Calculate a point estimate of the standard error of the sample means.
   (d) What distribution is used for the sampling distribution of the sample means?

This data was analysed in Exercises 3.1, Question 4, and Exercises 3.2, Question 3

4. The breaking strength of a fibre is tested in a laboratory. Forty samples of the fibre are tested and the breaking strengths (grams) are given below.

   2.143 2.143 2.148 2.158 2.137 2.137 2.147 2.140
   2.124 2.133 2.134 2.164 2.165 2.145 2.142 2.169
   2.168 2.170 2.162 2.130 2.133 2.162 2.137 2.156
   2.168 2.145 2.125 2.137 2.151 2.149 2.134 2.151
   2.150 2.146 2.122 2.149 2.156 2.161 2.168 2.131

   (a) Calculate a point estimate of the population mean.
   (b) Calculate a point estimate of the population standard deviation.
   (c) Calculate a point estimate of the standard error of the sample means.
   (d) What distribution is used for the sampling distribution of the sample means?
   (e) Find the probability that a sample mean falls within 0.005 g of the true mean breaking strength of all fibres.

8 Confidence intervals for a population mean

Objectives

At the end of this chapter you should be able to

- calculate and interpret a confidence interval for a population mean when the population standard deviation is known

- calculate and interpret a confidence interval for a population mean when the population standard deviation is estimated using a large sample

- calculate and interpret a confidence interval for a population mean when the population standard deviation is estimated using a small sample

8.1   Confidence Intervals

Read Chapter 7 before you read this chapter

A population parameter is a characteristic of the population

A point estimate is a single number which is used to estimate the value of a population parameter, e.g. the population mean. As we saw in Chapter 7, different samples from the same population are likely to provide different point estimates of the population parameter. A **confidence interval** (CI) represents a range of plausible values for the true value of the population parameter, based upon a point estimate of the parameter obtained from a sample.

CIs can be stated at various levels, commonly at 90%, 95% and 99%. The following definition is stated for an $\alpha\%$ CI.

If many samples of the same size n are taken from a population, then we would expect $\alpha\%$ of the CIs to contain the true value of the population parameter, i.e. the probability that an $\alpha\%$ CI contains the true value of the population parameter is $\alpha/100$.

Confidence intervals are very useful since they provide information on the precision of the estimates as well as on the estimated value of the population parameter. A CI which covers a small range of values implies that the population mean can be estimated more precisely than a CI which covers a wide range of values.

8.2

Confidence Interval for a population mean: population standard deviation known

Read Sections 7.5 and 7.7 before you read this section

In Section 7.7, we saw that if the population standard deviation, σ, is known, then the sampling distribution of the sample means is normally distributed with a mean μ and standard error $\sigma/\sqrt{n}$.

Figure 8.1 shows the sampling distribution of the sample means when the population standard deviation σ is known. The values of A and B in the figure are the lower and upper limits of an $\alpha\%$ CI, respectively, i.e. A and B are the values within which $\alpha\%$ of the sample means fall.

We need to find the values of A and B. In Chapter 6, we looked at the normal and standard normal distributions. Ninety per cent of the values in the standard normal distribution fall within the range -1.64 to $+1.64$, i.e. $P(-1.64 < Z < 1.64) = 0.9$. It can be shown that for any normal distribution, 90% of the values fall within $\mu - 1.64\sigma$ to $\mu + 1.64\sigma$. If the standard error of the sampling distribution of the sample means is denoted by $\sigma_{\bar{X}}$, then the values of A and B are:

$$A = \bar{x} - 1.64\sigma_{\bar{X}} \tag{8.1}$$

$$B = \bar{x} + 1.64\sigma_{\bar{X}} \tag{8.2}$$

Now $\sigma_{\bar{X}} = \sigma/\sqrt{n}$, thus [8.1] and [8.2] can be written as

$$A = \bar{x} - 1.64\frac{\sigma}{\sqrt{n}} \tag{8.3}$$

$$B = \bar{x} + 1.64\frac{\sigma}{\sqrt{n}} \tag{8.4}$$

Figure 8.1. Sampling distribution of the sample mean: population standard deviation known

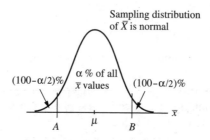

Sampling distribution of $\bar{X}$ is normal

$(100-\alpha/2)\%$ $\alpha \%$ of all $\bar{x}$ values $(100-\alpha/2)\%$

A μ B $\bar{x}$

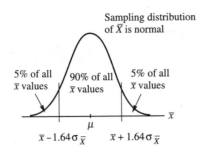

Figure 8.2. Ninety per cent confidence interval for μ when the population standard deviation is known

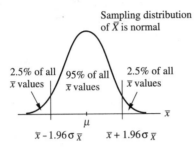

Figure 8.3. Ninety-five per cent confidence interval for μ when the population standard deviation is known

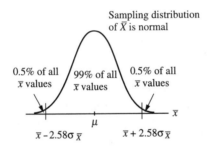

Figure 8.4. Ninety-nine per cent confidence interval for μ when the population standard deviation is known

KEY POINT

Thus a 90% CI for μ (Figure 8.2) is $\qquad \bar{x} \pm 1.64\dfrac{\sigma}{\sqrt{n}}$ $\qquad$ [8.5]

Similarly, 95% of values of a standard normal distribution fall in the range -1.96 to $+1.96$ and 99% of values fall within -2.58 to $+2.58$. The following two equations define the 95% (Figure 8.3) and 99% (Figure 8.4) CIs for μ:

KEY POINT

A 95% CI for μ is $\qquad \bar{x} \pm 1.96\dfrac{\sigma}{\sqrt{n}}$ $\qquad$ [8.6]

KEY POINT

A 99% CI for μ is $\qquad \bar{x} \pm 2.58\dfrac{\sigma}{\sqrt{n}}$ $\qquad$ [8.7]

Worked examples

8.1   (a) A sample of 40 items are taken from a population with standard deviation 10.3. Assuming that the mean of the sample is 3.6, find a

(i)   90% CI for the population mean μ
(ii)   95% CI for the population mean μ
(iii) 99% CI for the population mean μ.

Standard deviation = $\sqrt{\text{variance}}$

(b) A population is known to have a variance of 836.3664. For the following sample of ten items taken from this population, find a

(i)   90% CI for the population mean μ
(ii)   95% CI for the population mean μ
(iii) 99% CI for the population mean μ.

163.5 184.3 179.6 193.2 154.1 130.6 147.7 181.4 127.3 155.0

Solution   (a) Data summary: $\sigma = 10.3$, $\bar{x} = 3.6$, $n = 40$, $\sigma_{\bar{x}} = 10.3/\sqrt{40} = 1.6286$.

(i)   Using [8.5], a 90% CI for μ is

Use the normal distribution since σ is known

$$3.6 \pm 1.64 \times 1.6286 = 0.9291 \text{ to } 6.2709$$

(ii)   Using [8.6], a 95% CI for μ is

$$3.6 \pm 1.96 \times 1.6286 = 0.4079 \text{ to } 6.7921$$

(iii) Using [8.7], a 99% CI for μ is

$$3.6 \pm 2.58 \times 1.6286 = -0.6018 \text{ to } 7.8018$$

Use the normal distribution since σ is known, even though the sample is small ($n < 30$)

(b) Data summary: $\sigma^2 = 836.3664$, $\bar{x} = 161.67$, $n = 10$, $\sigma = \sqrt{836.3664} = 28.92$, $\sigma_{\bar{x}} = 28.92/\sqrt{10} = 9.1453$.

(i)   Using [8.5], a 90% CI for μ is

$$161.67 \pm 1.64 \times 9.1453 = 146.6717 \text{ to } 176.6683$$

(ii)   Using [8.6], a 95% CI for μ is

$$161.67 \pm 1.96 \times 9.1453 = 143.7452 \text{ to } 179.5948$$

(iii) Using [8.7], a 99% CI for μ is

$$161.67 \pm 2.58 \times 9.1453 = 138.0751 \text{ to } 185.2649$$

8.2   The data given below show the petrol consumption (miles per gallon (mpg)) of a new car in 20 independent circuits of a test track. From previous experience, the population standard deviation of the petrol consumption is 2.6 mpg.

46.3 47.2 44.9 51.7 50.1 49.4 51.7 45.1 42.8 46.0
44.9 43.2 43.6 47.3 45.1 44.5 49.4 48.3 50.2 52.0

Calculate, and interpret,

(a) a 90% CI for the mean petrol consumption μ
(b) a 95% CI for the mean petrol consumption μ
(c) a 99% CI for the mean petrol consumption μ.

Solution

Data summary: $n = 20$, $\Sigma x_i = 943.7$, $\Sigma x_i^2 = 44697.59$, $\sigma = 2.6$ mpg, $\bar{x} = 47.185$ mpg, $\sigma_{\bar{x}} = 2.6/\sqrt{20} = 0.5814$ mpg.

Use the normal distribution since σ is known, even though the sample is small ($n < 30$)

(a) Using [8.5], a 90% CI for μ is

$47.185 \pm 1.64 \times 0.5814 = 46.23$ to 48.14 mpg

We are 90% confident that the true mean petrol consumption lies in the range 46.23 mpg to 48.14 mpg.

(b) Using [8.6], a 95% CI for μ is

$47.185 \pm 1.96 \times 0.5814 = 46.05$ to 48.32 mpg

We are 95% confident that the true mean petrol consumption lies in the range 46.05 mpg to 48.32 mpg.

(c) Using [8.7], a 99% CI for μ is

$47.185 \pm 2.58 \times 0.5814 = 45.69$ to 48.69 mpg

We are 99% confident that the true mean petrol consumption lies in the range 45.69 mpg to 48.69 mpg.

Self-assessment questions 8.2

1. When the population standard deviation is known, which probability distribution is used in the calculation of the confidence interval for the population mean, μ?
2. State the equation which is used to calculate a 95% confidence interval for the population mean, μ, when the population standard deviation, σ, is known.

Exercises 8.2

1. A population is known to have a standard deviation of 76.53. A sample of 17 items, taken from this population, has a mean of 23.04.

   (a) Calculate the population standard error of the mean, $\sigma_{\bar{x}}$.
   (b) Calculate, and interpret, a 90% CI for the population mean μ.
   (c) Calculate, and interpret, a 95% CI for the population mean μ.
   (d) Calculate, and interpret, a 99% CI for the population mean μ.

2. A population has a variance of 400. A sample of 25 items taken from this population is given overleaf.

86.3 21.2 65.5 74.1 57.9 54.2 43.0 71.8 35.5 62.1
54.4 25.3 62.3 43.2 82.2 31.1 36.7 64.2 77.4 84.2
50.1 83.2 82.6 94.7 33.0

(a) Calculate the population standard error of the mean, $\sigma_{\bar{X}}$.
(b) Calculate, and interpret, a 90% CI for the population mean μ.
(c) Calculate, and interpret, a 95% CI for the population mean μ.
(d) Calculate, and interpret, a 99% CI for the population mean μ.

3. A survey is carried out on behalf of an electricity company to investigate the quarterly bills paid by domestic consumers. As part of this investigation, the company take a random sample of the bills of 600 domestic consumers in one town. The average of this sample is £127.62. Assuming that the standard deviation of all bills in this town is £52,

(a) calculate the population standard error of the mean, $\sigma_{\bar{X}}$,
(b) calculate a 90% CI for the population mean, μ,
(c) calculate a 95% CI for the population mean μ,
(d) calculate a 99% CI for the population mean μ.
(e) What do the CIs tell you about the average quarterly bills of all domestic consumers in this town?

8.3   Confidence interval for a population mean: large sample

Read Sections 7.5 and 7.7 before you read this section

In Section 7.7, we saw that if we take a large sample (30 or more items) the sampling distribution of the sample means can be approximated using a normal probability distribution. The population standard deviation can be estimated using the sample standard deviation s, where

$$s = \sqrt{\frac{\Sigma x_i^2 - n\bar{x}^2}{n-1}} \qquad [8.8]$$

The CIs in this case are the same as in Section 8.2, except that the population standard deviation is replaced by the sample standard deviation. For example, Figure 8.5 shows a 95% CI for the population mean μ based on a large sample. The equations used to calculate the CIs are given below.

KEY POINT

A 90% CI for μ is $\bar{x} \pm 1.64 \dfrac{s}{\sqrt{n}}$ \qquad [8.9]

Figure 8.5. Ninety-five per cent confidence interval for μ when the population standard deviation is estimated using a large sample

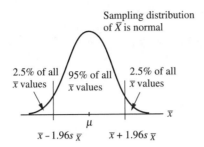

Sampling distribution of $\bar{X}$ is normal

2.5% of all $\bar{x}$ values   95% of all $\bar{x}$ values   2.5% of all $\bar{x}$ values

$\bar{x}$

μ

$\bar{x} - 1.96s\,\bar{x}$ $\bar{x} + 1.96s\,\bar{x}$

KEY POINT

A 95% CI for μ is $\qquad \bar{x} \pm 1.96 \dfrac{s}{\sqrt{n}}$ $\qquad$ [8.10]

KEY POINT

A 99% CI for μ is $\qquad \bar{x} \pm 2.58 \dfrac{s}{\sqrt{n}}$ $\qquad$ [8.11]

Worked examples

8.3   For the sample of data given below, calculate

(a) a 90% CI for the population mean μ,

(b)

   a 95% CI for the population mean μ,

(c) a 99% CI for the population mean μ.

```
27.8 33.2 16.3 31.4  9.9 21.1 40.5
35.7 32.5 34.4 46.7 21.8 34.5 13.7
57.9 16.6 45.9  6.1 42.3 18.2 38.2
20.7 45.6 12.3 61.6 24.4 53.8 23.1
37.0 32.1 59.3 27.3 39.5 24.2 33.2
```

Solution

Use the normal distribution since the sample is large ($n \geq 30$)

Data summary: $n = 35$, $\Sigma x_i = 1118.8$, $\Sigma x_i^2 = 42596.56$, $\bar{x} = 31.9657$, $s = 14.1767$, $s_{\bar{X}} = 14.1767/\sqrt{35} = 2.3963$.

(a) Using [8.9], a 90% CI for μ is

$31.9657 \pm 1.64 \times 2.3963 = 28.0358$ to 35.8956

(b) Using [8.10], a 95% CI for μ is

$31.9657 \pm 1.96 \times 2.3963 = 27.2690$ to 36.6624

(c) Using [8.11], a 99% CI for μ is

$31.9657 \pm 2.58 \times 2.3963 = 25.7832$ to 38.1482

8.4   The manager of a delicatessen conducted a survey of the value of sales in his shop on one day. The data given below show the values (£) of a sample of 32 sales made on one day.

6.49	8.90	22.95	13.39
18.63	4.44	24.99	4.44
34.98	8.12	8.99	6.99
21.25	24.99	1.26	9.97
9.98	3.99	4.35	12.49
2.19	7.75	11.99	1.69
4.65	4.50	9.85	13.89
10.45	7.49	29.97	2.77

Calculate and interpret
(a) a 90% CI for the population mean μ,
(b) a 95% CI for the population mean μ,
(c) a 99% CI for the population mean μ.

Solution   Data summary: $n = 32$, $\Sigma x_i = 358.78$, $\Sigma x_i^2 = 6339.5164$, $\bar{x} = £11.21$, $s = £8.65$, $s_{\bar{x}} = 8.65/\sqrt{32} = £1.53$.

Use the normal distribution since the sample size is large ($n \geq 30$)

(a) Using [8.9], a 90% CI for μ is

$$11.21 \pm 1.64 \times 1.53 = £8.70 \text{ to } £13.72$$

We are 90% confident that the true mean value of daily sales lies in the range £8.70. to £13.72.

(b) Using [8.10], a 95% CI for μ is

$$11.21 \pm 1.96 \times 1.53 = £8.21 \text{ to } £14.21$$

We are 95% confident that the true mean value of daily sales lies in the range £8.21 to £14.21.

(c) Using [8.11], a 99% CI for μ is

$$11.21 \pm 2.58 \times 1.53 = £7.26 \text{ to } £15.16$$

We are 99% confident that the true mean value of daily sales lies in the range £7.26 to £15.16.

Self assessment Questions 8.3

1. What is meant by a 'large sample'?
2. When a large sample is used to estimate the population standard deviation, which probability distribution is used in the calculation of the CI for the population mean μ?
3. State the equation which is used to calculate a 95% CI for the population mean μ when the population standard deviation is estimated from a large sample.

Exercises 8.3

1. The data below represent a random sample of 50 items taken from a very large population.

   (a) Calculate
       (i)   the sample mean $\bar{x}$,
       (ii) the sample standard deviation s,
       (iii) the estimated standard error of the sample means, $s_{\bar{x}}$.
   (b) Calculate a 90% CI for the population mean μ.
   (c) Calculate a 95% CI for the population mean μ.
   (d) Calculate a 99% CI for the population mean μ.

2.16	5.47	6.05	9.86	5.45	−0.01	3.27	8.88	4.51	6.24
2.79	5.30	1.66	8.54	2.47	6.36	4.33	1.23	2.20	7.87
9.17	8.26	−0.58	2.74	2.78	6.10	4.47	5.78	2.51	7.52
5.55	8.29	3.47	7.70	2.78	11.24	4.74	7.73	6.75	6.29
9.24	6.00	7.36	9.08	5.51	7.10	9.19	5.11	4.78	6.21

2. An advertising agency has conducted a pilot survey to investigate the average time spent by households watching television. A random sample of 40 households took part in the survey. The following data show the number of hours per week these households spent viewing the television.

35	4	28	49	26	10	41	15	43	41
29	25	32	37	8	36	14	25	30	29
21	31	15	39	30	38	40	20	45	11
28	7	27	12	35	32	34	34	27	24

   (a) Calculate
       (i)   the sample mean, $\bar{x}$,
       (ii) the sample standard deviation s,
       (iii) the estimated standard error of the sample means, $s_{\bar{x}}$.
   (b) Calculate a 90% CI for the population mean μ.
   (c) Calculate a 95% CI for the population mean μ.
   (d) Calculate a 99% CI for the population mean μ.
   (e) Clearly explain to the advertising agency what the CIs tell you about the average weekly time spent by households watching television.

8.4   Confidence interval for a population mean: small sample

Read Sections 7.5, 7.6 and 7.7 before you read this section

In Section 7.7, we saw that if we take a small sample (less than 30 items) then the sampling distribution of the sample means can be approximated

Figure 8.6. Approximate sampling distribution of the sample means using a small sample of data

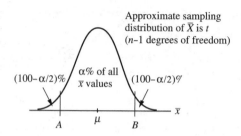

Figure 8.7. Ninety per cent confidence interval for μ when the population standard deviation is estimated using a small sample

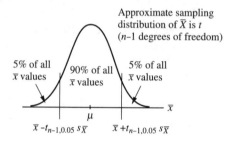

Figure 8.8. Ninety-five per cent confidence interval for μ when the population standard deviation is estimated using a small sample

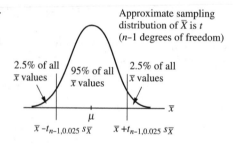

Figure 8.9. Ninety-nine per cent confidence interval for μ when the population standard deviation is estimated using a small sample

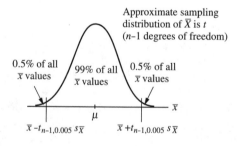

using a t distribution with $n - 1$ degrees of freedom, assuming that the population is normally distributed. Figure 8.6 shows this sampling distribution. The values of A and B in the diagram are the lower and upper limits of the $\alpha\%$ CI, respectively, i.e. A and B are the values within which $\alpha\%$ of the sample means fall. The format of the CI is the same as in Section 8.3, except that the t distribution with $n - 1$ degrees of freedom is used instead of the normal distribution. Thus the 90%, 95% and 99% CIs for the mean using a small sample (Figures 8.7–8.9) are as follows.

KEY POINT

A 90% CI for μ is

$$\bar{x} \pm t_{n-1,\,0.05} \times \frac{s}{\sqrt{n}} \qquad [8.12]$$

A 95% CI for μ is

$$\bar{x} \pm t_{n-1,\,0.025} \times \frac{s}{\sqrt{n}} \qquad [8.13]$$

A 99% CI for μ is

$$\bar{x} \pm t_{n-1,\,0.005} \times \frac{s}{\sqrt{n}} \qquad [8.14]$$

Worked examples

8.5 For the data given below, find

(a) a 90% CI for the population mean μ,
(b) a 95% CI for the population mean μ,
(c) a 99% CI for the population mean μ.

Use the *t* distribution since the sample size is small ($n < 30$)

2319 6237 3422 5601 7390 8125 5133
8218 6634 7340 1278 3195 7321 8830

Solution Data summary: $n = 14$, $\Sigma x_i = 81043$, $\Sigma x_i^2 = 543\,162\,959$, $\bar{x} = 5788.79$, $s = 2386.2168$, $s_{\bar{X}} = 2386.2168/\sqrt{14} = 637.7433$, degrees of freedom $= n - 1 = 13$. Note: we must assume that the population from which this sample was taken has a normal probability distribution.

(a) $t_{13,0.05} = 1.771$
Using [8.12], a 90% CI for μ is

$5788.79 \pm 1.771 \times 637.7433 = 4659.3466\text{–}6918.2333$

(b) $t_{13,0.025} = 2.160$
Using [8.13], a 95% CI for μ is

$5788.79 \pm 2.160 \times 637.7433 = 4411.2645\text{–}7166.3155$

(c) $t_{13,\,0.005} = 3.012$
Using [8.14], a 99% CI for μ is

$5788.79 \pm 3.012 \times 637.7433 = 3867.9072\text{–}7709.6728$

8.6 The following data represent a random sample of the percentage growth in sales of 11 chemists over the last year.

16.1   23.7   10.8   20.4   12.2   13.4   15.8   19.3   12.5   16.7   10.1

Calculate and interpret

(a) a 90% CI for the population mean μ,
(b) a 95% CI for the population mean μ,
(c) a 99% CI for the population mean μ.

Solution

Use the t distribution since the sample size is small ($n < 30$)

Data summary: $n = 11$, $\Sigma x_i = 171$, $\Sigma x_i^2 = 2841.38$, $\bar{x} = 15.5454\%$, $s = 4.2793\%$, $s_{\bar{x}} = 4.2793/\sqrt{11} = 1.2903\%$, degrees of freedom$= n - 1 = 10$. Note: we must assume that the population from which this sample was taken has a normal probability distribution.

(a) $t_{10,0.05} = 1.812$

Using [8.12], a 90% CI for μ is

$15.5454 \pm 1.812 \times 1.2903 = 13.21\%$ to 17.88%

We are 90% confident that the true mean annual percentage growth rate lies in the range 13.21% to 17.88%

(b) $t_{10,0.025} = 2.228$

Using [8.13], a 95% CI for μ is

$15.5454 \pm 2.228 \times 1.2903 = 12.67\%$ to 18.42%

We are 95% confident that the true mean annual percentage growth rate lies in the range 12.67% to 18.42%

(c) $t_{10,0.005} = 3.169$

Using [8.14], a 99% CI for μ is

$15.5454 \pm 3.169 \times 1.2903 = 11.46\%$ to 19.63%

We are 99% confident that the true mean annual percentage growth rate lies in the range 11.46% to 19.63%.

Self-assessment questions 8.4

1. What is meant by a 'small sample'?
2. When a small sample is used to estimate the population standard deviation, which probability distribution is used in the calculation of the confidence interval for the population mean μ?
3. State the equation which is used to calculate a 95% CI for the population mean, μ, when the population standard deviation is estimated from a small sample.
4. What must be assumed about the probability distribution of the population in order to be able to calculate a CI for the population mean, μ, using a small sample?

Exercises 8.4

1. The data given below represent a random sample of 16 items from a large population.

107.6   60.0   28.1   90.0   112.9   87.6   414.8   65.3
195.5   135.6   71.6   54.7   116.7   68.9   148.8   71.1

(a) Calculate
  (i)   the sample mean $\bar{x}$
  (ii) the sample standard deviation s
  (iii) the estimated standard error of the sample means, $s_{\bar{x}}$.
(b) Calculate a 90% CI for the population mean μ.
(c) Calculate a 95% CI for the population mean μ.
(d) Calculate a 99% CI for the population mean μ.

2. A new pesticide is designed to effectively control potato blight. Twenty-five one-acre plots are sown with potatoes. Each plot is sprayed with the new pesticide and the resulting yield (in tonnes) is given below.

735.60 2766.58 2340.13 1505.53   723.69 2787.88 2058.08
1854.26 1916.78 1111.86 2659.09 2921.48   914.18 2648.76
3083.11 2574.48 2008.27 1197.99 1123.79 2365.80 2474.73
1687.77 2999.32 2893.27 2567.65

(a) Calculate
  (i)   the sample mean $\bar{x}$
  (ii) the sample standard deviation s
  (iii) the estimated standard error of the sample means, $s_{\bar{x}}$.
(b) Calculate a 90% CI for the population mean μ.
(c) Calculate a 95% CI for the population mean μ.
(d) Calculate a 99% CI for the population mean μ.
(e) What do the CIs tell you about the average yield of potatoes when sprayed with this pesticide?
(f) What further information would you require in order to be able to assess how effective the new pesticide is compared to the standard pesticide?

Test exercises

1. A major chain store offers a store card (credit card to be used in the store). The Head Office have conducted a survey of 1500 store card users to estimate the average amount spent on the card. The following is a summary of the results of this survey.

Number of customers in sample = 1500
Mean amount spent using the store card = £372.67
Standard deviation of the amount spent using the store card = £135.21

(a) Calculate a 95% CI for the mean amount spent using the store card for all store card users. Clearly explain the meaning of this CI to the management of the chain store.

(b) Calculate a 99% CI for the mean amount spent using the store card for all store card users. Clearly explain the meaning of this CI to the management of the chain store.

2. The following data represent the annual amount spent by 50 British electronics companies on research and development expressed as a percentage of their annual turnover.

```
4.8  3.3  6.0  6.7  2.7  7.8  3.9  5.3  6.2  5.9
5.2  4.6  3.1  1.3  3.2  4.5  5.2  2.7  4.5  3.2
3.8  3.0  2.3  3.9  4.0  2.1  3.3  7.3  3.4  6.8
2.1  8.6  5.1  6.5  3.2  3.7  4.3  2.5  6.9  4.1
4.9  4.3  2.5  2.7  5.4  9.3  1.2  6.4  8.0  5.7
```

(a) Calculate the sample mean and standard deviation of the annual expenditure on research and development as a percentage of the annual turnover.
(b) Calculate 90%, 95% and 99% CIs for the mean annual expenditure on research and development by all British electronics companies.
(c) Using the CIs found in (b), comment on whether the mean annual expenditure on research and development could be 6% of the turnover of the company. Justify your answer.

3. A manufacturer frequently sends small packages to a customer in Germany using air freight. In many cases it is important for the package to reach the customer as soon as possible. The manufacturer currently uses ABC Shipping but they are considering Speedy Air Freight who claim that they deliver parcels significantly quicker than all other competitors. The average time currently taken by ABC Shipping to send packages to Germany is 10.2 hours. The manufacturer decides to test the claim of Speedy Air Freight by sending some of its packages to Germany using their service. A total of 237 packages were sent using Speedy over a one-month period. The average delivery time of this sample was 9.8 hours with a standard deviation of 2.7 hours.

(a) Calculate a 95% CI for the mean delivery time of all packages sent to Germany using Speedy Air Freight. Carefully explain the meaning of this CI to the manufacturer.
(b) Using the CI found in (a), does it appear that the claim made by Speedy Air Freight is justified, i.e. are they significantly quicker at delivering packages to Germany than ABC Shipping?

4. A housing federation provides luxury rented accommodation using a leasing agreement whereby the tenant pays a fixed rent and is responsible for all household bills. The average net monthly income to the federation is £280. The federation is considering a new type of leasing agreement whereby the tenant pays a higher rent but the federation pay the water, gas and electricity bills. It is believed that this will be an attractive option to tenants, but the federation is concerned about whether or not this new agreement will provide the same

average net monthly income as the existing agreement. The federation decided to test market the new agreement using a sample of 12 tenants over a six-month period. The average net monthly income of these 12 tenants was £255 with a standard deviation of £40.

(a) Calculate 90% and 95% CIs for the mean net monthly income from the new type of leasing agreement.
(b) Does this sample support the view that the new agreement provides the same mean net monthly income as the standard leasing agreement? Justify your answer.

5. The National Rivers Authority (NRA) is concerned about the amount of industrial pollutants being dumped in a certain part of a river. They believe that the health of the marine life is being adversely affected by these pollutants since they are reducing the amount of dissolved oxygen in the water. Some scientists believe that 10 parts per million is the maximum allowable level of pollutant which leaves enough dissolved oxygen in the water for the marine life to remain healthy. The following data show a random sample of the sewage readings (parts per million of water) taken from the same location on the river over a three-month period.

    9.98 12.61   7.32 6.81 8.15 11.51 7.94
    7.69 11.15 10.35 5.91 9.04   6.08

(a) Calculate the mean and standard deviation of this sample of sewage readings.
(b) Calculate 95% and 99% CIs for the mean sewage level in the river.
(c) Using the CIs found in (b), are the concerns of the NRA confirmed by this sample? Justify your answer.

6. The management of a factory with a large assembly line want to test a new assembly technique. Fifteen employees are randomly selected and the number of units assembled by each of them in one week is recorded. The same 15 employees are then trained to use the new assembly technique. The number of units assembled by each worker using the new technique over a one-week period is recorded. The following data show the difference in the number of units assembled by each employee using the two techniques (number of units assembled using the new technique – number of units assembled using the present technique).

Employee	1	2	3	4	5	6	7	8	9	10	11	12	13	14	15
Difference	−1	8	18	−4	11	14	15	6	5	10	−2	−7	9	3	7

(a) Calculate the mean and standard deviation of this sample of differences.
(b) Calculate 90%, 95% and 99% CIs for the mean difference in the number of units assembled by all workers using the two techniques.
(c) Using the CIs found in (b), advise the management on whether the new assembly technique should be used in preference to the present technique.

9 Hypothesis tests for a population mean

<table>
<tr><td>

Objectives

</td><td>

At the end of this chapter you should be able to

- state the null and alternative hypotheses
- perform two-tailed hypothesis tests for a population mean using a large sample
- perform two-tailed hypothesis tests for a population mean using a small sample
- perform one-tailed hypothesis tests for a population mean using a large sample
- perform one-tailed hypothesis tests for a population mean using a small sample

</td></tr>
</table>

Read Chapter 7 before you read this chapter

Hypothesis tests help us to make decisions about populations using a sample of data. For example, a sugar manufacturer sells sugar in bags with a stated weight of 500 g. If bags are sold which consistently weigh more or less than 500 g then this has implications for the manufacturer. If the bags are consistently under-weight then the manufacturer could be prosecuted by the Trading Standards Office. Bags which consistently are over-filled may result in loss of revenue. A sample of bags can be used to decide the average weight of all the bags.

9.1 Defining the problem – stating hypotheses

Hypothesis testing begins with determining a hypothesized value and stating two hypotheses; the null hypothesis and an alternative hypothesis. Let μ represent the population mean and μ_0 represent the hypothesized value of the population mean. The **null hypothesis** (H_0) is a suggestion about the value of the population parameter. The null hypothesis for a population mean is always stated as

$$H_0 : \mu = \mu_0$$

The **alternative hypothesis** (H_1) is the hypothesis of interest. There are two types of alternative hypothesis; **two-tailed alternative** and **one-tailed** alternative. A two-tailed alternative hypothesis is of the form

$$H_1 : \quad \mu \neq \mu_0$$

A one-tailed alternative hypothesis is of the form

$$H_1 : \quad \mu > \mu_0 \quad \text{or} \quad H_1 : \quad \mu < \mu_0$$

In a given situation, one of these alternative hypotheses must be selected. The alternative hypothesis is chosen by focusing on what is to be shown using the sample. The sample mean must not be used to determine the alternative hypothesis. An example of each type of alternative hypothesis is given in the following three worked examples.

Worked examples

9.1 Consider the weight of sugar example discussed earlier. State the null and alternative hypotheses.

Solution Let μ represent the average weight of the bags of sugar (g). The null hypothesis states that the true mean weight of the bags is 500 g, i.e.

g represents grams

$$H_0 : \quad \mu = 500 \text{ g}$$

The manufacturer needs to establish whether the bags are being over-filled or under-filled with sugar. Thus we need to decide whether the mean weight is not 500 g, i.e.

$$H_1 : \quad \mu \neq 500 \text{ g}$$

This is an example of a two-tailed alternative hypothesis.

9.2 A new design for the body of a racing car is being tested. The designer claims that it is more energy efficient and will make the car travel at least 5 miles per hour (mph) faster than a conventionally shaped car. State the null and alternative hypotheses.

Solution Let μ represent the average increase in speed of the car with the new body shape relative to the speed of the conventionally shaped car.

The null hypothesis states that, on average, the new shaped car is 5 mph faster than the conventionally shaped car, i.e.

$$H_0 : \quad \mu = 5 \text{ mph}$$

The alternative hypothesis states that, on average, the new car will travel at least 5 mph faster than the conventionally shaped car, i.e.

$$H_1 : \quad \mu > 5 \text{ mph}$$

This is an example of a one-tailed alternative hypothesis.

9.3 A new method of producing a video component has been developed. It is claimed that it is cheaper to use the new method to produce the component. State the null and alternative hypotheses.

Solution   Let μ represent the average decrease in the cost of producing the component using the new method compared to the standard method. The null hypothesis states that, on average, the new method costs the same as the standard method, i.e.

$$H_0 : \quad \mu = £0$$

The alternative hypothesis states that, on average, the new method costs less than the standard method, i.e.

$$H_1 : \quad \mu < £0$$

This is an example of a one-tailed alternative hypothesis.

Self-assessment questions 9.1

1. What is a null hypothesis?
2. What is an alternative hypothesis?
3. How are the null and alternative hypotheses determined?
4. State, in general terms, the null hypothesis which is always used for testing a population mean.
5. State the three alternative hypotheses which can be used for testing a population mean.

Exercises 9.1

1. An advertising agency has conducted a pilot survey to investigate the average time spent by households watching television. A random sample of 40 households took part in the survey. The following data shows the number of hours per week these households spent watching the television. The agency want to test whether, on average, households spend less than 35 hours watching the television. State the most appropriate null and alternative hypotheses for this situation.

You may have calculated a data summary of this data in Exercises 8.3, Question 2

35	4	28	49	26	10	41	15	43	41
29	25	32	37	8	36	14	25	30	29
21	31	15	39	30	38	40	20	45	11
28	7	27	12	35	32	34	34	27	24

2. A survey is carried out on behalf of an electricity company to investigate the quarterly bills paid by domestic consumers. As part of this investigation, the company take a random sample of the bills of 600 domestic consumers in one town. The average of this sample is £127.62. The company want to investigate whether or not the average quarterly bills of all domestic consumers in this town is £135. Assuming that the standard deviation of all bills in this town is £52, state the most appropriate null and alternative hypotheses for this situation.

You may have calculated the standard error of the sample means in Exercises 8.2, Question 3

You may have calculated
a data summary of this
data in Exercises 8.4,
Question 2

3. A new pesticide is designed to effectively control potato blight. Twenty-five one-acre plots are sown with potatoes. Each plot is sprayed with the new pesticide and the resulting yield (in tonnes) is given below. It is claimed that the new pesticide will produce at least 1750 tonnes of potatoes. State the most appropriate null and alternative hypotheses for this situation.

735.60	2766.58	2340.13	1505.53	723.69	2787.88	2058.08
1854.26	1916.78	1111.86	2659.09	2921.48	914.18	2648.76
3083.11	2574.48	2008.27	1197.99	1123.79	2365.80	2474.73
1687.77	2999.32	2893.27	2567.65			

9.2   Making a decision

Hypotheses are tested in order to make decisions about a population using a sample of data. Since a sample of data is used, hypothesis tests will never prove or disprove a hypothesis. However, they can be used to 'indicate' whether a null hypothesis should be rejected. A decision is made depending on the results of the hypothesis test. A test will result in one of two outcomes;

Do not reject H_0 or   Reject H_0.

Examples

9.1 Refer to the weight of bags of sugar example (Worked Example 9.1). The hypotheses were

$H_0 : \quad \mu = 500$ g
$H_1 : \quad \mu \neq 500$ g

If the test indicates that H_0 should not be rejected then the sample indicates that the average weight of the bags could be 500 g.

If the test indicates that H_0 should be rejected, then this implies that the alternative hypothesis should be adopted, i.e. the sample indicates that the average weight of the sugar bags is not 500 g. The sample mean can then be used to indicate whether, on average, the bags weighed more or less than 500 g. For example, if the sample mean is 488 g, then the manufacturer could be in danger of prosecution from the Trading Standards Office for selling bags which consistently weighed less than the stated amount. If the sample mean was 517 g, the manufacturer is over-filling his bags and this may result in lost revenue.

Examples

9.2 Refer to the racing car body example (Worked Example 9.2). The hypotheses were

$$H_0 : \quad \mu = 5 \text{ mph}$$
$$H_1 : \quad \mu > 5 \text{ mph}$$

If the test indicates that H_0 should not be rejected, then the sample indicates that, on average, the new shaped car is 5 mph faster than the conventionally shaped car.

If the test indicates that H_0 should be rejected, then this implies that the alternative hypothesis should be adopted, i.e. the sample indicates that the new shaped car is at least 5 mph faster, on average, than the conventionally shaped car. The sample mean can be used to estimate the amount by which the new shaped car is faster.

9.3 Refer to the video component example (Worked Example 9.3). The hypotheses were

$$H_0 : \quad \mu = £0$$
$$H_1 : \quad \mu < £0$$

If the test indicates that H_0 should not be rejected, then the sample indicates that, on average, the new method costs the same as the standard method.

If the test indicates that H_0 should be rejected, then the sample indicates that the alternative hypothesis, H_1, should be adopted, i.e. the sample indicates that, on average, it costs less to produce a component using the new method than it does using the standard method.

Exercises 9.2

1. Consider the hypotheses determined for the hours spent watching television data (Exercises 9.1, Question 1).
   (a) If the sample mean is 48.6 hours, then the null hypothesis will not be rejected. What does this mean in practice?
   (b) If the sample mean is 26.93 hours, then the null hypothesis will be rejected. What does this mean in practice?
2. Consider the hypotheses determined for the electricity company data (Exercises 9.1, Question 2).
   (a) If the sample mean is £129.90, then the null hypothesis will not be rejected. What does this mean in practice?
   (b) If the sample mean is £120.05, then the null hypothesis will be rejected. What does this mean in practice?

3. Consider the hypotheses determined for the potato yield data (Exercises 9.1, Question 3).
   (a) If the sample mean is 2000 tonnes, then the null hypothesis will not be rejected. What does this mean in practice?
   (b) If the sample mean is 2100 tonnes, then the null hypothesis will be rejected. What does this mean in practice?

9.3   Choosing between the decisions

The purpose of a hypothesis test is to use a sample of data to make decisions about a population. To illustrate how we can choose bteween the hypotheses, assume that we are testing a two-sided alternative hypothesis ($H_1 :$ $\mu \neq \mu_0$). Figure 9.1 shows the sampling distribution of the sample means (assuming the population standard deviation is known). If the sample mean, $\bar{x}$, is similar to the hypothesized value of the population mean, μ_0, then the sample is consistent with the null hypothesis. Values of the sample mean such as $\bar{x}_a$ and $\bar{x}_b$ in Figure 9.1 are reasonably close to μ_0 and are therefore consistent with the hypothesis that μ_0 could be the true value of the population mean, i.e. the null hypothesis would not be rejected. Values of the sample mean such as $\bar{x}_c$ and $\bar{x}_d$ in Figure 9.1 are not consistent with the hypothesis that the population mean is μ_0 and would lead to the rejection of this hypothesis in favour of the alternative hypothesis. We need to find the largest and smallest values of the sample mean at which the sample will stop being consistent with H_0. These points are known as the **critical values**. The critical values separate the sampling distribution of the sample means into regions; the **acceptance region** and the **rejection regions**. Figure 9.2 shows the acceptance and rejection regions for a two-sided alternative hypothesis.

Figure 9.1. Sampling distribution of the sample means assuming the population standard deviation is known

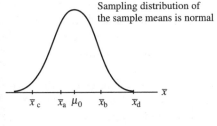

Sampling distribution of the sample means is normal

Figure 9.2. Acceptance and rejection regions of the sampling distribution of the sample means for $H_1 : \mu \neq \mu_0$

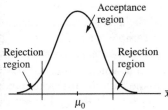

Acceptance region

Rejection region

Rejection region

The **acceptance region** contains the values of the sample mean which are consistent with the null hypothesis, i.e. the values of the sample mean which are reasonably similar to the hypothesized value of the population mean, μ_0. If the sample mean falls in this region, then the sample provides no evidence to reject the null hypothesis.

The **rejection regions** contain the values of the sample mean which are inconsistent with the null hypothesis, i.e. the values of the sample mean which are not reasonably similar to the hypothesized value of the population mean, μ_0. If the sample mean falls in either of these regions, then the sample provides some evidence to reject the null hypothesis in favour of the alternative hypothesis.

The area of the sampling distribution covered by the acceptance and rejection regions depends on the type of alternative hypothesis being tested. Figures 9.3 and 9.4 show the acceptance and rejection regions for the two types of one-sided alternative hypotheses.

Figure 9.3. Acceptance and rejection regions of the sampling distribution of the sample means for $H_1 : \mu > \mu_0$

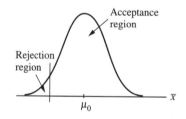

Figure 9.4. Acceptance and rejection regions of the sampling distribution of the sample means for $H_1 : \mu < \mu_0$

To perform a hypothesis test, we first need to define the acceptance and rejection regions. The rejection region is defined to be a certain percentage of the sampling distribution. Usually the rejection region covers 5% or 1% of the tails of the sampling distribution, i.e. the very low or very high values of the sample mean. This percentage is known as the **significance level** of the test. The shape of the sampling distribution (i.e. normal or t) can then be used to find the critical value and thus define the acceptance and rejection regions. For example, if we are testing the two-sided alternative hypothesis at the 5% significance level based upon the normal distribution, the critical values are -1.96 and $+1.96$ (Figure 9.5).

The shape of the sampling distribution of the sample means $\bar{x}$ is discussed in section 7.7

Having defined the acceptance and rejection regions, we need to find whether or not the sample mean is consistent with the null hypothesis. This is done using a **test statistic**. A test statistic is a number calculated from the sample of data which is directly compared to the critical value.

If the test statistic falls in the acceptance region, then the sample provides no evidence to reject the null hypothesis. If the test statistic falls

Figure 9.5. Critical values for a two-sided alternative hypothesis at the 5% significance level based on the normal distribution

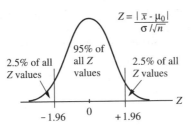

$$Z = \frac{|\bar{x} - \mu_0|}{\sigma / \sqrt{n}}$$

95% of all Z values

2.5% of all Z values

2.5% of all Z values

− 1.96   0   + 1.96

Z

in the rejection region, then the sample provides evidence to reject the null hypothesis in favour of the alternative hypothesis. The strength of the evidence to reject the null hypothesis can be determined by looking at the difference between the sample mean, $\bar{x}$, and the hypothesized population mean, μ_0. The greater the difference, the stronger the evidence to reject the null hypothesis. This procedure involves decreasing the significance level of the test, e.g. from 5% to 1%. In this way, we are looking at ever more extreme values of the sample mean.

If the significance level of the test is set at 5% and the data provide evidence to reject H_0, then we say that there is **some evidence to reject** H_0. If the significance level of the test is set at 1% and the data provide evidence to reject H_0, then we say that there is **strong evidence to reject** H_0.

9.4   A summary of the hypothesis testing procedure

There are seven main steps in performing a hypothesis test.

1. State the null and alternative hypotheses.
2. Decide on an appropriate test to use. This depends on what is known about the population:
   (a) population standard deviation, σ, is known;
   (b) population standard deviation, σ, is unknown and is estimated using a large sample of data (30 or more items);
   (c) population standard deviation, σ, is unknown and is estimated using a small sample of data (less than 30 items).
3. Specify the significance level of the test.
4. Find the critical value and thus the acceptance and rejection regions.
5. Calculate the test statistic using the sample of data.
6. Compare the test statistic with the critical value to decide whether the test statistic falls in the acceptance or rejection region.
7. State the conclusions of the test in plain English.

Sections 9.5–9.7 give the tests corresponding to the three cases given in step 2 above.

9.5   Hypothesis test for a population mean where population standard deviation is known

Read Sections 7.5 and 7.7 before you read this section

In Section 7.7 we saw that if the population standard deviation, σ, is known, then the sampling distribution of the sample means is normally distributed with mean μ and standard error $\sigma/\sqrt{n}$, where n is the size of the sample. Figures 9.6–9.8 show the critical values of the standard normal distribution for testing $H_1: \mu \neq \mu_0$, $H_1: \mu > \mu_0$ and $H_1: \mu < \mu_0$ respectively at the 5% and 1% significance levels.

Figure 9.6. Critical values for testing $H_1: \mu \neq \mu_0$ at the (a) 5% and (b) 1% significance levels

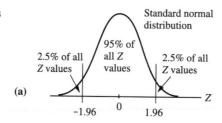

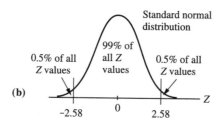

Figure 9.7. Critical values for testing $H_1: \mu > \mu_0$ at the (a) 5% and (b) 1% significance levels

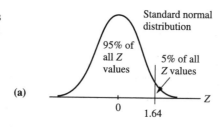

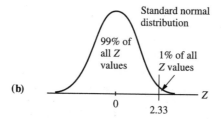

Figure 9.8. Critical values for testing $H_1 : \mu < \mu_0$ at the (a) 5% and (b) 1% significance levels

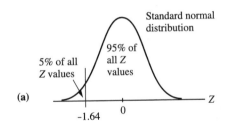

(a)

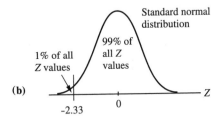

(b)

Testing the alternative hypothesis H_1: $\mu \neq \mu_0$

KEY POINT

Hypotheses: $H_0 : \mu = \mu_0$
                $H_1 : \mu \neq \mu_0$

Test statistic : $Z = \dfrac{|\bar{x} - \mu_0|}{\sigma/\sqrt{n}}$ [9.1]

where $\bar{x}$ represents the sample mean, μ_0 represents the hypothesized value of the population mean, σ represents the population standard deviation and n represents the size of the sample. Note: the modulus sign is used to always make the test statistic positive when testing a two-sided alternative hypothesis.

Decisions:
If $Z < 1.96$ then the null hypothesis is not rejected at the 5% level, i.e. there is no evidence to reject the null hypothesis.

If $Z > 1.96$ then the null hypothesis is rejected at the 5% level, i.e. there is some evidence to reject the null hypothesis in favour of H_1.

If $Z > 2.58$ then the null hypothesis is rejected at the 1% level, i.e. there is strong evidence to reject the null hypothesis in favour of H_1.

Worked example

9.4   A sample of 40 items is taken from a population with standard deviation 10.3. Assuming that the mean of the sample is 3.6, perform a test of the hypotheses

$$H_0 : \quad \mu = 2$$
$$H_1 : \quad \mu \neq 2$$

Solution

Use the normal distribution since σ is known

In this case we are testing a two-sided alternative hypothesis and we know that the population standard deviation is 10.3. Thus we use the test described on page 139.

Using [9.1], the test statistic is:

$$Z = \frac{|3.6 - 2|}{10.3/\sqrt{40}} = 0.9824$$

Comparing this with the critical values gives

5% significance level $Z = 0.9824 < 1.96$

Thus the null hypothesis is not rejected at the 5% level of significance, i.e. the sample suggests that the population mean could be 2.

Testing the alternative hypothesis $H_1: \mu > \mu_0$

KEY POINT

Hypotheses: $H_0 : \quad \mu = \mu_0$
                $H_1 : \quad \mu > \mu_0$

Test statistic: $Z = \dfrac{\bar{x} - \mu_0}{\sigma/\sqrt{n}}$ [9.2]

where $\bar{x}$ represents the sample mean, μ_0 represents the hypothesized value of the population mean, σ represents the population standard deviation and n represents the size of the sample.

Decisions:

If $Z < 1.64$ then the null hypothesis is not rejected at the 5% level, i.e. there is no evidence to reject the null hypothesis.

If $Z > 1.64$ then the null hypothesis is rejected at the 5% level, i.e. there is some evidence to reject the null hypothesis in favour of H_1.

If $Z > 2.33$ then the null hypothesis is rejected at the 1% level, i.e. there is strong evidence to reject the null hypothesis in favour of H_1.

Worked example

9.5   A sample of 40 items is taken from a population with standard deviation 10.3. Assuming that the mean of the sample is 3.6, perform a test of the hypotheses

$$H_0 : \quad \mu = 1$$
$$H_1 : \quad \mu > 1$$

Solution

Use the normal distribution since σ is known

In this case we are testing a greater than alternative hypothesis and we know that the population standard deviation is 10.3. Thus we use the test described on page 140.

Using [9.2], the test statistic is:

$$Z = \frac{3.6 - 1}{10.3/\sqrt{40}} = 1.5965$$

Comparing this with the critical values gives

5% significance level $Z = 1.5965 < 1.64$

Thus the null hypothesis is not rejected at the 5% level of significance, i.e. the sample suggests that the population mean could be 1.

Testing the alternative hypothesis $H_1: \mu < \mu_0$

KEY POINT

Hypotheses: $H_0 : \mu = \mu_0$
$H_1 : \mu < \mu_0$

Test statistic: $Z = \dfrac{\bar{x} - \mu_0}{\sigma/\sqrt{n}}$ [9.3]

where $\bar{x}$ represents the sample mean, μ_0 represents the hypothesized value of the population mean, σ represents the population standard deviation and n represents the size of the sample.

Decisions:

If $Z > -1.64$ then the null hypothesis is not rejected at the 5% level, i.e. there is no evidence to reject the null hypothesis.

If $Z < -1.64$ then the null hypothesis is rejected at the 5% level, i.e. there is some evidence to reject the null hypothesis in favour of H_1.

If $Z < -2.33$ then the null hypothesis is rejected at the 1% level, i.e. there is strong evidence to reject the null hypothesis in favour of H_1.

Worked examples

9.6   A sample of 40 items is taken from a population with standard deviation 10.3. Assuming that the mean of the sample is 3.6, perform a test of the hypotheses

$$H_0 : \mu = 8$$
$$H_1 : \mu < 8$$

Solution

Use the normal distribution since σ is known

In this case we are testing a less than alternative hypothesis and we know that the population standard deviation is 10.3. Thus we use the test described above.

Using [9.3], the test statistic is

$$Z = \frac{3.6 - 8}{10.3/\sqrt{40}} = -2.7018$$

Comparing this with the critical values gives

5% significance level $Z = -2.7018 < -1.64$
1% significance level $Z = -2.7018 < -2.33$

Thus the null hypothesis is rejected at the 5% and 1% levels of significance, i.e there is strong evidence that the population mean is not 8. The sample indicates that the population mean is significantly less than 8 and may be as low as 3.6.

9.7 Consider the weight of the sugar bags data given in Worked Example 9.1. The hypotheses are

$$H_0 : \quad \mu = 500 \text{ g}$$
$$H_1 : \quad \mu \neq 500 \text{ g}$$

where μ represents the mean weight (g) of the sugar bags. The standard deviation of the weights of all bags of sugar is 5 g. The data given below represent the weights of a random sample of 20 bags of sugar. Use this sample of data to test the hypotheses stated above.

489.6 493.7 503.1 499.3 507.8 502.5 498.2 495.3
497.4 488.6 507.7 501.0 491.1 489.2 492.3 510.8
496.6 495.5 504.0 493.4

Solution

Use the normal distribution since σ is known, even though the sample size is small ($n < 30$)

We want to test a two-sided alternative hypothesis and we know that the population standard deviation is 5 g. Thus the test described on page 139 will be used.

First calculate the sample mean: $n = 20$ and $\Sigma x_i = 9957.1$, so sample mean $\bar{x} = \frac{3957.1}{20} = 497.855$ g

Next calculate the test statistic using [9.1]:

$$Z = \frac{|497.855 - 500|}{5/\sqrt{20}} = 1.9185$$

Comparing this with the critical values gives

5% significance level $Z = 1.9185 < 1.96$

The sample provides no evidence to reject the null hypothesis at the 5% significance level.

The mean weight of all sugar bags could be 500 g, i.e. the bags are not consistently under-filled or over-filled. This implies that the manufacturer does not need to adjust the production line.

Self-assessment questions 9.5

1. When the population standard deviation is known, which probability distribution is used to find the acceptance and rejection regions?
2. State the equations used to calculate the test statistic for each of the three types of alternative hypothesis when the population standard deviation is known.

Exercises 9.5

1. A population is known to have a standard deviation of 76.53. A sample of 17 items taken from this population has a mean of 23.04.
   (a) Test the following hypotheses:
      (i) $H_0 : \mu = 25$
            $H_1 : \mu \neq 25$
      (ii) $H_0 : \mu = 50$
            $H_1 : \mu < 50$
      (iii) $H_0 : \mu = 0$
            $H_1 : \mu > 0$
   (b) Comment on the range of possible values of the population mean in the light of the results of the hypothesis tests performed in (a).

2. Consider the electricity company data given in Exercises 9.1, Question 2. The company want to investigate whether or not the average quarterly bills are £135. Test these hypotheses assuming that the standard deviation of all electricity bills in this town is £52.

9.6   **Hypothesis test for a population mean: large sample**

Read Sections 7.5 and 7.7 before you read this section

In Section 7.7 we saw that if the population standard deviation, σ, is unknown and is estimated using a large sample (30 or more items), then the sampling distribution of the sample means is normally distributed with mean, μ, and estimated standard error, $s/\sqrt{n}$, where s is the sample standard deviation and n is the size of the sample. Figures 9.6–9.8 show the critical values of the standard normal distribution for testing $H_1 : \mu \neq \mu_0$, $H_1 : \mu > \mu_0$ and $H_1 : \mu < \mu_0$ respectively at the 5% and 1% significance levels.

Testing the alternative hypothesis H_1: $\mu \neq \mu_0$

Hypotheses:	H_0 : $\mu = \mu_0$
	H_1 : $\mu \neq \mu_0$
Test statistic:	$Z = \dfrac{|\bar{x} - \mu_0|}{s/\sqrt{n}}$ [9.4]

where $\bar{x}$ represents the sample mean, μ_0 represents the hypothesized value of the population mean, s represents the sample standard deviation and n represents the size of the sample. Note that the modulus sign is used to always make the test statistic positive when testing a two-sided alternative hypothesis.

Decisions:

If $Z < 1.96$ then the null hypothesis is not rejected at the 5% level, i.e. there is no evidence to reject the null hypothesis.

If $Z > 1.96$ then the null hypothesis is rejected at the 5% level, i.e. there is some evidence to reject it in favour of H_1.

If $Z > 2.58$ then the null hypothesis is rejected at the 1% level, i.e. there is strong evidence to reject it in favour of H_1.

Worked example

9.8 For the sample of data given below perform a test of the hypotheses
H_0 : $\mu = 37$
H_1 : $\mu \neq 37$

This data was analysed in Worked Example 8.3

27.8	33.2	16.3	31.4	9.9	21.1	40.5
35.7	32.5	34.4	46.7	21.8	34.5	13.7
57.9	16.6	45.9	6.1	42.3	18.2	38.2
20.7	45.6	12.3	61.6	24.4	53.8	23.1
37.0	32.1	59.3	27.3	39.5	24.2	33.2

Solution Data summary: $n = 35$, $\Sigma x_i = 1118.8$, $\Sigma x_i^2 = 42596.56$, $\bar{x} = 31.9657$, $s = 14.1767$. In this case we are testing a two-sided alternative hypothesis and we have estimated the standard deviation using a large sample. Thus we use the test described above.

Use the normal distribution since the sample size is large ($n > 30$)

Using [9.4], the test statistic is

$$Z = \frac{|31.9657 - 37|}{14.1767/\sqrt{35}} = 2.1009$$

Comparing this with the critical values gives

5% significance level	$Z = 2.1009 > 1.96$
1% significance level	$Z = 2.1009 < 2.58$

Thus the null hypothesis is rejected at the 5% level of significance but not at the 1% level, i.e. there is some evidence that the population mean is not 37. This sample suggests that the mean is approximately 32.

Testing the alternative hypothesis $H_1: \mu > \mu_0$

KEY POINT

Hypotheses: $H_0: \quad \mu = \mu_0$
               $H_1: \quad \mu > \mu_0$

Test statistic: $Z = \dfrac{\bar{x} - \mu_0}{s/\sqrt{n}}$ [9.5]

where $\bar{x}$ represents the sample mean, μ_0 represents the hypothesized value of the population mean, s represents the sample standard deviation and n represents the size of the sample.

Decisions:

If $Z < 1.64$ then the null hypothesis is not rejected at the 5% level, i.e. there is no evidence to reject the null hypothesis.

If $Z > 1.64$ then the null hypothesis is rejected at the 5% level, i.e. there is some evidence to reject the null hypothesis in favour of H_1.

If $Z > 2.33$ then the null hypothesis is rejected at the 1% level, i.e. there is strong evidence to reject the null hypothesis in favour of H_1.

Worked example

9.9   For the sample of data given in Worked Example 9.8, perform a test of the hypotheses

$H_0: \quad \mu = 25$
$H_1: \quad \mu > 25$

Solution

Use the normal distribution since the sample size is large ($n > 30$)

In this case we are testing a greater than alternative hypothesis and we have estimated the standard deviation using a large sample. Thus we use the test described above.

Using [9.5], the test statistic is

$$Z = \frac{31.9657 - 25}{14.1767/\sqrt{35}} = 2.9069$$

Comparing this with the critical values gives:

5% significance level $Z = 2.9069 > 1.64$
1% significance level $Z = 2.9069 > 2.33$

Thus the null hypothesis is rejected at the 5% and 1% levels of significance, i.e. there is strong evidence that the population mean is not 25. This sample suggests that the population mean is greater than 25 and is approximately 32.

Testing the alternative hypothesis H_1: $\mu < \mu_0$

KEY POINT

Hypotheses: H_0 : $\mu = \mu_0$
               H_1 : $\mu < \mu_0$

Test statistic: $Z = \dfrac{\bar{x} - \mu_0}{s/\sqrt{n}}$ [9.6]

where $\bar{x}$ represents the sample mean, μ_0 represents the hypothesized value of the population mean, s represents the sample standard deviation and n represents the size of the sample.

Decisions:

If $Z > -1.64$ then the null hypothesis is not rejected at the 5% level, i.e. there is no evidence to reject the null hypothesis.

If $Z < -1.64$ then the null hypothesis is rejected at the 5% level, i.e. there is some evidence to reject the null hypothesis in favour of H_1.

If $Z < -2.33$ then the null hypothesis is rejected at the 1% level, i.e. there is strong evidence to reject the null hypothesis in favour of H_1.

Worked examples

9.10 For the sample of data given in Worked Example 9.8, perform a test of the hypotheses

H_0 : $\mu = 33$
H_1 : $\mu < 33$

Solution In this case we are testing a less than alternative hypothesis and we have estimated the standard deviation using a large sample. Thus we use the test described above.

Use the normal distribution since the sample size is large $(n > 30)$

Using [9.6], the test statistic is

$$Z = \frac{31.9657 - 33}{14.1767/\sqrt{35}} = -0.4316$$

Perform the test at the 5% level of significance:

$$Z = -0.4316 > -1.64$$

Thus the null hypothesis is not rejected at the 5% level of significance. This sample indicates that the population mean could be 33.

9.11 Consider the speed of the racing car example (Worked Example 9.2). The hypotheses are

H_0 : $\mu = 5$
H_1 : $\mu > 5$

where μ represents the mean increase in the speed of the car with the new body shape relative to the conventional body shape. The following data represents a random sample of the increase in speed for 36 independent circuits of a test track. Using this sample of data, test the hypotheses stated above.

6.0	4.7	6.1	5.8	5.3	6.2	3.8	7.2	5.0
5.1	5.6	6.0	5.3	6.4	6.3	7.1	4.8	5.1
4.9	5.5	5.1	5.2	7.0	6.2	6.3	7.2	7.0
5.7	4.5	4.8	6.9	5.7	5.4	7.3	6.3	5.6

Solution

We want to test a greater than alternative hypothesis and we are estimating the population standard deviation using a large sample. Thus the test described on page 145 will be used.

First calculate the sample mean and sample standard deviation: $n = 36$, $\Sigma x_i = 208.4$ and $\Sigma x_i^2 = 1232.98$ so

$$\bar{x} = \frac{208.4}{36} = 5.7889 \qquad s = 0.8714$$

Next calculate the test statistic using [9.5]:

$$Z = \frac{5.7889 - 5}{0.8714/\sqrt{36}} = 5.4319$$

Comparing this with the critical values gives

| 5% significance level | $Z = 5.4319 > 1.64$ |
| 1% significance level | $Z = 5.4319 > 2.33$ |

The sample provides evidence to reject the null hypothesis at the 5% and 1% significance levels, i.e. there is strong evidence to reject H_0 in favour of H_1. The sample suggests that the new body shape is at least 5 mph faster than the conventionally shaped car. This sample suggests that the mean increase in speed is 5.79 mph.

Use the normal distribution since the sample size is large ($n > 30$)

Self-assessment questions 9.6

1. What is meant by a 'large' sample?
2. When a large sample is used to estimate the population standard deviation, which probability distribution is used to find the acceptance and rejection regions?
3. State the equations which are used to calculate the test statistic for each of the three types of alternative hypothesis when a large sample is used to estimate the population standard deviation.

Exercises 9.6

1. The data below represent a random sample of 50 items taken from a very large population.

You may have calculated a data summary for this data in Exercises 8.3, Question 1

2.16	5.47	6.05	9.86	5.45	−0.01	3.27	8.88	4.51	6.24
2.79	5.30	1.66	8.54	2.47	6.36	4.33	1.23	2.20	7.87
9.17	8.26	−0.58	2.74	2.78	6.10	4.47	5.78	2.51	7.52
5.55	8.29	3.47	7.70	2.78	11.24	4.74	7.73	6.75	6.29
9.24	6.00	7.36	9.08	5.51	7.10	9.19	5.11	4.78	6.21

(a) Test the following hypotheses:
  (i) $H_0 : \mu = 4$
        $H_1 : \mu \neq 4$
  (ii) $H_0 : \mu = 3$
        $H_1 : \mu > 3$
  (iii) $H_0 : \mu = 6$
        $H_1 : \mu < 6$

(b) Comment on the range of possible values of the population mean in the light of the results of the hypothesis tests performed in (a).

2. Consider the television viewing data given in Exercises 9.1, Question 1. The agency want to test whether or not, on average, households spend less than 35 hours watching the television. Use the sample of data to test these hypotheses.

9.7   Hypothesis test for a population mean: small sample

Read Sections 7.5, 7.6 and 7.7 before you read this section

In Section 7.7 we saw that if the population standard deviation σ is unknown and is estimated using a small sample (less than 30 items), then the sampling distribution of the sample means approximately follows a t distribution with $n - 1$ degrees of freedom, where n is the size of the sample. Note that we have to assume that the population is normally distributed. Figures 9.9–9.11 show the critical values of a t distribution with $n - 1$ degrees of freedom for testing $H_1 : \mu \neq \mu_0$, $H_1 : \mu > \mu_0$ and $H_1 : \mu < \mu_0$ respectively at the 5% and 1% significance levels.

Testing the alternative hypothesis $H_1: \mu \neq \mu_0$

KEY POINT

Hypotheses: $H_0 : \mu = \mu_0$
               $H_1 : \mu \neq \mu_0$

Test statistic: $T = \dfrac{|\bar{x} - \mu_0|}{s/\sqrt{n}}$ [9.7]

where $\bar{x}$ represents the sample mean, μ_0 represents the hypothesized value of the population mean, s represents the sample standard deviation and n represents the size of the sample. Note: the modulus sign is used to always

Figure 9.9. Critical values for testing $H_1 : \mu \neq \mu_0$ at the (a) 5% and (b) 1% significance levels

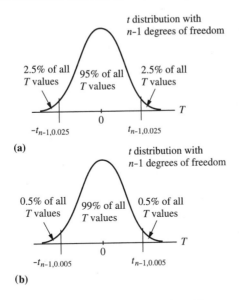

t distribution with *n*-1 degrees of freedom

2.5% of all *T* values   95% of all *T* values   2.5% of all *T* values

$-t_{n-1,0.025}$ 0 $t_{n-1,0.025}$

(a)

t distribution with *n*-1 degrees of freedom

0.5% of all *T* values   99% of all *T* values   0.5% of all *T* values

$-t_{n-1,0.005}$ 0 $t_{n-1,0.005}$

(b)

Figure 9.10. Critical values for testing $H_1 : \mu > \mu_0$ at the (a) 5% and (b) 1% significance levels

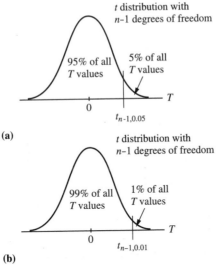

t distribution with *n*-1 degrees of freedom

95% of all *T* values   5% of all *T* values

0    $t_{n-1,0.05}$

(a)

t distribution with *n*-1 degrees of freedom

99% of all *T* values   1% of all *T* values

0    $t_{n-1,0.01}$

(b)

make the test statistic positive when testing a two-sided alternative hypothesis.

Decisions:

If $T < t_{n-1,\,0.025}$ then the null hypothesis is not rejected at the 5% level, i.e. there is no evidence to reject the null hypothesis.

If $T > t_{n-1,0.025}$ then the null hypothesis is rejected at the 5% level, i.e. there is some evidence to reject the null hypothesis in favour of H_1.

If $T > t_{n-1,0.005}$ then the null hypothesis is rejected at the 1% level, i.e. there is strong evidence to reject the null hypothesis in favour of H_1.

Figure 9.11. Critical values for testing $H_1 : \mu < \mu_0$ at the (a) 5% and (b) 1% significance levels

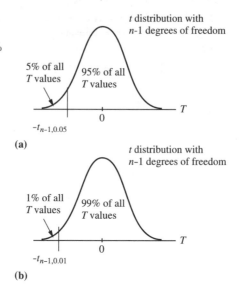

(a)

(b)

Worked example

9.12   For the sample of data given below, perform a test of the hypotheses

$$H_0 : \quad \mu = 8000$$
$$H_1 : \quad \mu \neq 8000$$

This data was analysed in Worked Example 8.5

| 2319 | 6237 | 3422 | 5601 | 7390 | 8125 | 5133 |
| 8218 | 6634 | 7340 | 1278 | 3195 | 7321 | 8830 |

Solution

Use the t distribution since the sample size is small ($n < 30$)

Data summary: $n = 14$, $\Sigma x_i = 81043$, $\Sigma x_i^2 = 543\,162\,959$, $\bar{x} = 5788.7857$, $s = 2386.2168$. In this case we are testing a two-sided alternative hypothesis and we have estimated the standard deviation using a small sample. Thus we use the test described on page 148.

Using [9.7], the test statistic is

$$T = \frac{|5788.7857 - 8000|}{2386.2168/\sqrt{14}} = 3.4672$$

The degrees of freedom are $14 - 1 = 13$. Comparing the value of T with the critical values of a t_{13} distribution gives

5% significance level $t_{13,0.025} = 2.160$

$$T = 3.4672 > 2.160$$

1% significance level $t_{13,0.005} = 3.012$

$$T = 3.4672 > 3.012$$

Thus the null hypothesis is rejected at the 5% and 1% levels of significance, i.e. there is strong evidence that the population mean is not 8000. This sample suggests that the population mean is approximately 5789.

Testing the alternative hypothesis H_1: $\mu > \mu_0$

Hypotheses:	$H_0 :\ \mu = \mu_0$ $H_1 :\ \mu > \mu_0$
Test statistic:	$T = \dfrac{\bar{x} - \mu_0}{s/\sqrt{n}}$ [9.8]

where $\bar{x}$ represents the sample mean, μ_0 represents the hypothesized value of the population mean, s represents the sample standard deviation and n represents the size of the sample.

Decisions:

If $T < t_{n-1,0.05}$ then the null hypothesis is not rejected at the 5% level, i.e. there is no evidence to reject it.

If $T > t_{n-1,0.05}$ then the null hypothesis is rejected at the 5% level, i.e. there is some evidence to reject it in favour of H_1.

If $T > t_{n-1,0.01}$ then the null hypothesis is rejected at the 1% level, i.e. there is strong evidence to reject it in favour of H_1.

Worked example

9.13 For the sample of data given in Worked Example 9.12, perform a test of the hypotheses

$$H_0 :\ \mu = 3500$$
$$H_1 :\ \mu > 3500$$

Solution In this case we are testing a greater than alternative hypothesis and we have estimated the standard deviation using a small sample. Thus we use the test described above.

Use the t distribution since the sample size is small ($n < 30$)

Using [9.8], the test statistic is

$$T = \frac{5788.7857 - 3500}{2386.2168/\sqrt{14}} = 3.5889$$

The degrees of freedom are $14 - 1 = 13$. Comparing T with the critical values of a t_{13} distribution gives

5% significance level $t_{13,0.05} = 1.771$

$T = 3.5889 > 1.771$

1% significance level $t_{13,0.01} = 2.650$

$T = 3.5889 > 2.650$

Thus the null hypothesis is rejected at the 5% and 1% levels of significance, i.e. there is strong evidence that the population mean is not 3500. The sample indicates that the population mean is significantly greater than 3500 and is approximately 5789.

Testing the alternative hypothesis $H_1: \mu < \mu_0$

KEY POINT

Hypotheses: $H_0 : \quad \mu = \mu_0$
                  $H_1 : \quad \mu < \mu_0$

Test statistic: $T = \dfrac{\bar{x} - \mu_0}{s/\sqrt{n}}$ [9.9]

where $\bar{x}$ represents the sample mean, μ_0 represents the hypothesized value of the population mean, s represents the sample standard deviation and n represents the size of the sample.

Decisions:

If $T > -t_{n-1,0.05}$ then the null hypothesis is not rejected at the 5% level, i.e. there is no evidence to reject the null hypothesis.

If $T < -t_{n-1,0.05}$ then the null hypothesis is rejected at the 5% level, i.e. there is some evidence to reject the null hypothesis in favour of H_1.

If $T < -t_{n-1,0.01}$ then the null hypothesis is rejected at the 1% level, i.e. there is strong evidence to reject the null hypothesis in favour of H_1.

Worked examples

9.14   For the sample of data given in Worked Example 9.12, perform a test of the hypotheses

$$H_0 : \quad \mu = 7200$$

$$H_1 : \quad \mu < 7200$$

Solution   In this case we are testing a less than alternative hypothesis and we have estimated the standard deviation using a small sample. Thus we use the test described above.

Use the t distribution since the sample size is small ($n < 30$)

Using [9.9], the test statistic is

$$T = \frac{5788.7857 - 7200}{2386.2168/\sqrt{14}} = -2.2128$$

The degrees of freedom are $14 - 1 = 13$. Comparing T with the critical values from a t_{13} distribution gives

5% significance level $-t_{13,0.05} = -1.771$

$T = -2.2128 < -1.771$

1% significance levels $-t_{13,0.01} = -2.650$

$T = -2.2128 > -2.650$

Thus the null hypothesis is rejected at the 5% level of significance but not the 1% level, i.e. there is some evidence that the population mean is not

7200. The sample indicates that the population mean is less than 7200 and is approximately 5789.

9.15 Consider the cost of producing a video component example (Worked Example 9.3). The hypotheses are

$$H_0 : \quad \mu = \text{£}0$$
$$H_1 : \quad \mu < \text{£}0$$

where μ represents the mean difference in the cost of producing the component using the new and standard methods. The data given below represent a random sample of the differences in cost for 15 components. Test the hypotheses stated above using the sample of data.

−0.13	0.37	−0.83	−0.05	−0.96
−0.74	−1.23	−0.31	−1.06	−0.27
−0.67	−0.45	0.71	−0.50	0.53

Solution We want to test a less than alternative hypothesis and we are estimating the population standard deviation using a small sample. Thus the test described on page 152 will be used.

Use the t distribution since the sample size is small ($n < 30$)

First calculate the sample mean and sample standard deviation: $n = 15$, $\Sigma x_i = -5.59$ and $\Sigma x_i^2 = 6.8063$ so

$$\text{Sample mean } \bar{x} = \frac{-5.59}{15} = -0.3727$$

$$\text{Sample standard deviation } s = \sqrt{\frac{6.8063 - (15 \times (-0.37))^2}{14}}$$

$$= 0.5827$$

Next calculate the test statistic using [9.9]:

$$T = \frac{-0.3727 - 0}{0.5827/\sqrt{15}} = -2.4772$$

The degrees of freedom are $15 - 1 = 14$. Comparing this with the critical values of a t_{14} distribution gives:

5% significance level $-t_{14,0.05} = -1.761$

$T = -2.4772 < -1.761$

1% significance level $-t_{14,0.01} = -2.624$

$T = -2.4772 > -2.624$

The sample provides evidence to reject the null hypothesis at the 5% significance level but not at the 1% significance level, i.e. there is some evidence to reject H_0 in favour of H_1.

The sample provides some evidence that, on average, it is cheaper to use the new method to produce the video component than the standard method. This sample suggests that it is 37p cheaper to use the new method than the standard.

Self-assessment questions 9.7

1. What is meant by a 'small' sample?
2. When a small sample is used to estimate the population standard deviation, which probability distribution is used to find the acceptance and rejection regions?
3. State the equations which are used to calculate the test statistic for each of the three types of alternative hypothesis when a small sample is used to estimate the population standard deviation.
4. What must be assumed about the probability distribution of the population in order to be able to perform a hypothesis test for a population mean using a small sample?

Exercises 9.7

You may have calculated a data summary for this data in Exercises 8.4, Question 1

1. The data given below represent a random sample of 16 items from a large population.

| 107.6 | 60.0 | 28.1 | 90.0 | 112.9 | 87.6 | 414.8 | 65.3 |
| 195.5 | 135.6 | 71.6 | 54.7 | 116.7 | 68.9 | 148.8 | 71.1 |

(a) What assumptions must be made in order to be able to perform a hypothesis test for the population mean using this sample?

(b) Test the following hypotheses:
  (i) $H_0 : \mu = 80$
        $H_1 : \mu \neq 80$
  (ii) $H_0 : \mu = 150$
        $H_1 : \mu > 150$
  (iii) $H_0 : \mu = 170$
        $H_1 : \mu < 170$

(c) Comment on the range of possible values of the population mean in the light of the results of the hypothesis test performed in (a).

2. Consider the potato yield data given in Exercises 9.1, Question 3. It is claimed that the new pesticide will produce at least 1750 tonnes of potatoes. Test these hypotheses using the sample of data.

Test exercises

You may have analysed this data in Chapter 8, Test Exercises, Question 1

1. A major chain store offers a store card (credit card to be used in the store). The Head Office have conducted a survey of 1500 store card users to estimate the average amount spent on the card. The following is a summary of the results of this survey.

   Number of customers in sample = 1500
   Mean amount spent using the store card = £372.67
   Standard deviation of the amount spent using the store card = £135.21

   The Head Office believe that on average, store card users buy at least £360 of goods using their store card.

   (a) State the null and alternative hypotheses that can be used to test the belief of the Head Office.
   (b) Perform a test of the hypotheses stated in (a). Clearly state the conclusions of the test.

2. The following data represent the annual amount spent by 50 British electronics companies on research and development expressed as a percentage of their annual turnover.

You may have analysed this data in Chapter 8, Test Exercises, Question 2

4.8	3.3	6.0	6.7	2.7	7.8	3.9	5.3	6.2	5.9
5.2	4.6	3.1	1.3	3.2	4.5	5.2	2.7	4.5	3.2
3.8	3.0	2.3	3.9	4.0	2.1	3.3	7.3	3.4	6.8
2.1	8.6	5.1	6.5	3.2	3.7	4.3	2.5	6.9	4.1
4.9	4.3	2.5	2.7	5.4	9.3	1.2	6.4	8.0	5.7

   (a) Calculate the sample mean and standard deviation of the annual expenditure on research and development as a percentage of the annual turnover.
   (b) The average percentage spent on research and development by similar Japanese electronics companies is 5.2%. Use a hypothesis test to decide whether the average amount spent by British companies is the same as that spent by Japanese companies. Clearly state the hypotheses and conclusions of the test.

You may have analysed this data in Chapter 8 Test Exercises, Question 3

3. A manufacturer frequently sends small packages to a customer in Germany using air freight. In many cases it is important for the package to reach the customer as soon as possible. The manufacturer currently uses ABC Shipping but they are considering Speedy Air Freight who claim that they deliver parcels significantly quicker than all other competitors. The average time currently taken by ABC Shipping to send packages to Germany is 10.2 hours. The manufacturer decides to test the claim of Speedy Air Freight by sending some of its packages to Germany using their service. A total of 237 packages were sent using Speedy over a one-month period. The average delivery time of this sample was 9.8 hours with a standard deviation of 2.7 hours.

(a) State the hypotheses which can be used to test the claim of Speedy Air Freight that they deliver packages significantly quicker than their competitors.

(b) Perform a hypothesis test to decide whether the claim made by Speedy Air Freight is valid.

(c) Advise the manufacturer on which company should be used to deliver their packages to Germany.

You may have analysed this data in Chapter 8, Test Exercises, Question 4

4. A housing federation provides luxury rented accommodation using a leasing agreement whereby the tenant pays a fixed rent and is responsible for all household bills. The average net monthly income to the federation is £280. The federation is considering a new type of leasing agreement whereby the tenant pays a higher rent but the federation pay the water, gas and electricity bills. It is believed that this will be an attractive option to tenants, but the federation is concerned about whether or not this new agreement will provide the same average net monthly income as the existing agreement. The federation decided to test market the new agreement using a sample of 12 tenants over a six-month period. The average net monthly income of these 12 tenants was £255 with a standard deviation of £40.

(a) Test whether or not the two types of leasing agreement provide the same mean net monthly income. Clearly state the hypotheses and conclusions of this test.

(b) Does this sample support the view that the new agreement provides the same mean net monthly income as the standard leasing agreement? Justify your answer.

You may have analysed this data in Chapter 8, Test Exercises, Question 5

5. The National Rivers Authority (NRA) is concerned about the amount of industrial pollutants being dumped in a certain part of a river. They believe that the health of the marine life is being adversely affected by these pollutants since they are reducing the amount of dissolved oxygen in the water. Some scientists believe that ten parts per million is the maximum allowable level of pollutant which leaves enough dissolved oxygen in the water for the marine life to remain healthy. The following data show a random sample of the sewage readings (parts per million of water) taken from the same location on the river over a three-month period.

9.98	12.61	7.32	6.81	8.15	11.51	7.94
7.69	11.15	10.35	5.91	9.04	6.08	

(a) Calculate the mean and standard deviation of this sample of sewage readings.

(b) State the hypotheses that can be used to test the concern of the NRA that this river contains dangerous levels of pollutants.

(c) Use a hypothesis test to decide whether the concerns of the NRA are justified.

You may have analysed this data in Chapter 8 Test Exercises, Question 6

6. The management of a factory with a large assembly line want to test a new assembly technique. Fifteen employees are randomly selected and

the number of units assembled by each of them in one week is recorded. The same 15 employees are then trained to use the new assembly technique. The number of units assembled by each worker using the new technique over a one-week period is recorded. The following data show the difference in the number of units assembled by each employee using the two techniques (number of units assembled using the new technique – number of units assembled using the present technique). The management believe that more units can be assembled using the new rather than the present technique.

Employee	1	2	3	4	5	6	7	8	9	10	11	12	13	14	15
Difference	−1	8	18	−4	11	14	15	6	5	10	−2	−7	9	3	7

(a) Calculate the mean and standard deviation of this sample of differences.
(b) State the hypotheses that can be used to test the management's belief.
(c) Use a hypothesis test to advise the management on whether the new assembly technique should be used in preference to the present technique.

10 Correlation and simple linear regression

Objectives	When you have read this chapter you should be able to
	• recognize a linear relationship between two variables, X and Y, by drawing a scatter diagram
	• calculate a correlation coefficient and interpret it
	• determine the equation of the least squares regression line of best fit
	• use the least squares line to make predictions when appropriate

10.1   Introduction to correlation and regression

Business decisions are often based upon the relationships between two or more variables. If there are relationships then it may be possible to predict a variable from one or more other variables. For example it may be possible to predict the number of sales of a product from the amount spent on advertising.

The statistical procedures in this chapter concentrate on investigating the simplest relationship between just two variables, a linear relationship. However, they can be extended to take into account more variables and non-linear relationships.

The procedures discussed in this chapter include correlation analysis, which investigates the strength of the linear relationship between our two variables, and simple linear regression analysis. Simple linear regression analysis is used to develop an equation of the straight line that relates our two variables. The variable we are interested in predicting is usually called the **dependent** variable and is denoted by Y, and the variable used to predict Y is usually called the **independent** variable and is denoted by X. So, for example, if the amount spent on advertising is used to predict the number of sales of a product, then the amount spent on advertising is our independent variable X and number of sales is our dependent variable Y.

The data we collect on our two variables is usually taken from past records, sampling or experimentation. They will be in the form of n pairs of X and Y values, $(x_1, y_1), (x_2, y_2), \ldots, (x_n, y_n)$.

Self-assessment questions 10.1

1. Explain the meaning of the following terms:
   (a) dependent variable,
   (b) independent variable.
2. What do we aim to do in simple linear regression?

Exercise 10.1

As part of an investigation into the salaries of their employees, a company is interested in the relationship between employees' age and their current salary. Which of these two variables, age and salary, would be the dependent variable and which would be the independent variable?

10.2   The scatter diagram

A **scatter diagram** should always be used as a preliminary investigation to give an overview of a set of data and to ensure that the data does follow approximately a linear relationship. We plot the independent variable, X, on the horizontal axis and the dependent variable, Y, on the vertical axis.

Worked example

10.1 The marketing department of a large chain of department stores wants to investigate whether there is a relationship between the income from the January sale and the amount spent on advertising the sale. Data was collected from ten similar branches of the store, in terms of size, yearly sales and situation, for the previous January sale. The data is given below.

Expenditure on advertising (£000s)	5.0	8.2	6.1	5.3	7.6	7.9	5.6	6.3	6.8	7.4
Income from sale (£0000s)	10.82	18.93	15.32	13.45	17.59	16.97	12.37	14.23	13.53	17.42

Investigate, using a scatter diagram, any relationship between the income from the January sale and the amount spent on advertising the sale.

Solution The marketing department will be interested in trying to predict income from the sale from the amount spent on advertising to determine whether it is beneficial to spend more on advertising. The dependent variable, Y, is the income from the January sale, and the independent variable, X, is the amount spent on advertising. Figure 10.1 shows the scatter diagram for the set of data. The diagram shows us that as the amount spent on

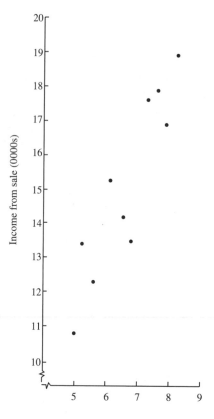

Figure 10.1. Scatter diagram to investigate the relationship between the income from the January sale and the amount spent on advertising the sale

Expenditure on advertising (000s)

advertising increases then so does the income from the sale, and the relationship appears to be fairly linear.

Self-assessment questions 10.2

1. Why do we use a scatter diagram?
2. What do we plot on the horizontal and vertical axes?

Exercises 10.2

1. For the scatter diagrams shown in Figure 10.2 (page 162) comment on whether there appears to be a linear relationship between X and Y.

2. Draw a scatter diagram of the following data and comment on the strength of the linear relationship between X and Y.

X	4	8	11	16	18	21
Y	3	6	9	12	18	19

3. The company described in Exercise 10.1 has collected the following data on their employees' ages and salaries. Draw a scatter diagram of the data and comment on the strength of the relationship between an employee's age and their salary.

Age (Years)	23	32	49	57	48	48	39	25	57	33
Salary (£000s)	14	17	32	36	30	28	25	17	32	19

4. A manufacturing company wants to investigate the relationship between the size of order of a particular component and the cost of producing the order. The following data have been recorded for different sized orders. Draw a scatter diagram of the data and comment on the relationship.

Size of order	115	140	160	180	200	230	280	325	350
Production cost (£s)	1900	2600	3100	3300	3400	3700	3800	3900	3950

5. A small engineering firm believes that there is a linear relationship between the hourly rate an employee is paid and the amount of overtime they undertake, with the lowest paid undertaking the most overtime. The following data have been collected for 12 of the employees. Draw a scatter diagram of the data and comment on whether there is the linear relationship they believe.

Hourly rate (£s)	2.50	4.00	3.25	3.25	2.75	3.75	4.50	4.00	4.50	2.50	3.25	3.00
Average weekly overtime (hours)	12	4	7	8	11	8	4	6	5	9	9	9

6. Students on a particular course are required to take two accountancy exams; Accounts I in the first year and Accounts II in the second year. The tutor wants to investigate the relationship between the results obtained in the two exams for 20 of his students to determine whether the Accounts II result can be predicted from the Accounts I result. Carry out a preliminary investigation of the data to determine if there is a linear relationship between the two results.

Accounts I (%)	12	38	27	41	49	46	89	70	84	50	61	15	50	53	90	60	30	79	44	60
Accounts II (%)	41	54	49	60	52	50	73	48	60	37	77	25	57	60	87	64	31	66	45	46

Figure 10.2. Scatter diagrams for Exercises 10.2, Question 1

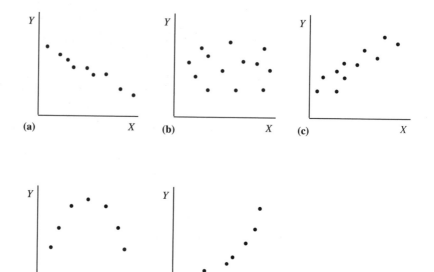

(a) (b) (c) (d) (e)

The correlation coefficient

The **correlation coefficient** provides a measure of the strength of the linear relationship that exists between two variables, X and Y, and is denoted by the letter r. Unlike simple linear regression it does not require dependent and independent variables, so it can be used in more applications. For example, the correlation coefficient could be used to measure the strength of the linear relationship between height and weight without referring to one of them as the dependent variable.

The correlation coefficient should be calculated and interpreted in conjunction with the scatter diagram and used as a preliminary investigation of a set of data.

Calculation of the correlation coefficient

Appendix B discusses the Σ notation

For n pairs of values on two variables, X and Y, (x_i, y_i) for $i = 1, \ldots, n$, the correlation coefficient is calculated as shown below.

The correlation coefficient

KEY POINT

$$r = \frac{\Sigma xy - (\Sigma x \times \Sigma y)/n}{\sqrt{\Sigma x^2 - (\Sigma x)^2/n} \times \sqrt{\Sigma y^2 - (\Sigma y)^2/n}}$$

[10.1]

Figure 10.3. The range of values of the correlation coefficient

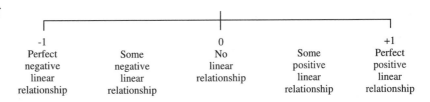

Follow Worked Example 10.2 on how to calculate *r*

Interpretation of the correlation coefficient

In practice, values of *r* which are exactly −1, 0 or +1 are rare so for strong linear relationships we are looking for values of *r* close to −1 and +1.

The correlation coefficient, *r*, always lies in the range −1 to +1 and its value within this range indicates the strength of the linear relationship between *X* and *Y*. Figure 10.3 illustrates the range of values of the correlation coefficient.

The following points should be taken into consideration when interpreting the correlation coefficient.

1. The closer *r* is to −1 or +1, the stronger the linear relationship between *X* and *Y*.
2. A value of *r* close to 0 indicates that there is very little 'linear' relationship between *X* and *Y*, it could indicate that there is no relationship or that there is a non-linear relationship between *X* and *Y*.
3. If *r* = −1 or *r* = +1 there is a perfect linear relationship between *X* and *Y*; all of the points on the scatter diagram lie on a straight line.
4. If *r* = 0 then there is no 'linear' relationship between *X* and *Y*; a non-linear, curved relationship between *X* and *Y* could have a zero correlation.
5. The sign of *r* indicates the 'direction' of the linear relationship. If *r* lies between 0 and 1 then we say that there is a positive correlation. This implies that as the values of the *X* variable increase then so do the values of the *Y* variable. If *r* lies between −1 and 0 then we say that there is a negative correlation. This implies that as the values of the *X* variable increase then the values of the *Y* variable decrease. Figure 10.4 shows examples of positive and negative correlations.

Note that a non-linear relationship could have a high correlation so the scatter diagram must be used in conjunction with the correlation. The scatter diagram in Figure 10.5 shows a curved relationship between *X* and *Y*, but the correlation coefficient *r* is −0.91.

Figure 10.4. (a) Positive $(0 < r \le 1)$ and (b) negative $(-1 \le r < 0)$ correlations

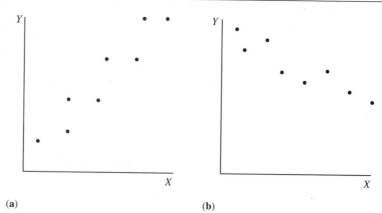

(a)   (b)

Figure 10.5. Graph to show a curved relationship with a high correlation

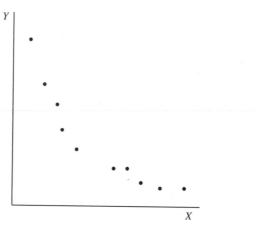

Worked example

10.2   In Worked Example 10.1 we used a scatter diagram to show that there was a linear relationship between the income from the January sale and the amount spent on advertising the sale. Calculate the correlation coefficient for this data and comment on the strength of the linear relationship.

Solution X is the amount spent on advertising, Y is the income from the January sale. Data summary: $n = 10$, $\Sigma x = 66.2$, $\Sigma x^2 = 449.76$, $\Sigma y = 150.63$, $\Sigma y^2 = 2330.44$, $\Sigma xy = 1021.64$.

The correlation coefficient is found using [10.1]:

$$r = \frac{1021.64 - (66.2 \times 150.63)/10}{\sqrt{449.76 - (66.2)^2/10} \times \sqrt{2330.44 - (150.63)^2/10}}$$

$$= \frac{1021.64 - 997.1706}{\sqrt{11.516} \times \sqrt{61.50031}}$$

$$= 0.92$$

The interpretation of this is that there is a strong positive correlation between the amount of income from the January sale and the amount spent on advertising the sale. This means that as the expenditure on advertising increases then the amount of income from the January sale increases. This confirms our interpretation of a good linear relationship on the scatter diagram.

Self-assessment questions 10.3

1. Explain why we calculate a correlation coefficient.
2. How would you interpret a correlation coefficient close to
   (a) 1, (b) −1 and (c) 0?
3. Why do we need to consider the correlation coefficient in conjunction with the scatter diagram?

Exercises 10.3

1. The correlation coefficients for the scatter diagrams in Exercises 10.2, Question 1, have been calculated as follows: (a) −0.99, (b) 0.12, (c) 0.8, (d) 0 and (e) 0.9. Comment on the strength of the linear relationship between X and Y using the correlation coefficients and the scatter diagrams.
2. Calculate the correlation coefficient for the data in Exercises 10.2, Question 2, and comment on the strength of the linear relationship.
3. Calculate the correlation coefficient for the data in Exercises 10.2, Question 3, and comment on the strength of the linear relationship.
4. Calculate the correlation coefficient for the data in Exercises 10.2, Question 4, and comment on the strength of the linear relationship (consider the relationship shown on the scatter diagram).
5. Calculate the correlation coefficient for the data in Exercises 10.2, Question 5, and comment on the strength of the linear relationship.
6. Calculate the correlation coefficient for the data in Exercises 10.2, Question 6, and comment on the strength of the linear relationship.

10.4   Simple linear regression

Once the scatter diagram and correlation have been used to investigate the strength of the linear relationship between the variables X and Y, simple

Figure 10.6. Graph to show the equation of a straight line: a, intercept with the Y axis; b, slope of the line

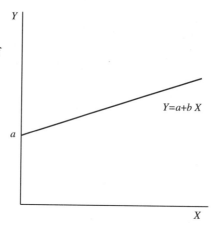

linear regression can be used to carry out a more detailed investigation of the relationship. In simple linear regression we find the equation of a straight line that best represents the linear relationship between X and Y. This equation can be used to predict the dependent variable, Y, given the value of the independent variable, X.

The equation of a straight line

The general equation of a straight line, illustrated in Figure 10.6, is given by

KEY POINT

$$Y = a + bX \qquad\qquad [10.2]$$

where a is the point at which the line intercepts the vertical axis and b is the gradient of the line, i.e. the steepness of the slope of the line.

In order to find the values of a and b that give the equation of the line that is the best relationship between our two variables X and Y, a method called **least squares** is used.

The method of least squares

Consider the scatter diagram in Figure 10.7. If the straight line shown on the scatter diagram is the best line that can be drawn through the data points, then the distances d_i of the data points from the line will be the smallest possible. In other words, the best line through a set of data points is the one that minimizes the distances d_i of the data points from the line. There are points above and below the best line and to minimize the

Figure 10.7. Scatter diagram to illustrate the method of least squares

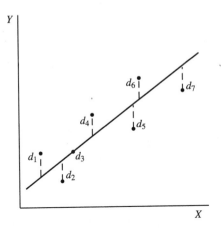

distances of these points from the best line we have to minimize the sum of the squares of the differences,

$$\Sigma d_i^2 = d_1^2 + d_2^2 + \cdots + d_n^2 \qquad [10.3]$$

Appendix B discusses the Σ notation

The method used to minimize Σd_i^2 is beyond the scope of this text, but it produces the following values of a and b for the best line that can be calculated from our n pairs of data values.

Least squares estimates for a and b

KEY POINT

$$b = \frac{\Sigma xy - (\Sigma x \times \Sigma y)/n}{\Sigma x^2 - (\Sigma x)^2/n} \qquad [10.4]$$

$$a = \frac{\Sigma y - b\Sigma x}{n} \qquad [10.5]$$

The line that has these values of a and b in its equation is called the **least squares line** and the values a and b are called the **least squares estimates**.

Using the least squares line for prediction

Once we have calculated the equation of the least squares line we can consider using it to predict our dependent variable Y. To predict values of Y we substitute values of our independent variable X into the equation. The values predicted for Y from the equation are called the **predicted values** and are usually denoted by $\hat{y}_i$, i.e.

$$\hat{y}_i = a + bx_i \qquad [10.6]$$

where $\hat{y}_i$ is the predicted value, x_i is the value of the independent variable used to predict y_i and a and b are the least squares estimates of the intercept and slope. The values we obtain will only be good predictions if our sample data set is representative of all possible data sets that could be collected for the variables X and Y, and shows a strong linear relationship from the scatter diagram and correlation analysis. The predicted values can be used to plot the least squares line on our scatter diagram, the line should 'look like' the best line through the data points.

Note that when predicting values of our dependent variable Y we should only use values of our independent variable X which lie within the range of the data set used to find the least squares equation. For any values above the maximum X or below the minimum X we do not know if the relationship between X and Y is still linear. More data should be obtained outside the range for further investigation.

Worked example

10.3 In Worked Examples 10.1 and 10.2 we used a scatter diagram and correlation coefficient to show that there was a linear relationship between the income from the January sale and the amount spent on advertising the sale.

(a) Calculate the least squares estimates for the data and hence the least squares line.

(b) Find, if appropriate, predictions of the income from the January sale when the amount spent on advertising is (i) £7000, (ii) £10000.

Solution (a) X is the amount spent on advertising, Y is the income from the January sale. Data summary: $n = 10$, $\Sigma x = 66.2$, $\Sigma x^2 = 449.76$, $\Sigma y = 150.63$, $\Sigma xy = 1021.64$. The least squares estimates are

$$b = \frac{1021.64 - (66.2 \times 150.63)/10}{449.76 - (66.2)^2/10}$$

$$= \frac{1021.64 - 997.1706}{11.516}$$

$$= 2.125$$

$$a = \frac{150.63 - 2.125 \times 66.2}{10}$$

$$= 0.9955$$

The equation of the least squares line is

$$\hat{y}_i = 0.9955 + 2.125 \times x_i$$

where $\hat{y}_i$ is the fitted/predicted value of the income from the January sale and x_i is the amount spent on advertising.

(b) (i) The prediction of income when the amount spent on advertising is £7000 is

$$\hat{y} = 0.9955 + 2.125 \times 7.0$$
$$= 15.87$$

The predicted income from the January sale is £158700.

(ii) The income when the amount spent on advertising is £10000 cannot be predicted. The amount spent on advertising is outside the range of our data set as the maximum amount spent is £8000. We cannot be sure that the relationship between income from the January sale and amount spent on advertising will continue to be linear for amounts spent over £8000, the income could start to level off at this point or even increase at a faster rate. Therefore, it is not appropriate to predict income for this amount spent on advertising.

Self-assessment questions 10.4

1. State and explain what each of the terms represent in the general equation of a straight line.
2. What does the least squares line represent?
3. When will the least squares line give good predictions for the dependent variable?
4. Why should we not use the least squares equation to predict Y for values of X outside the range of the data given?

Exercises 10.4

1. Calculate the least squares estimates and line for the data in Exercises 10.2, Question 2, and draw the line on the scatter diagram.
2. Calculate the least squares estimates and line for the data in Exercises 10.2, Question 3. Predict, if possible, an employee's salary at age 30 and age 65.
3. Discuss why we should not calculate the least squares estimates and line for the data in Exercises 10.2, Question 4.
4. Calculate the least squares estimates and line for the data in Exercises 10.2, Question 5, and draw the line on the scatter diagram.
5. Calculate the least squares estimates and line for the data in Exercises 10.2, Question 6, and draw the line on the scatter diagram. Predict, if possible, a student's result for Accounts II if they achieve 55% in Accounts I.

Test exercises

1. For the following set of data:

   (a) draw a scatter diagram of the data and comment on the linear relationship between X and Y;
   (b) calculate the correlation coefficient and comment;

(c) find, if appropriate, the least squares estimates and line, and plot the line on the scatter diagram;

(d) predict, if possible, the value of Y when $X = 25$ and when $X = 40$.

X	9	12	14	17	19	22	24	26	29	30	32	35
Y	89.5	92	90.5	89.5	93	95.5	91.5	95	99	93	96.5	100

2. The following data represent the monthly output and associated labour costs of a factory. Investigate the relationship between the output and labour costs by drawing a scatter diagram, calculating a correlation coefficient and finding the least squares line. Comment at each stage.

Monthly output (tonnes $\times$ 10^3)	Labour cost (£000s)
66	48
74	53
78	64
70	52
81	64
90	80
87	77
85	68

3. A supermarket chain is considering reducing the price of some of its own brand products. An experiment has been carried out to investigate how changing the price of one product affects the demand for the product. Eight supermarkets in the chain were selected and different prices were assigned randomly to each. The same advertising was used for all eight and the sales of the product recorded the following week. The price and sales are recorded below. Carry out a preliminary investigation of the data and, if appropriate, find the least squares line. Predict, if possible, the sales for prices of £1.12 and 90p.

Price (£s)	0.95	1.00	1.05	1.10	1.15	1.20	1.25	1.30
Sales (£s)	1120	999	932	884	807	760	701	621

4. Draw a scatter diagram of the following data and comment on the linear relationship between X and Y. Calculate the correlation coefficient and comment. Find, if appropriate, the least squares estimates and line.

X	87	73	78	70	83	80	80	82	75	85	76
Y	37	17	20	17	31	22	24	27	18	32	20

11 Time series analysis and forecasting

Objectives

When you have read this chapter you should be able to

- recognize time series data

- draw a time series plot

- understand the four components of a time series

- find estimates of the trend and seasonal components

- forecast using the trend and seasonal estimates

- use exponential smoothing

Time series represent data that are measured over time, e.g. yearly trade figures, quarterly fuel consumption, monthly sales figures or daily temperatures. In a time series analysis we use time series data collected to investigate patterns in a variable of interest, called the Y variable, over a period of time measured at intervals T, e.g. yearly, monthly or daily. It may be possible to use these patterns in the past data to predict future values; this method of prediction is called **forecasting.**

Time series can show very complex patterns. This chapter will consider only the simplest patterns to look for in a time series, these are called the **components of a time series**. Example 11.1 below shows how a set of time series data may be presented and this method will be used throughout the chapter.

Example

11.1 A manufacturer of a compact disc (CD) player wants to analyse the countrywide sales of its CD player over the past four years, so it can plan production more efficiently in the future. The data available are presented overleaf and represent a time series measured at quarterly time intervals (every three months).

Year	Quarter	Sales (000s)
1	1	4.1
	2	3.1
	3	2.8
	4	4.2
2	1	4.5
	2	3.8
	3	3.2
	4	4.8
3	1	5.4
	2	4.0
	3	3.6
	4	5.5
4	1	5.8
	2	4.3
	3	3.9
	4	6.0

11.1   The components of a time series

A time series can be thought of as consisting of four separate components. These components are the

trend (TR)
seasonal variation (S)
cyclical variation (C)
irregular activity (I)

The analysis of a set of time series data consists of breaking down the data into the above components and trying to find an estimate for each of them. The components will be discussed in detail below, and Section 11.2 will consider how we estimate the components.

Plot of a time series

As a preliminary investigation into the components of a time series, the data should be plotted. The variable of interest, Y, is plotted on the vertical axis and time, T, is plotted on the horizontal axis. As the points are in ascending order of time they are usually connected by lines.

Example

11.2   The data presented in Example 11.1 have been represented in a time series plot in Figure 11.1.

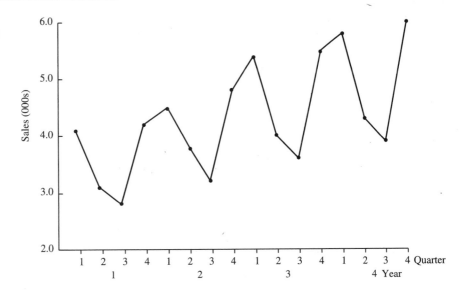

Figure 11.1. Time series plot of the quarterly sales of a compact disc player

Trend component

The trend component considers the overall pattern in the time series. There will be fluctuations in the time series data between the time points, but the trend looks for a long-term increase or decrease in the time series. The trend may represent changes in such things as the economy, the population or consumer preferences. Figure 11.2 shows a time series plot with an overall increasing trend.

If we consider Examples 11.1 and 11.2 on the sales of a CD player, overall there appears to be an increase in the number of sales, but the number of sales fluctuates between the quarters. This overall increase could be due to various reasons, such as a decreasing price of the player and the CDs or increased marketing and preference for CDs rather than records.

The overall trend can take on various patterns. Here we will concentrate on when the trend is a straight line, called a linear trend, and will use the methods discussed in Chapter 10.

Seasonal variation

Many time series show regular patterns of variability over a one-year time period, which are called seasonal effects. For example, sales of tennis rackets will be highest in spring and summer, whereas household fuel consumption will peak during the winter months.

Although we tend to think of seasonal effects as occurring over a one-year period, any regular patterns of variability occurring over a shorter period of time can be represented by the seasonal component. For

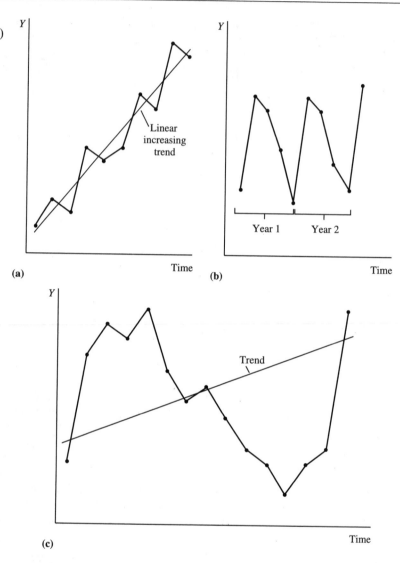

Figure 11.2. Time series plots showing (a) trend, (b) seasonal and (c) cyclical components

example, the number of travellers on the London Underground will peak during the early morning and evening rush hours. Figure 11.2 shows a time series plot with a seasonal component.

Example 11.1 considers the sales of a CD player, the plot of this data in Figure 11.1 shows us that quarters 1 and 4 have the maximum sales, quarter 1 probably representing the January sales period and quarter 4 the Christmas period.

Cyclical variation

The cyclical component of a time series takes into account regular patterns in the data over long periods, more than one year, and can usually be detected by alternating sequences of points above and below the trend line. A lot of cyclical movement in business time series represents economic activity, periods of expansion and recession. To be able to recognize and measure cyclical variation a lot of data needs to be available, many cycles last up to ten years, hence 20 years worth of data may only show two cycles. Figure 11.2 shows a time series plot with a cyclical component.

Irregular activity

This component accounts for any variation or activity in a time series that cannot be accounted for by the other three components. It does not contain any obviously predictable pattern, and consists of random and unpredictable events. For example, natural disasters, such as earthquakes and floods, and accidents can have unpredictable effects on our variable of interest.

Self-assessment questions 11.1

1. What does the trend component of a time series measure?
2. How do we recognize seasonal variation?
3. What is the difference between cyclical and seasonal components?
4. What does the irregular activity component measure?

Exercises 11.1

1. A company is investigating the number of orders (thousands) of four of its products, A, B, C and D, and has quarterly data available for the past three years. Draw a time series plot of the data for each of the four products and comment on the trend and seasonal components.

		Product			
Year	Quarter	A	B	C	D
1990	1	84	5	2.0	30
	2	90	8	2.4	46
	3	112	9	1.8	28
	4	107	10	1.6	37
1991	1	88	14	2.1	18
	2	95	17	2.3	14
	3	118	18	1.7	29
	4	116	22	1.6	35
1992	1	98	24	2.0	50
	2	106	24	2.3	29
	3	128	27	1.8	20
	4	124	28	1.7	47

2. The following sales data has been collected three times a year over four years. Draw a time series plot of the data and comment on any trend and seasonal components.

Year	Month	Sales
1	April	620
	August	660
	December	850
2	April	560
	August	640
	December	750
3	April	540
	August	550
	December	720
4	April	480
	August	500
	December	630

3. A supplier of a certain fertilizer recorded its quarterly sales figures, in thousands of tons, for the years 1988–91: Draw a time series plot of the data and comment on the trend and seasonal components.

	Quarter			
Year	1	2	3	4
1988	48	52	16	35
1989	50	46	22	40
1990	68	34	26	35
1991	73	56	16	45

4. A travel agent is interested in promoting a particular foreign holiday resort and has collected monthly figures over three years of the number of tourists flying into the resort. Draw a time series plot of the data and comment on any seasonal differences and overall trend in the data.

	Year		
Month	1	2	3
January	0.8	1.0	0.8
February	0.5	0.4	0.3
March	2.5	2.0	1.8
April	9.1	7.0	6.5
May	5.4	5.4	5.2

June	6.5	6.0	6.0
July	14.5	13.0	12.4
August	20.5	19.5	17.2
September	15.1	14.8	14.0
October	6.3	6.0	5.1
November	3.1	3.5	2.7
December	8.8	8.3	8.9

11.2   Combining the components of a time series

The components of a time series can be combined in various ways, the most common being

(i) the **additive form**, the sum of the components,

KEY POINT

$$Y = TR + S + C + I \qquad\qquad [11.1]$$

(ii) the **multiplicative form**, the product of the components,

KEY POINT

$$Y = TR \times S \times C \times I \qquad\qquad [11.2]$$

This chapter will only be concerned with finding estimates of the trend (TR) and seasonal (S) components. The additive form given by equation [11.1] assumes that the seasonal component for each season remains the same regardless of the trend effect, whereas the multiplicative form allows the seasonal effect to increase or decrease according to the underlying trend.

It has been observed that the multiplicative form is the most appropriate for business applications, especially for sales data, where an increase in sales usually means increased seasonal differences in sales, so this text will concentrate on the multiplicative form.

Self-assessment questions 11.2

1. How do the additive and multiplicative forms combine the components of a time series?
2. Why is the multiplicative form most appropriate for business applications?

| 11.3 | **Measuring the components of a time series** |

Breaking down a time series and calculating estimates of the components is usually called the **decomposition of a time series**. As a large amount of data is required to investigate cyclical variation and the irregular activity is impossible to predict, we will concentrate on the trend and seasonal components of a time series, then any variation remaining can be attributed to the cyclical and irregular activity components. Each step in the decomposition of a time series will be demonstrated using the data on the sales of a CD player given in Example 11.1.

Step 1: Moving averages

In order to isolate the seasonal component from the time series and to be able to investigate the trend more accurately, we use a method called **moving averages**. This method removes the seasonal component and also **smooths** the data by taking out some of the irregular activity.

The sales data in Example 11.1 is quarterly, so to remove the seasonal component we calculate what are called four-point moving averages.

Four-point moving averages

Calculate the average of the first four values in the data, i.e. those for the first four quarters. Move one value down and calculate the average of these four values. Continue moving one value down the data and calculating the average until the last quarter value has been used to calculate an average.

Each average is calculated from four values, one from each quarter, the first is calculated from year 1 quarters 1, 2, 3 and 4, the second from year 1 quarters 2,3 and 4, and year 2 quarter 1, etc.

For Example 11.1 the first three moving averages have been calculated below and are identified in Table 11.1.

$$\frac{4.1 + 3.1 + 2.8 + 4.2}{4} = \frac{14.2}{4} = 3.55$$

$$\frac{3.1 + 2.8 + 4.2 + 4.5}{4} = \frac{14.6}{4} = 3.65$$

$$\frac{2.8 + 4.2 + 4.5 + 3.8}{4} = \frac{15.3}{4} = 3.825$$

In general, for time series data $y_1, y_2, \ldots, y_n$ the following equations can used to calculate i-point moving averages.

KEY POINT

$$\frac{y_1 + y_2 + \cdots + y_i}{i}$$

$$\frac{y_2 + y_3 + \cdots + y_{i+1}}{i} \quad \text{and so on to} \qquad\qquad [11.3]$$

$$\frac{y_{n-i+1} + y_{n-i+2} + \cdots + y_n}{i}$$

Table 11.1. Quarterly sales of a CD player: moving averages

Year	Quarter	Sales (thousands)	Total	Moving average (total/4)	Centred moving average
1	1	4.1			
	2	3.1			
			14.2	3.550	
	3	2.8			3.6000
			14.6	3.650	
	4	4.2			3.7375
			15.3	3.825	
2	1	4.5			3.8750
			15.7	3.925	
	2	3.8			4.0000
			16.3	4.075	
	3	3.2			4.1875
			17.2	4.300	
	4	4.8			4.3250
			17.4	4.350	
3	1	5.4			4.4000
			17.8	4.450	
	2	4.0			4.5375
			18.5	4.625	
	3	3.6			4.6750
			18.9	4.725	
	4	5.5			4.7625
			19.2	4.800	
4	1	5.8			4.8375
			19.5	4.875	
	2	4.3			4.9375
			20.0	5.000	
	3	3.9			
	4	6.0			

It is important to lay out the data correctly in a table, as shown in Table 11.1. The moving averages should be positioned at the centre of the values that are used to calculate them. Table 11.1 shows the four-point moving averages for Example 11.1 positioned correctly, the first lying between quarters 2 and 3 of year 1, the second between quarters 3 and 4 of year 1 etc. To be able to use these moving averages we need to be able to associate them with just one quarter, rather than them lying between two quarters. We again calculate moving averages, this time only two point moving averages. These new moving averages are called **centred moving averages** because they correspond to just one quarter. For Example 11.1 the first two centred moving averages will be

$$\frac{3.55 + 3.65}{2} = 3.60$$

and

$$\frac{3.65 + 3.825}{2} = 3.7375$$

All of the centred moving averages are given in Table 11.1. Note that if our data has an odd number of values for each year, e.g. only three values per year, then the moving averages will already correspond to just one quarter and we do not need to calculate centred moving averages.

Step 2: Estimating the seasonal component

The centred moving averages represent the data with the seasonal and irregular activity components smoothed out. By dividing the values in the time series by their corresponding centred moving average we can find joint estimates of the seasonal and irregular activity components.

For Example 11.1, the estimate of the joint seasonal and irregular activity component for year 1 quarter 3 will be 2.8/3.6 = 0.7778. All of these components are given in Table 11.2, notice that the components for quarters 1 and 4 are all greater than 1, this indicates that there are above average sales for these quarters.

If we consider the seasonal effects for quarter 1, 1.1613, 1.2273 and 1.1990, the year-to-year differences can most likely be attributed to the irregular activity in the time series. If we calculate the average of these values we can determine an overall estimate of the seasonal component for quarter 1.

For Example 11.1 the seasonal components for each quarter will be

$$\text{Quarter 1} \qquad \frac{1.1613 + 1.2273 + 1.1990}{3} = 1.1959$$

$$\text{Quarter 2} \qquad \frac{0.9500 + 0.8815 + 0.8709}{3} = 0.9008$$

Table 11.2. Quarterly sales of a CD player: seasonal components and deseasonalized data

Year	Quarter	Sales (thousands)	Centred moving average (CMA)	Seasonal components (sales/CMA)	Deseasonalized sales (sales/seasonal)
1	1	4.1			3.426
	2	3.1			3.439
	3	2.8	3.6000	0.7778	3.630
	4	4.2	3.7375	1.1237	3.715
2	1	4.5	3.8750	1.1613	3.760
	2	3.8	4.0000	0.9500	4.215
	3	3.2	4.1875	0.7642	4.149
	4	4.8	4.3250	1.1098	4.246
3	1	5.4	4.4000	1.2273	4.512
	2	4.0	4.5375	0.8815	4.437
	3	3.6	4.6750	0.7701	4.667
	4	5.5	4.7625	1.1549	4.866
4	1	5.8	4.8375	1.1990	4.846
	2	4.3	4.9375	0.8709	4.770
	3	3.9			5.056
	4	6.0			5.308

Quarter 3 $\dfrac{0.7778 + 0.7642 + 0.7701}{3} = 0.7707$

Quarter 4 $\dfrac{1.1237 + 1.1098 + 1.1549}{3} = 1.1295$

One final adjustment may be required as the sum of the seasonal components should be equal to the number of seasons. For Example 11.1 they should sum to 4 as there are four quarters. The sum of the four seasonal components is

$$1.1959 + 0.9008 + 0.7707 + 1.1295 = 3.9969$$

so we should adjust each of them by multiplying by 4/(sum of the components).

The adjusted seasonal components for the sales of a CD player are

Quarter 1 $1.1959 \times \dfrac{4}{3.9969} = 1.1959 \times 1.008 = 1.1969$

Quarter 2 $0.9008 \times \dfrac{4}{3.9969} = 0.9008 \times 1.008 = 0.9015$

Quarter 3 $0.7707 \times \dfrac{4}{3.9969} = 0.7707 \times 1.008 = 0.7713$

Quarter 4 $1.1295 \times \dfrac{4}{3.9969} = 1.1295 \times 1.008 = 1.1304$

Step 3: Estimating the trend component

Deseasonalizing the data

To estimate the trend more accurately we can remove the seasonal component from the time series data, this is called **deseasonalizing** the data. We do this by dividing each value in the time series by its corresponding seasonal component. For Example 11.1 we divide all the quarter 1 sales by the seasonal component for quarter 1, 1.1969. The deseasonalized data is given in Table 11.2.

Method of least squares

If we plot the deseasonalized data against the corresponding time points, with the deseasonalized data on the vertical axis, and they show an approximately linear relationship then we can use the method of least squares described in Chapter 10 to estimate the trend.

The time points are represented by a variable t, with $t = 1$ being the first time point, and are equivalent to the X variable in simple linear regression. For Example 11.1, $t = 1, 2, 3, \ldots, 16$ where $t = 1$ represents

Figure 11.3. Plot of the deseasonalized data and trend line for the quarterly sales of a compact disc player

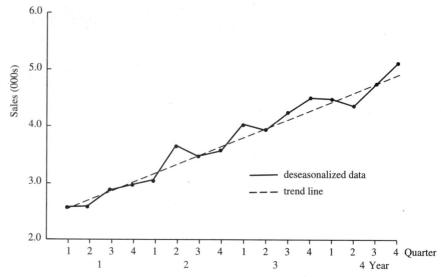

year 1, quarter 1, and $t = 16$ represents year 4, quarter 4. Using the method of least squares we get the following estimate of the trend:

KEY POINT

$$TR = a + bt \qquad\qquad [11.4]$$

where TR represents the trend, t represents the time point, a represents the intercept and b represents the gradient of the trend. The deseasonalized data for Example 11.1 has been plotted in Figure 11.3 and shows an approximate linear trend, therefore the method of least squares can be used on the data and is laid out below.

Chapter 10 discusses the method of least squares

Time point (t)	1	2	3	4	5	6	7	8
Deseasonalized data (y)	3.426	3.439	3.630	3.715	3.760	4.215	4.149	4.246

Time point (t)	9	10	11	12	13	14	15	16
Deseasonalized data (y)	4.512	4.437	4.667	4.866	4.846	4.770	5.056	5.308

Method of least squares
$X = t$ and $Y =$ deseasonalized data
$n = 16$ $\Sigma x = 136$ $\Sigma x^2 = 1496$ $\Sigma y = 69.042$ $\Sigma xy = 628.408$

$$b = \frac{\Sigma xy - (\Sigma x \times \Sigma y)/n}{\Sigma x^2 - (\Sigma x)^2/n} = \frac{628.408 - (136 \times 69.042)/16}{1496 - 136^2/16} = 0.1222$$

$$a = \frac{\Sigma y - b\Sigma x}{n} = \frac{69.042 - (0.1222 \times 136)}{16} = 3.2764$$

Hence

$$TR = 3.2764 + 0.1222t$$

This indicates that the sales of the CD player are increasing at an average rate of 122.2 per quarter. The trend line has been plotted on Figure 11.3.

Summary of the decomposition of a time series: multiplicative form

Draw a time series plot of the data and comment. Draw up a table of the data.

Step 1

Calculate moving averages and if necessary centred moving averages. Position correctly in the table.

Step 2

Divide the Y variable data by their corresponding moving averages. Calculate an average of these values for each season to give the seasonal components. Adjust if the seasonal components do not sum to the number of seasons.

Step 3

Deseasonalize the Y variable data by dividing by their corresponding seasonal component. Plot deseasonalized data against the time points and if there is a linear relationship use the method of least squares to estimate the trend.

Self-assessment questions 11.3

1. Explain what is meant by the decomposition of a time series.
2. Why do we calculate moving averages?
3. When do we need to calculate centred moving averages?
4. How do we calculate the seasonal components using the centred moving averages?
5. What value should the seasonal components sum to?
6. Why do we need to plot the deseasonalized data?
7. If the trend is linear, which method can be used to estimate the trend?

Exercises 11.3

1. Use the data given for product A in Exercises 11.1, Question 1.

    (a) Draw up a table of the data and calculate moving averages and centred moving averages.

(b) Calculate the seasonal components and adjust if necessary.
(c) Deseasonalize the data. Plot the deseasonalized values against the time points and comment on the relationship.
(d) If the relationship in (c) is approximately linear, use the method of least squares to estimate the trend.

2. Use the sales data in Exercises 11.1, Question 2.

(a) Draw up a table of the data and calculate moving averages. Do these moving averages need to be centred?
(b) Calculate the seasonal components and adjust if necessary.
(c) Deseasonalize the data. Plot the deseasonalized values against the time points and comment on the relationship.
(d) If the relationship in (c) is approximately linear, use the method of least squares to estimate the trend.

3. For the fertilizer sales data in Exercises 11.1, Question 3, calculate the seasonal components and find an estimate of the trend.

4. The seasonal components for the travel agent's data in Exercises 11.1, Question 4, have been calculated for January to December as follows: 0.123, 0.0485, 0.268, 0.9605, 0.758, 0.8595, 1.832, 2.669, 2.001, 0.8305, 0.4505, 1.1655. What should these components sum to? Comment on what the unadjusted seasonal components tell us about the numbers of tourists flying into the resort.

11.4   Forecasting using the trend and seasonal components

We have seen how to find estimates of the seasonal and trend components for the multiplicative form of a time series, now we can use them to forecast future values. We do however need to be aware of the dangers of forecasting future values from past data. We have only estimated the seasonal and trend components, there could be long-term cyclical variation in the data, it is virtually impossible to forecast irregular activity and we will not even be certain that the linear trend will continue in the future. Forecasting, however, is a valuable source of information for planning in the future.

There are many methods of forecasting, but we will concentrate on using the estimates of the seasonal and trend components. There are two steps:

1. extend the trend line for the deseasonalized data across to the time point to be forecast,
2. multiply the above trend forecast by the corresponding seasonal component.

Table 11.3. Quarterly
sales of a CD player:
forecasts for year 5

Year	Quarter	Time point (t)	Trend estimate using least squares line	Seasonal component	Forecast
5	1	17	$3.2764 + 0.1222 \times 17 = 5.3538$	1.1969	6.408
	2	18	$3.2764 + 0.1222 \times 18 = 5.4760$	0.9015	4.937
	3	19	$3.2764 + 0.1222 \times 19 = 5.5982$	0.7713	4.318
	4	20	$3.2764 + 0.1222 \times 20 = 5.7204$	1.1304	6.466

For Example 11.1 the forecasts for the quarterly sales of a CD player for
year 5 are shown in the final column of Table 11.3.

Self-assessment questions 11.4

1. What are the dangers of forecasting using the methods discussed
    in this chapter so far?
2. Describe the two steps for forecasting using the seasonal and
    trend components.

Exercises 11.4

1. Forecast the number of orders of product A for the four quarters
    of 1993 using the results in Exercises 11.3, Question 1.
2. Forecast the sales for August in year 5 using the results in
    Exercises 11.3, Question 2.
3. Forecast the sales of fertilizer in 1992 using the results in
    Exercises 11.3, Question 3.

11.5   Simple exponential smoothing

In the previous sections we have looked at using centred moving averages
to smooth a time series. There are many other methods of smoothing and
one often used is **simple exponential smoothing**. This method uses all the
preceding values in the time series data to determine a smoothed value at a
particular time point or to forecast a future time point. It works well for
time series that do not have a trend component, these are called **stationary**
time series.

The method places more emphasis on recent values in the time series
than values further in the past, and begins by letting the first smoothed
value for time $t = 1$ equal the first value in the time series. If we let y_t be
the time series value at time point t and s_t be the smoothed value at time

point t, then

$$s_1 = y_1$$

$$s_2 = cy_2 + (1 - c)s_1$$

$$s_3 = cy_3 + (1 - c)s_2$$

$$s_4 = cy_4 + (1 - c)s_3$$

and so on, where c is called the **smoothing constant** and lies between 0 and 1.

In general,

KEY POINT

$$s_i = cy_i + (1 - c)s_{i-1} \qquad\qquad [11.5]$$

Values of c nearer to 1 put more emphasis on the time series value, and should be used when the time series is fairly stable. Smaller values of c should be used for time series with a lot of irregular activity, as the emphasis is on past time series values rather than the corresponding value.

To forecast with exponential smoothing use the previous smoothed value as the forecast, i.e. use s_t to forecast y_{t+1}.

Worked example

11.1   The following data has been collected for the sales of a product over 12 months. Plot the data and calculate the smoothed values using exponential smoothing, with $c = 0.3$ and $c = 0.5$. Which value of c appears to be most appropriate? Forecast the sales for the thirteenth month using the most appropriate value of c.

Month	Sales
1	210
2	240
3	225
4	210
5	195
6	225
7	250
8	245
9	205
10	185
11	205
12	215

Solution   The plot of the data can been seen in Figure 11.4, there does not appear to be an overall trend in the data. The smoothed values are calculated using

[11.4], so, with $c = 0.3$,

$$s_1 = y_1 = 210$$

$$s_2 = 0.3y_2 + (1 - 0.3)s_1$$

$$= (0.3)(240) + (0.7)(210)$$

$$= 219$$

and so on.

All the smoothed values for $c = 0.3$ and $c = 0.5$ are shown in Table 11.4. The smoothed value at the previous time point is used to forecast, and when $c = 0.5$ the smoothed values provide slightly closer forecasts of the actual data points, so this value seems most appropriate.

To forecast we use the previous smoothed value, so, with $c = 0.5$,

$$y_{13} = s_{12} = 209.62$$

Figure 11.4. Plot of the sales data for exponential smoothing

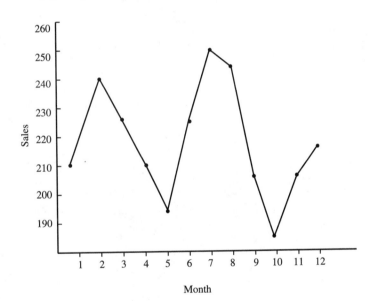

Month

Table 11.4. Smoothed values of the sales data using exponential smoothing

Month	Sales	$0.3y_i$	$s_i = 0.3y_i + 0.7s_{i-1}$	$0.5y_i$	$s_i = 0.5y_i + 0.5s_{i-1}$
1	210		210.00		210.00
2	240	72.0	219.00	120.0	225.00
3	225	67.5	220.80	112.5	225.00
4	210	63.0	217.56	105.0	217.50
5	195	58.5	210.79	97.5	206.25
6	225	67.5	215.05	112.5	215.63
7	250	75.0	225.54	125.0	232.81
8	245	73.5	231.38	122.5	238.91
9	205	61.5	223.46	102.5	221.95
10	185	55.5	211.92	92.5	203.48
11	205	61.5	209.85	102.5	204.24
12	215	64.5	211.39	107.5	209.62

Self-assessment questions 11.5

1. When does exponential smoothing work well?
2. How do we choose values of the smoothing constant, c?
3. Which value would you use to forecast y_{t+1}?

Exercises 11.5

1. The following sales data has been recorded daily over 16 days. Plot the data and use exponential smoothing with a smoothing constant $c = 0.6$.

Day	1	2	3	4	5	6	7	8	9	10	11	12	13	14
Sales	17	22	25	19	18	22	24	18	16	22	20	25	20	17

Day	15	16
Sales	21	22

2. Data has been recorded on the number of orders for a product placed weekly over a 12-week period. Plot the data and use exponential smoothing, with $c = 0.2$ and $c = 0.3$, to calculate smoothed values. Which value of c appears to give the best values? Forecast the number of orders for week 13.

Week	Number of orders
1	117
2	121
3	119
4	123
5	118
6	116
7	120
8	118
9	122
10	120
11	115
12	122

Test exercises

1. Describe, using sketches of time series plots where helpful, the four components of a time series.
2. The quarterly electricity bills (£) for a company have been given below.

    (a) Plot the data and comment on any trend and seasonal components.
    (b) Calculate moving averages and, if necessary, centred moving

averages and use these to find estimates of the seasonal components. Comment on the seasonal components.

(c) Deseasonalize the data and find an estimate of the trend. Comment on the trend.

(d) Forecast the quarterly bills for 1993.

Bill	Quarter			
(£)	1	2	3	4
1989	626	662	712	790
1990	686	718	821	846
1991	743	779	827	876
1992	805	842	876	908

3. A company believes that the sales of its products are affected by the time of year and that there has been an overall trend. The following sales data was recorded three times a year over four years. Investigate, in detail, the effect of the time of year and any overall trend. Comment on both of these components.

Sales	Year			
	1	2	3	4
January–April	84	92	94	100
May–August	121	140	148	161
September–December	67	81	83	95

4. The profits made from the sales of a product are not affected by the time of year and do not seem to have increased or decreased overall in the past few years. Plot the profit data below and use exponential smoothing, with $c = 0.3$ and $c = 0.4$, to calculate smoothed values. Which value of c appears to give the best values? Forecast the profit for month 13.

Month	Profit (£000s)
1	270
2	292
3	298
4	264
5	271
6	289
7	275
8	297
9	300
10	272
11	261
12	283

12 Index numbers

<table>
<tr><td>**Objectives**</td><td>When you have read this chapter you should be able to

- calculate index numbers for any given set of data

- link different sets of index numbers together

- understand how the Retail Price Index is constructed

- construct price indices

- construct quantity indices

- calculate a value index</td></tr>
</table>

If we want to represent changes over time, a simple way of describing these changes is by using index numbers. This means expressing our new value as a percentage of some existing value, called a **base value**. The base value is associated with a base period, which is chosen for no reason other than the fact that it is a typical period for the data. The index number given to the base period is 100. An index number for the nth period, I_n, is calculated using

KEY POINT

$$I_n = \frac{V_n}{V_0} \times 100 \qquad\qquad [12.1]$$

where V_n represents the value in the nth period and V_0 represents the value in the base period.

Worked example

12.1 The value of a company's stock at the end of each of 6 months is given below.

Month	Jan	Feb	Mar	Apr	May	Jun
Stock value (£)	7220	7400	7450	7610	7910	7650

Express the stock values as index numbers based on April as the base period.

Solution As April is the base period, April $= 100$. The other index numbers can be found using [12.1]. For example, for January the index number represented by I_1 will be

$$I_1 = \frac{7220}{7610} \times 100 = 94.9$$

Similarly, the index numbers for the 6 months are given below.

	Jan	Feb	Mar	Apr	May	Jun
n	1	2	3	4	5	6
Index number I_n	94.9	97.2	97.9	100	103.9	100.5

If the change we are trying to represent is related to the base period, the percentage change is simply the difference in the corresponding index numbers. For instance, from Worked Example 12.1, the stock value in May is 3.9% greater than the stock value in April, and the stock value in March is 2.1% less than that in April.

12.1   The Retail Price Index

The Retail Price Index (RPI) is the most commonly used method of measuring the rate of inflation. It measures the change, from month to month, of a representative selection of goods and services. The actual goods and services selected are chosen as being relevant to a typical household. Worked Example 12.2 gives the RPI for January 1987 to January 1993.

Worked example

12.2

Year	1987	1988	1989	1990	1991	1992	1993
RPI	100	103.3	111.0	119.5	130.2	135.6	137.9

Source: Employment Gazette, October 1993

Find the change in the RPI from
(a) January 1987 to January 1988,
(b) January 1987 to January 1989.

Solution The RPI represents index numbers with January 1987 as the base, hence January 1987 $= 100$. As January 1987 is the base period, the change in the RPI from January 1987 to any subsequent time is simply the difference in the index numbers.

(a) The change in the RPI from January 1987 to January 1988, expressed as a percentage, is

$$103.3 - 100 = 3.3\%$$

(b) The change in the RPI from January 1987 to January 1989, expressed as a percentage, is

$$111.0 - 100 = 11.0\%$$

These results tell us that the rise in the RPI from January 1987 to January 1988 was 3.3% and the rise in the RPI from January 1987 to January 1989 was 11%.

If we wish to find the change between two periods with index numbers I_i and I_j which do not involve the base period, we must express the difference as a percentage of I_i using the following equation:

KEY POINT

$$\text{Percentage change} = \frac{I_j - I_i}{I_i} \times 100 \qquad [12.2]$$

Worked example

12.3 Consider the RPI data given in Worked Example 12.2. Calculate the percentage change in the RPI from January 1988 to January 1989.

Solution The percentage change in the RPI for the period, using [12.2], is

$$\frac{110.0 - 103.3}{103.3} \times 100 = 7.45\%$$

This means that the rise in the RPI from January 1988 to January 1989 was 7.45%. Note that even though the actual change in the RPI from January 1988 to January 1989 was 7.7, this represents an increase of only 7.45% as the RPI at the start of this period is 103.3 and not 100.

12.2   Chain-basing

From time to time it becomes necessary to update the base period for a series of index numbers. This may be because the original base period is no longer typical, the index numbers are becoming too large or the base period is too far into the past. Any index number I_n can be translated from a new series into an old series to give I_n' by a technique known as **chain-basing**. In order to perform this technique, we need to know the index number of the new base value in the old series, I_B. Any index number can be chain-based to the old series using the following equation.

KEY POINT

$$I'_n = \frac{I_n}{100} \times I_B \qquad\qquad [12.3]$$

where n represents the number of periods after the base period. An index number from the old series, I'_n, can be translated into the new series by expressing it as a percentage of I_B using the following equation.

KEY POINT

$$I_n = \frac{I'_n}{I_B} \times 100 \qquad\qquad [12.4]$$

where n represents the number of periods after the base period.

Worked example

12.4 Until recently, the base period for the RPI was January 1974. The base period, for convenience, has now been changed to January 1987. The following table gives the RPI for January 1980 to January 1987, with January 1974 as the base.

Year	1980	1981	1982	1983	1984	1985	1986	1987
RPI	245.3	277.3	310.6	325.9	342.6	359.8	379.7	394.5

Source: Employment Gazette, January 1988

Chain-base the RPI figure for January 1988, which is 103.3, based on January 1987, back to January 1974.

Solution The figure for 1987, based on January 1974 = 100, is 394.5, i.e. $I_B = 394.5$. To chain-base the figure for January 1988 back to January 1974, we use [12.3] with n equal to 1, since 1988 is one year after the base year. I_1 equals 103.3 (this is given in Worked Example 12.2); so

$$I'_1 = \frac{103.3}{100} \times 394.5 = 407.5$$

12.3   Construction of the Retail Price Index

The RPI is designed to show the change in the cost of living for a typical household. Each month, usually on the Tuesday nearest to the middle of the month, prices are collected for a whole range of goods and services, from a sample of retail outlets in different areas. A large number of households, representing all economic groups, other than those at the extremes of income distribution, are included in the survey. An average

Table 12.1. The 14 main categories and weights used in the RPI in 1993

Category	Weight	Index number
Food	144	128.8
Catering	45	151.7
Alcoholic drink	78	151.0
Tobacco	35	150.0
Housing	164	151.6
Fuel and light	46	127.1
Household goods	79	125.8
Household services	47	139.8
Clothing and footwear	58	114.9
Personal goods and services	39	144.7
Motoring expenditure	136	137.9
Fares and other travel	21	148.6
Leisure goods	46	121.3
Leisure services	62	153.6
Total weight	1000	

price is calculated for each item, and the items are grouped into one of 14 main categories. Index numbers can then be calculated for each category in exactly the same way as the RPI is calculated.

Each January the categories are assigned a weighting to reflect the overall importance of that category in the family budget. These weightings are used to calculate the RPI for the remainder of the year. The weightings are updated on an annual basis. All calculations involving these weightings work on the same principle as Worked Example 12.2.

The 14 main categories, and the weights assigned to each in 1993, are shown in Table 12.1, together with the index numbers, by category, for January 1993.

Each main category is subdivided into smaller groups. For instance, food is divided into seasonal and non-seasonal food, with weights 21 and 123 respectively. An increase in the cost of non-seasonal food will, therefore, obviously affect the RPI much more than the same increase in the cost of seasonal food.

Worked example

12.5 Using Table 12.1, what change in the RPI would be caused by
(a) a 10% increase in the housing index,
(b) a 5% decrease in the food index?

Solution   (a) The housing index is stated as 151.6 with a weighting of 164 units (out of 1000). A 10% increase will therefore increase the RPI by

$$\frac{164 \times 15.16}{1000} = 2.5 \text{ units}$$

Note that this is an actual not a percentage increase.

(b) The food index is 128.8 with a weighting of 144 units (out of 1000). A 5% decrease will therefore reduce the RPI by

$$\frac{144 \times 6.44}{1000} = 0.9 \text{ units}$$

Self-assessment questions 12.3

1. How can a set of data be translated into index numbers?
2. Describe the technique known as 'chain-basing'.
3. What does the RPI represent?

Exercises 12.3

1. A woman invested £1000 in a savings plan in January 1989. By January 1992 the value of her savings had increased to £1250. Use the table in Worked Example 12.2 to determine whether or not the increase in the value of her savings had matched the increase in the RPI.
2. The following data shows the total output for a sweet manufacturer for each month of 1993.

Month	Output (kg)
January	1760
February	1950
March	2050
April	2100
May	1975
June	1850
July	1800
August	1800
September	1900
October	1925
November	1975
December	2200

Express the output figures as index numbers using January 1993 as the base period.

3. The main categories and weights used to calculate the RPI in 1993 are shown in Table 12.1. The index numbers for January 1993 for each main category are also shown in this table. If taxes were raised so that the alcoholic drink index increased by 10%, the tobacco index increased by 20% and the motoring expenditure index increased by 15%, what would be the resulting increase in the RPI? (In Worked Example 12.2, the RPI for January 1993 was given as 137.9.)

Price indices

The total amount spent on a product will generally be due to both the unit price of the product and the quantity of the product purchased. A **price index** attempts to measure the amount of change which is due to the change in the **price** of the product, rather than the change in the quantity purchased.

The most common form of price index is the Laspeyre price index, which was named after its originator. The Paasche price index, also named after its originator, is also often used.

The Laspeyre price index

The **Laspeyre price index** is calculated from the total value of a 'basket' of goods in some base year and the value of the same goods in some subsequent year. The index is calculated by expressing the new value as a percentage of the base value. The Laspeyre price index is given by

KEY POINT

$$L_p = \frac{\Sigma q_0 p_n}{\Sigma q_0 p_0} \times 100 \qquad\qquad [12.5]$$

where p_0 represents the base year price, p_n represents the price in year n, q_0 represents the base year quantity and n represents the nth year after the base year. To calculate $\Sigma q_0 p_0$ take each item of goods bought in the base year. Multiply the quantity of that item purchased in the base year by the base year price of that item. This will give a value of $q_0 p_0$ for each item. Summing these individual values of $q_0 p_0$ will give $\Sigma q_0 p_0$. This is the value of the whole 'basket' of goods, with the goods valued at base year prices.

To calculate $\Sigma q_0 p_n$, we repeat the above process, but using prices for year n. $\Sigma q_0 p_n$ can be found for all years after the base year. For one year after the base year ($n = 1$) we would find $\Sigma q_0 p_1$ using year 1 prices. For two years after the base year ($n = 2$) we would find $\Sigma q_0 p_2$ using year 2 prices.

Referring to [12.5], quantities are the same from year to year; prices change from year to year. The change in the value of the 'basket' of goods is therefore due to a change in *prices*, hence the term price index.

- Quantity is used as a 'weight' for a price index. The actual quantity used for each item reflects the importance of that item within the 'basket'

Worked example

12.6   Consider a company which uses four different types of fuel to provide its energy. The number of units of each fuel used, together with costs per unit, for each of two years, are shown below. Calculate the Laspeyre price index for 1993.

| | 1992 | | 1993 | |
Type of fuel	Quantity q_0	Price p_0	Quantity q_1	Price p_1
Coal	450	1.28	550	1.25
Electricity	800	0.90	700	0.98
Gas	900	0.60	1000	0.66
Oil	750	0.67	800	0.78

Solution   In this example, 1992 is the base year. 1993 is one year after the base year so n is 1. The cost of fuel in 1992, the base year, was

$$(450 \times 1.28) + (800 \times 0.90) + (900 \times 0.60) + (750 \times 0.67) = £2338.50,$$

i.e. $\Sigma q_0 p_0 = £2338.50$.

The cost of the same fuel a year later, in 1993, would be

$$(450 \times 1.25) + (800 \times 0.98) + (900 \times 0.66) + (750 \times 0.78) = £2525.50,$$

i.e. $\Sigma q_0 p_1 = £2525.50$. Using [12.5], the Laspeyre price index is

$$L_p = \frac{2525.50}{2338.50} \times 100 = 108.0$$

In practice, a significant increase in the cost of an item will often lead to a reduction in the amount of that item purchased. The Laspeyre price index will therefore often overstate the effect of any price rises. An alternative approach is to consider a Paasche price index.

The Paasche price index

The **Paasche price index** is calculated from the total value of a 'basket' of goods in the current year and compares this with the value of the same goods in the base year. The index is calculated by expressing the current year value as a percentage of the base year value. The Paasche price index is given by

KEY POINT

$$P_p = \frac{\Sigma q_n p_n}{\Sigma q_n p_0} \times 100 \qquad [12.6]$$

Quantity is again used as a 'weight', but we are now using current year quantities. This might reflect changing trends

where p_0 represents the base year price, p_n represents the price in year n, q_n represents the quantity in year n and n represents the nth year after the base year. To calculate $\Sigma q_n p_n$, take each item of goods bought in the nth year. Multiply the quantity of that item purchased in the nth year by the price of that item in year n. This will give a value of $q_n p_n$ for each item. Summing these individual values of $q_n p_n$ will give $\Sigma q_n p_n$. This is the value of the whole 'basket' of goods, with the goods valued at year n prices. This can be applied for all years after the base year. When $n = 1$ we would use p_1 and q_1, when $n = 2$ we would use p_2 and q_2 etc.

To calculate $\Sigma q_n p_0$ we repeat the above process, but using prices for the base year. $\Sigma q_n p_0$ can be found for all years after the base year. When $n = 1$ we would use q_1, when $n = 2$ we would use q_2 etc.

Worked example

12.7   Using the fuel data given in Worked Example 12.6, calculate the Paasche price index for 1993.

Solution   The cost of fuel in 1993 was

$$(550 \times 1.25) + (700 \times 0.98) + (1000 \times 0.66) + (800 \times 0.78) = £2657.50,$$

i.e. $\Sigma q_1 p_1 = £2657.50$. The cost of the same fuel if it had been bought in 1992 would have been

$$(550 \times 1.28) + (700 \times 0.90) + (1000 \times 0.60) + (800 \times 0.67) = £2470.00,$$

i.e. $\Sigma q_1 p_0 = £2470.00$. Using [12.6], the Paasche price index is given by

$$P_p = \frac{2657.50}{2470.00} \times 100 = 107.6$$

In the same way that the Laspeyre index tends to overstate the effect of price increases, the Paasche index will normally understate them. The Paasche index has the disadvantage of using current year quantities, which often may not be available until well into the following year.

12.5   Quantity indices

A **quantity** index attempts to measure the change which is due to the change in the quantity of the product purchased rather than the change in price. A quantity index is also referred to as a **volume index**. We can calculate a quantity index using either a Laspeyre or a Paasche index, but again the more common form is the Laspeyre index.

The Laspeyre quantity index

The **Laspeyre quantity index** is calculated from the total value of a 'basket' of goods in some base year, as for the Laspeyre price index. A second value is found by calculating the value of the goods bought in some subsequent year, but pricing them at base year prices. The index is calculated by expressing the new value as a percentage of the base value. The Laspeyre quantity index is given by

KEY POINT

$$L_q = \frac{\Sigma p_0 q_n}{\Sigma p_0 q_0} \times 100 \qquad [12.7]$$

Price is used as a 'weight' for a quantity index

where p_0 represents the base year price, q_0 represents the base year quantity, q_n represents the quantity in year n and n represents the nth year after the base year. $\Sigma p_0 q_0$ is found as for the Laspeyre price index (refer to Section 12.4). $\Sigma p_0 q_n$ is found using base year prices together with quantities purchased in year n.

Referring to [12.7], prices are the same from year to year; quantities change from year to year. The change in the value of the 'basket' of goods is therefore due to a change in quantity, hence the term **quantity index**.

Worked example

12.8   Calculate the Laspeyre quantity index for 1993 using the fuel data given in Worked Example 12.6.

Solution   In Worked Example 12.6 we found that the cost of the fuel bought in the base year, 1992, was

$$\Sigma p_0 q_0 = £2338.50$$

The cost of the quantity of fuel purchased in 1993, but at 1992 prices, was

$$(550 \times 1.28) + (700 \times 0.90) + (1000 \times 0.60) + (800 \times 0.67) = £2470.00,$$

i.e. $\Sigma p_0 q_1 = £2470.00$. Using [12.7], the Laspeyre quantity index is

$$L_q = \frac{2470.00}{2338.50} \times 100 = 105.6$$

The Paasche quantity index

The **Paasche quantity index** is given by

KEY POINT

$$P_q = \frac{\Sigma p_n q_n}{\Sigma p_n q_0} \times 100 \qquad [12.8]$$

Price is again used as a 'weight', but for a Paasche index we use current year prices

where p_n represents the price in year n, q_0 represents the base year quantity, q_n represents the quantity in year n and n represents the nth year after the base year. $\Sigma p_n q_n$ is found as for the Paasche price index (refer to Section 12.4). $\Sigma p_n q_0$ is found using base year quantities together with year n prices.

Worked example

12.9   Calculate the Paasche quantity index for 1993 using the fuel data given in Worked Example 12.6.

Solution   In Worked Example 12.7 we found that $\Sigma q_1 p_1 = 2657.50$. In Worked Example 12.6 we found that $\Sigma q_0 p_1 = 2525.50$. Using [12.8], the Paasche quantity index is

$$P_q = \frac{2657.50}{2525.50} \times 100 = 105.2$$

12.6   The value index

The **value index** expresses the **value** of the total goods bought in some subsequent year as a percentage of the value of the total goods bought in the base year

KEY POINT

$$V = \frac{\Sigma p_n q_n}{\Sigma p_0 q_0} \times 100 \quad \text{(laspeyre's)}$$ [12.9]

where p_0 represents the base year price, p_n represents the price in year n, q_0 represents the base year quantity, q_n represents the quantity in year n and n represents the nth year after the base year. $\Sigma p_0 q_0$ is found as for the Laspeyre price index (p. 196) and $\Sigma p_n q_n$ is found as for the Paasche price index (p. 197).

Worked example

12.10   Calculate the value index for 1993 using 1992 as base year for the fuel data given in Worked Example 12.6.

Solution   In Worked Example 12.7 we found that $\Sigma q_1 p_1 = 2657.50$. In Worked Example 12.6 we found that $\Sigma q_0 p_0 = 2338.50$. Using [12.9], the value index for 1993 is

$$V = \frac{2657.50}{2338.50} \times 100 = 113.6$$

Self-assessment questions 12.6

1. What does a price index, a quantity index and a value index attempt to measure?

2. How does a Laspeyre index differ from a Paasche index?
3. What are the advantages of using a Laspeyre index rather than a Paasche index?

Exercise 12.6

The number of staff employed in each of three departments of a company are given in Table 12.2, together with the average salaries for each of the years 1991 to 1993. Using the number of staff as quantity and the average salary as price, find

(a) a Laspeyre price index for 1992 and 1993 based on 1991,
(b) a Paasche quantity index for 1992 and 1993 based on 1991,
(c) a value index for 1992 and 1993 based on 1991.
(d) Explain the meaning of your answer to (c).

Table 12.2. The number of staff and average salary (£) of staff employed in three departments of a company for 1991–1993

| | 1991 | | 1992 | | 1993 | |
Department	Number of staff	Average salary (£)	Number of staff	Average salary (£)	Number of staff	Average salary (£)
Personnel	12	10000	14	10400	14	10650
Computing	31	19500	32	21000	36	22750
Maintenance	8	9500	8	9950	6	10200

Test exercises

1. Table 12.3 gives the average annual salary for manual workers at Strong plc, together with the average RPI for the years 1989 to 1992.

(a) Tabulate the percentage increases on the previous year for both average salary and the RPI. What does this tell you about average salary increases on an annual basis compared to the increase in the RPI for the same year?
(b) Construct index numbers for average salary and the RPI, based on 1989 = 100. What does this tell you about the average salary

Table 12.3. The average annual salary for manual workers at Strong plc and the average RPI for 1989–1992

Year	Average salary	Retail Price Index (1987 = 100)
1989	9900	115.2
1990	10450	126.1
1991	10890	133.5
1992	11340	138.5

Source: Employment Gazette, October 1993

increases over the three-year period compared with the increase in the RPI over the same time?

(c) If salary increases had kept pace with the increase in the RPI over the three-year period, what would the average salary have been in 1992?

2. Variation plc manufactures a number of electrical items which use four common components. Each item has a differing component requirement, and since the number of items produced each year varies, the total component requirement varies also. Table 12.4 shows the quantity of each component purchased, together with the average cost price per component, for 1991 to 1993.

(a) Determine the Laspeyre price indices for 1992 and 1993, based on 1991, for Variation's purchases.

(b) Determine the Paasche price indices for 1992 and 1993, based on 1991, for Variation's purchases.

(c) Using your answers to (a) and (b), discuss the advantages and disadvantages of a Laspeyre price index compared with a Paasche price index.

Table 12.4. The price and quantity of four components used by Variation plc for manufacturing electrical items in 1991, 1992 and 1993

	1991		1992		1993	
Component	Price (£)	Quantity	Price (£)	Quantity	Price (£)	Quantity
P	4.95	75	5.25	80	5.30	80
Q	11.95	46	11.90	52	12.90	60
R	7.46	115	7.42	115	7.45	125
S	1.27	250	1.30	275	1.30	300

13 Linear programming

Objectives	When you have read this chapter you should be able to

- formulate a maximization linear programming problem
- formulate a minimization linear programming problem
- solve linear programming problems involving two unknowns by graphical methods
- perform elementary sensitivity analysis
- calculate shadow prices for resources

A linear function is one in which all variables are to the power 1, e.g.
$5x + 4y$ is linear,
$x^2 + y$ is not linear,
$x + xy$ is not linear,
$x + \sqrt{y}$ is not linear

Many problems in business fall into the general class of maximizing or minimizing some function of variables subject to inequality constraints. The techniques used to solve these problems fall under the heading **mathematical programming**, and when the inequality constraints are linear we have the sub-class known as **linear programming**.

In linear programming, we maximize or minimize a linear function of variables subject to linear constraints on the variables, and subject to none of the variables being allowed to take negative values. The general term for maximizing, or minimizing, is **optimizing**, and the function to be optimized is the **objective function**. The value of this objective function is usually denoted by π.

13.1   Defining the problem

There are four steps involved in setting up a linear programming problem:

KEY POINT

Step 1	Defining the decision variables
Step 2	Defining the objective function
Step 3	Defining the constraints
Step 4	Stating the linear programming problem

Worked Examples 13.1 and 13.2 overleaf illustrate a maximization problem and a minimization problem respectively.

Worked example

13.1   A specialist toy manufacturer produces two versions of a particular toy. The 'deluxe' model uses 5 units of material, three hours of machine time and two hours of unskilled labour time. The 'standard' model uses 4 units of material, two hours of machine time and three hours of unskilled labour time. In an attempt to keep the deluxe version more exclusive, the manufacturer has decided to produce no more than 50 of these in any week. Each week he is able to allocate 400 units of material, 200 hours of machine time and 250 hours of unskilled labour time to the production of the two versions of the toy.

Every unit of the deluxe model that is made and sold produces a profit of £12, and every unit of the standard model that is made and sold produces a profit of £4. If the manufacturer is able to sell all he makes of both versions of the toy, how should he formulate a linear programming problem so that he can arrange production in order to maximize profit, whilst satisfying all the constraints?

Solution

Step 1   Defining the decision variables

Defining the decision variables first makes the problem easier to formulate

The **objective** of the manufacturer is to allocate his production in such a way that he is able to **maximize** his **profit**. The manufacturer will do this by deciding upon the number of deluxe and standard models he should make in order to achieve this. These are the **unknowns**, over which the manufacturer has control, and are known as the **decision variables**.

Let the number of deluxe models made be x and the number of standard models made be y. The remainder of the problem formulation can now be written in terms of x and y only.

Step 2   Defining the objective function

The profit from every unit of the deluxe model is £12, and the manufacturer intends to make x units of this model. The total profit from all the deluxe models produced will therefore be £12x. Similarly, the profit from every unit of the standard model is £4, and the manufacturer intends to make y units of this model. The total profit from all the standard models produced will therefore be £4y. The combined profit for the deluxe and standard models will be £$(12x + 4y)$.

The manufacturer's objective is to maximize this profit. The objective function is

$$\text{maximize } \pi = 12x + 4y$$

(we understand that the units are £s).

Step 3   Defining the constraints

In theory the manufacturer would like x and y to be as large as possible. However, there are restrictions on the number of units that can be produced due to the limited amounts of material, machining time and unskilled labour time that is available in any week. There is also the added, self-imposed, restriction being placed on the number of deluxe models made. These restrictions place **constraints** on the objective function. The constraints are that the amount of any resource actually being used is less than, or equal to, the amount of that resource available. In this example there are four constraints to consider: the material constraint, the machining constraint, the labour constraint and the exclusivity constraint.

The material constraint

Five units of material are being used in every unit of the deluxe model. As x units of the deluxe model are being made, $5x$ units of material are being used to make all the deluxe models. Similarly, 4 units of material are being used in every unit of the standard model. As y units of the standard model are being made, $4y$ units of material are being used to make all the standard models. The amount of material being used in total is therefore $5x + 4y$ units. The total amount of material available is 400 units, so the material constraint is

$$5x + 4y \leq 400,$$

i.e. the amount of material used must be less than or equal to the amount of material available. (The **units** on **both sides** of the inequality **should always be the same**, and can therefore be disregarded.)

The machining and labour constraints are formatted in exactly the same way.

The machining constraint

The amount of machining time needed to produce one deluxe model is three hours, so to produce x deluxe models will take $3x$ hours. In the same way, if two hours of machining time is needed to produce one standard model then $2y$ hours will be needed to produce y standard models.

The total machining time needed to produce both versions of the toy is $3x + 2y$ hours. The total amount of machining time available is 200 hours, so the machining constraint is

$$3x + 2y \leq 200$$

(units on both sides would be hours).

The labour constraint

The amount of labour time needed for each of the x deluxe models is two hours, giving a total labour requirement of $2x$ hours for all the deluxe models. Similarly, the amount of labour time needed for each of the y standard models is three hours, giving a total labour requirement of $3y$ hours for all the standard models. The total labour requirement for both versions of the toy is $2x + 3y$ hours, which must be less than or equal to

250 hours, the total time available. The labour constraint is therefore

$$2x + 3y \leq 250$$

(units on both sides would be hours).

The exclusivity constraint

We have an additional constraint that the manufacturer is imposing in an attempt to keep the deluxe version exclusive. The constraint is that no more than 50 units of the deluxe version are produced in any week. The actual number being produced is x, so the additional constraint is

$$x \leq 50$$

Step 4   Stating the linear programming problem

We have now completely formulated the linear programming problem, and can write it as follows.

Maximize	$\pi = 12x + 4y$	objective function
subject to	$5x + 4y \leq 400$	material constraint
	$3x + 2y \leq 200$	machining constraint
	$2x + 3y \leq 250$	labour constraint
	$x \leq 50$	exclusivity constraint

We have the added restrictions that

$$x \geq 0 \quad \text{and} \quad y \geq 0$$

since we cannot produce negative quantities.

On many occasions, rather than trying to maximize some profit function, we will instead be trying to minimize some function, such as a cost function. A minimization problem is formulated in exactly the same way as a maximization problem.

Worked example

13.2   An office furniture company is planning its production of 'basic', 'super' and 'luxury' desks for the coming year. It operates two machines which are both capable of producing the three desks, though in varying amounts and at different production costs.

Machine A can produce 1 unit of the 'basic' desk, 3 units of the 'super' desk, and 4 units of the 'luxury' desk in each hour, and has an operating cost of £15 per hour. Machine B can produce 3 units of 'basic' desk, 2 units of 'super' desk and 2 units of 'luxury' desk in each hour, and has an operating cost of £14 per hour.

The company has orders for the coming week of 30 units of 'basic', 48 units of 'super' and 50 units of 'luxury' desk. At least enough units of each product must be produced in order to satisfy these orders.

Produce a linear programming problem that will allow the company to plan its production in order to meet the required production levels at minimum cost The information is summarized in the following table.

	Production rate per hour			Operating cost per hour (£)
	Basic	Super	Luxury	
Machine A	1	3	4	15
Machine B	3	2	2	14
Minimum requirement	30	48	50	

Solution

Step 1   Defining the decision variables

The company's **objective** in this case is to **minimize** the total cost of producing the required number of each type of desk. The **decision variables** are the number of hours each of the machines should be operated for. These are the unknowns, over which the company has control. Let the number of hours machine A operates for be x and the number of hours machine B operates for be y. The remainder of the formulation can again be written in terms of x and y only.

Step 2   Defining the objective function

If machine A operates for x hours, at a cost of £15 per hour, the total cost involved is £15x. If machine B operates for y hours, at a cost of £14 per hour, the total cost involved is £14y. The overall production cost is therefore £$(15x + 14y)$. The company's **objective** is to minimize this overall production cost, so the objective for the problem is to

$$\text{Minimize} \quad \pi = 15x + 14y$$

Step 3   Defining the constraints

The **constraints** being imposed upon this objective function are that the company must produce at least 30 units of 'basic', 48 units of 'super' and 50 units of 'luxury' desk. Thus there are three constraints: the 'basic' constraint, the 'super' constraint and the 'luxury' constraint.

The 'basic' constraint

Machine A produces 1 unit of 'basic' per hour, and operates for x hours. The number of units of 'basic' produced by machine A will therefore be $1x = x$ units. Similarly, machine B produces 3 units of 'basic' per hour, and operates for y hours. The number of units of 'basic' produced by machine B will therefore be $3y$ units. The number of units of 'basic' produced in total will be $x + 3y$. The requirement is for at least 30 units of 'basic', so the constraint is

$$x + 3y \geq 30,$$

i.e. the number of units produced must be greater than or equal to the number of units required.

The 'super' constraint

Machine A produces 3 units of 'super' per hour, so in x hours it produces $3x$ units. Machine B produces 2 units of 'super' per hour, so in y hours it produces $2y$ units. The number of units of 'super' produced in total will be $3x + 2y$, and as the requirement for 'super' is 48 units, the constraint is

$$3x + 2y \geq 48$$

The 'luxury' constraint

Machine A produces 4 units of 'luxury' per hour, so in x hours it produces $4x$ units. Machine B produces 2 units of 'luxury' per hour, so in y hours it produces $2y$ units. The number of units of 'luxury' produced in total is $4x + 2y$, and as the requirement is for at least 50 units, the constraint is

$$4x + 2y \geq 50$$

Step 4   Stating the linear programming problem

We have now completely formulated the linear programming problem, and can write it as follows.

Minimize	$\pi = 15x + 14y$	objective function
subject to	$x + 3y \geq 30$	'basic' constraint
	$3x + 2y \geq 48$	'super' constraint
	$4x + 2y \geq 50$	'luxury' constraint

We have the added restrictions that

$$x \geq 0 \text{ and } y \geq 0$$

since we cannot operate the machine for a negative amount of time.

Self-assessment questions 13.1

1. What is the aim of linear programming?
2. What are decision variables?
3. What does the objective function give?
4. Why are constraints imposed?

Exercises 13.1

1. A manufacturer produces two products, A and B, with profit of £400 per unit and £300 per unit respectively. The resource

requirements and the resource availability for each product are shown below. The aim is to maximize profit. Formulate this as a linear programming problem.

	Labour requirement (hours)	Component requirement (units)	Packaging requirement (hours)
Product A	5	6	3
Product B	5	10	8
Resource availability	40	60	40

2. A company wants to increase its available shelving space. It has £2400 available to spend. It will buy only type X shelves, which cost £4 each and provide 4 m of shelving, and type Y shelves, which cost £3 each and provide 2 m of shelving. A total of at least 1800 m of shelving is required. Because of the shape of the area to be shelved, at least as many type Y shelves must be purchased as type X. Installation problems are such that the company wishes to minimize the total number of shelves it buys. Formulate this as a linear programming problem.

13.2   Graphical solutions of linear programming problems

For linear programming problems involving only two unknowns, we can represent all possible combinations for the two unknowns by points on a graph. This makes a graphical method of solution possible. This method consists of two steps:

KEY POINT

Step 1   Find the region consisting of all the combinations for the two unknowns which satisfy all the constraints

Step 2   Find the point in this region at which the objective function is optimized. This point is known as the **solution point**

Worked example

13.3   Consider the maximization problem formulated in Worked Example 13.1. The problem is stated as follows.

Maximize $\pi = 12x + 4y$
subject to $5x + 4y \leq 400$
                 $3x + 2y \leq 200$
                 $2x + 3y \leq 250$
                 $x \leq 50$
                 $x \geq 0 \quad y \geq 0$

Determine the values of x and y in order to maximize the objective function subject to the given constraints.

Solution

Step 1   Determine the feasible region

The inequalities $x \geq 0$ and $y \geq 0$ restrict us to the first quadrant, including its boundary lines.

The constraint $5x + 4y \leq 400$ restricts us to one side of the line $5x + 4y = 400$. We first of all draw the line $5x + 4y = 400$. (The easiest way is to find the value of y when $x = 0$ and then to find the value of x when $y = 0$. This gives two points, $(0,100)$ and $(80,0)$. As we are drawing a straight line, these are the only points we need.) We next have to test which side of the line satisfies the inequality. The easiest way to do this is by selecting a single point and testing whether or not the constraint is satisfied. The best point to choose is normally the origin, $x = 0$, $y = 0$. In this case $x = 0$, $y = 0$ satisfies the constraint as

$$(5 \times 0) + (4 \times 0) = 0 \leq 400.$$

Because the constraints involve '$\leq$' and not '$<$', the boundary lines themselves form part of the feasible region.

We can therefore shade away the side of the line which does not contain the origin as this part of the graph can never contain the solution point. This is illustrated in Figure 13.1. We can then repeat the process for the other constraints to leave a region containing no shading as in Figure 13.2. This region is the only part of the graph which satisfies all the constraints, and is known as the **feasible region.** The solution point must lie somewhere in the feasible region.

Step 2   Determine the solution point

We now need to find the point in the feasible region which maximizes our objective function $\pi = 12x + 4y$.

Figure 13.1. The line $5x + 4y = 400$. Unshaded region indicates the constraint has been satisfied. Shaded region does not satisfy the inequality

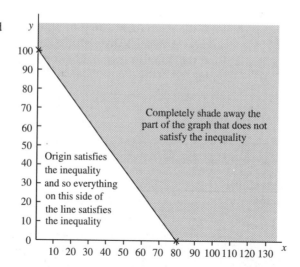

Figure 13.2. Feasible region for the profit maximization problem in Worked Example 13.3. The feasible region is the unshaded region together with its boundary lines. All other parts of the graph violate at least one constraint

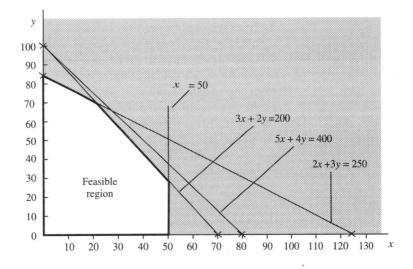

Figure 13.3. Solution point of the profit maximization problem in Worked Example 13.3

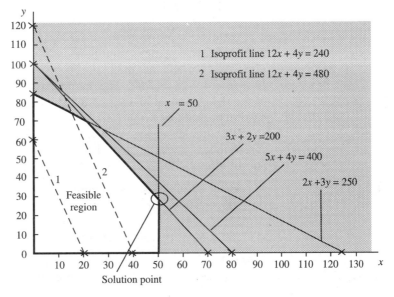

For any given value of π, all the points on the line $\pi = 12x + 4y$ give the same profit. We call the line $\pi = 12x + 4y$ the **isoprofit line**. We can draw the isoprofit line by selecting any value for π we choose. It makes sense to choose a value of π into which both coefficients of x and y in the objective function (in this case 12 and 4) will divide. It also helps if the magnitude of π is such that the isoprofit line fits well onto the feasible region. In this example, the coefficients of the objective function are 12 and 4. It therefore makes sense to use a multiple of 48 as our value of π. Values of 240 and 480 produce lines which fit well onto the scale of Figure 13.2. Figure 13.3 shows the two isoprofit lines $12x + 4y = 240$ and $12x + 4y = 480$ drawn onto Figure 13.2. From Figure 13.3 we can see that the isoprofit lines we have drawn are different members of a family of parallel straight lines. The larger the value of π, the further from the origin the line is drawn. Hence the line $12x + 4y = 480$ is further from the origin than $12x + 4y = 240$. If the value of π we had chosen were greater than 480, we would have another parallel line drawn still further from the origin. As we are maximizing $\pi = 12x + 4y$, we want the line to be as far from the origin as possible. We are, however, restricted to the feasible region for our solution point. If we place a ruler along the line closest to the origin, $12x + 4y = 240$, and slide it away from the origin, parallel to the other line $12x + 4y = 480$, this represents an infinite number of parallel straight lines. The last intersection of the ruler with the feasible region as it moves away from the origin gives the largest possible value of $12x + 4y$ within the feasible region. This point of intersection represents the solution point. The solution point will always be given by a vertex of the feasible region, and can be estimated from the graph or found by solving the equations of the intersecting lines simultaneously.

In this example, the solution point is the intersection of the two lines

$$3x + 2y = 200$$

$$x = 50$$

Solving these equations simultaneously, or reading the solution from Figure 13.3, tells us that $x = 50$, $y = 25$. The maximum profit is $12 \times 50 + 4 \times 25 = £700$. The manufacturer should therefore make 50 of the deluxe model and 25 of the standard model, in order to make a maximum profit of £700.

We should always substitute our solution point back into the constraints as a check, and also to see what resources have been used. Substituting $x = 50$, $y = 25$ into the four constraints, in turn, gives

$$350 \leq 400 \qquad \text{from constraint 1}$$
$$200 \leq 200 \qquad \text{from constraint 2}$$
$$175 \leq 250 \qquad \text{from constraint 3}$$
$$50 \leq 50 \qquad \text{from constraint 4}$$

This tells us that all four constraints are satisfied and gives additional information about each of the resources:

Constraint 1 tells us that of the 400 units of material, 50 units are not used.
Constraint 2 tells us that all the machining time is used.
Constraint 3 tells us that 75 hours of labour time remains unused.
Constraint 4 tells us that we have produced the maximum number of deluxe models allowed.

Worked example

13.4   Consider the minimization problem formulated in Worked Example 13.2. The problem is stated as follows.

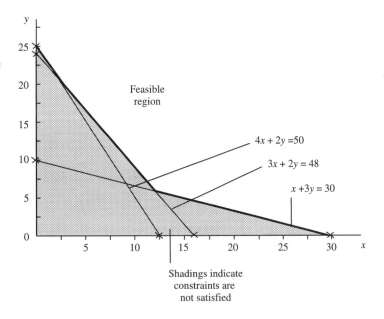

Figure 13.4. Feasible region for the cost minimization problem in Worked Example 13.4 The feasible region is the unshaded area, together with its boundary lines.

Feasible region

$4x + 2y = 50$

$3x + 2y = 48$

$x + 3y = 30$

Shadings indicate constraints are not satisfied

Minimize $\pi = 15x + 14y$
subject to $x + 3y \geq 30$
                        $3x + 2y \geq 48$
                        $4x + 2y \geq 50$
                        $x \geq 0 \quad y \geq 0$

Determine the values of x and y in order to minimize the objective function subject to the given constraints.

Solution

Step 1   Determine the feasible region

The feasible region is shown in Figure 13.4. (Again the origin is used to decide which side of the line satisfies each of our constraints.) We again draw an isoprofit line; in this case let $\pi = 315$. Our line is therefore $15x + 14y = 315$ and is shown as a broken line on Figure 13.5.

Step 2   Determine the solution point

Since we want to **minimize** our objective function, the solution point in this case will be the last intersection of the isoprofit line with the feasible region as it moves **towards** the origin. The solution point is given by the intersection of the lines

$$x + 3y = 30$$

and

$$3x + 2y = 48$$

Solving these equations simultaneously, or reading the solution from Figure 13.5, gives $x = 12$, $y = 6$. The minimum value of the function is

Figure 13.5. Solution point of the cost minimization problem in Worked Example 13.4. The solution point is the last intersection of the isoprofit line with the feasible region as the line moves towards the origin

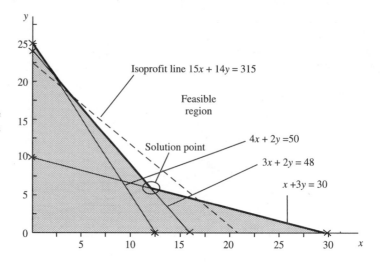

$15 \times 12 + 14 \times 6 = £264$, i.e. machine A should be run for 12 hours and machine B should be run for six hours. The total operating costs would be £264.

Again we ensure that our solution point satisfies all the constraints substituting $x = 12$, $y = 6$ into each constraint in turn gives

$30 \geq 30$ from the 'basic' constraint
$48 \geq 48$ from the 'super' constraint
$60 \geq 50$ from the 'luxury' constraint

This tells us that we have produced exactly the required number of 'basic' and 'super' and have produced ten more than the minimum requirement for 'luxury'.

Worked example

13.5   A company manufactures two products, X and Y. Product X has a labour requirement of five minutes per unit while product Y has a labour requirement of four minutes per unit. There is a total of 30 hours labour available. Each unit of product X produces a profit of £1, while a unit of product Y produces a profit of £2. There is a requirement to produce at least 100 units of each product.

(a) Formulate the problem as a linear programming problem and solve it graphically.
(b) If the method of production is such that the number of product X produced should be at least half the number of product Y produced, what difference will this make to the company's profit?

Solution   (a) The company needs to decide the number of each product it should produce. Let x be the number of product X produced and y be the number of product Y produced. The company's objective is to

Figure 13.6. Feasible region and solution point of the profit maximization problem in Worked Example 13.5(a). Light shading indicates that all constraints other than one are satisfied, dark shading indicates that two constraints are not satisfied

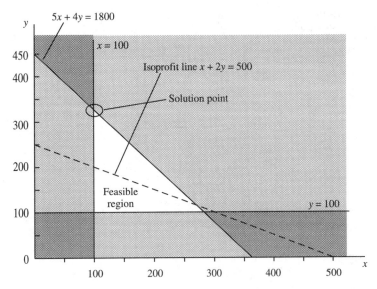

maximize profit, i.e.

maximize $\pi = x + 2y$

The constraints are imposed by the limited labour time available and by the requirement to produce at least 100 units of each product. The constraints are

$5x + 4y \leq 1800$	labour time	
$x \geq 100$	product X requirement	
$y \geq 100$	product Y requirement	

Note that the limit of the labour time constraint is written in units of minutes to match the labour time requirement. The linear programming problem is to

Maximize	$\pi = x + 2y$
subject to	$5x + 4y \leq 1800$
	$x \geq 100$
	$y \geq 100$

(The final two constraints mean that the requirements for $x \geq 0$ and $y \geq 0$ are not needed since the last two constraints already state this.) The feasible region and the isoprofit line are shown in Figure 13.6. The solution point is the intersection of the two lines

$$x = 100$$

and

$$5x + 4y = 1800$$

Solving these equations simultaneously gives $x = 100$ and $y = 325$. Substituting these values into the objective function, $x + 2y$, tells us

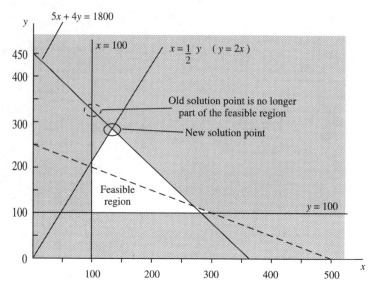

Figure 13.7. Feasible region and solution point of the profit maximization problem in Worked Example 13.5(b)

that the maximum profit will be £750. Check: Substituting the solution into each constraint in turn gives

$$1800 \leq 1800$$
$$100 \geq 100$$
$$325 \geq 100$$

and hence all constraints are satisfied.

(b) The additional constraint will be

$$x \geq y/2$$

Since the origin lies on this line you should choose any point other than the origin to test the inequality

Including this constraint gives a new feasible region shown in Figure 13.7. The new solution point is given by the intersection of the two lines

$$x = y/2$$

and

$$5x + 4y = 1800$$

Solving these equations simultaneously will give the solution $x = 138.46$, and $y = 276.92$. Substituting these values into the objective function gives a profit of £692.31, which is a reduction of £57.69 in the company's profit.

Check: This solution substituted into the constraints gives

$$1800 \leq 1800$$
$$138.46 \geq 100$$
$$276.92 \geq 100$$
$$138.46 \geq 138.46$$

and again all constraints are satisfied. Note: In practice, the actual number of each product produced would be given by integer values.

To ensure that the solution produces integer values involves **integer programming**, which is beyond the scope of this book. In general, rounding the values down will give a sensible answer and ensure that the constraints are satisfied.

Self-assessment questions 13.2

1. What is a 'feasible region'?
2. How is the value π of an isoprofit line determined?
3. What is meant by a 'solution point'?
4. How are the number of surplus units of resource determined?
5. If the linear program solution results in non-integer values for the decision variables, should the results be rounded up or down to the nearest integer? Explain your answer.

Exercises 13.2

1. For the problem formulated in Exercises 13.1, Question 1,

   (a) plot a graph and identify the feasible region on this graph,
   (b) find the point in the feasible region which maximizes the objective function,
   (c) calculate the manufacturer's profit and determine how much of each resource remains unused.

2. Consider the problem formulated in Exercises 13.1, Question 2.

   (a) Use a graphical method of solution to determine the number of each type of shelf to be bought.
   (b) What will be the total cost to the company?

| 13.3 | Introduction to sensitivity analysis |

In the business world, prices of materials, goods, labour costs etc. are constantly changing, as are the quantities of these items that are available at any one time.

   Sensitivity analysis looks at how changes in the coefficients of the objective function, or in the quantities of resources which are available, affect the optimal solution.

Changes to the objective coefficients

Once we have identified the feasible region, the exact solution point is found by sliding the isoprofit line in the appropriate direction. It is the

Figure 13.8. Solution point for new objective function: maximize $4x + 4y$

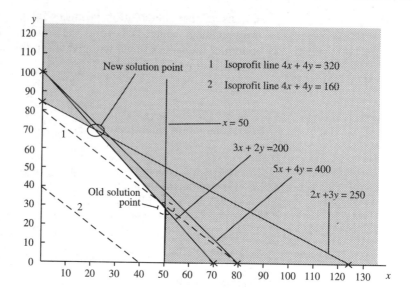

slope of the isoprofit line that determines which vertex of the feasible region is the solution point. It is important, therefore, to know what changes in the objective coefficients will lead to new solution points, and what changes will lead to the original solution point being retained. If a very small change in one coefficient would lead to a new optimal product mix, it is vital that the coefficients have been calculated accurately. It is less important if even quite large changes leave the solution point unchanged.

Refer to the profit maximization problem given in Worked Example 13.3. In Figure 13.3, we see that the solution point is given by the intersection of $3x + 2y = 200$ and $x = 50$. As long as the slope of the isoprofit line remains between the slopes of these two lines, the solution point remains unchanged. If the slope were to change so that it were no longer between the slopes of these two lines, the solution point would change also. For example, if the objective function in Worked Example 13.3 became

Maximize $\pi = 4x + 4y$

the solution point would be found according to Figure 13.8. We observe that the solution point is now the intersection of the lines $2x + 3y = 250$ and $3x + 2y = 200$. Thus changing the slope of the isoprofit line so that it no longer lies between the lines $3x + 2y = 200$ and $x = 50$ has produced a change in the solution point. Returning to the original problem with objective function $\pi = 12x + 4y$, let line A represent the line $3x + 2y = 200$ and line B represent the line $x = 50$. The solution remains unchanged provided

KEY POINT

slope of line B $\leq$ slope of isoprofit line $\leq$ slope of line A

Figure 13.9. The slope of the original isoprofit line together with $3x + 2y = 200$ and $x = 50$

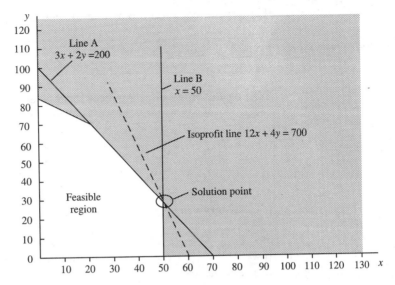

Note that the inequality is written in this order because all the slopes are negative.

Figure 13.9 illustrates how the slope of the isoprofit line lies between the slopes of line A and line B. If one of the lines of intersection is vertical, as line B is in this case, that line can be disregarded provided that the coefficients of the objective function are positive. This is because the slope of the line will always be negative and therefore cannot go beyond this vertical line. In this case we are then able to say that the solution point will remain unchanged provided

KEY POINT

slope of isoprofit line $\leq$ slope of line A

Now line A is given by the equation $3x + 2y = 200$. If we re-write this equation in terms of y, the line will be in its slope/intercept form. This gives

Equation of a straight line is $y = mx + c$ where m is the slope and c is the intercept with the y axis

$$y = -\frac{3}{2}x + 100$$

slope of line A   intercept of line A
on the y axis

So for our solution point to remain unchanged,

$$\text{slope of isoprofit line} \leq -\frac{3}{2}$$

The general equation of an isoprofit line is

KEY POINT

$$c_1 x + c_2 y = \pi$$

c_1 is the coefficient of x, usually the profit per unit for x. c_2 is the coefficient of y, usually the profit per unit for y

Writing this in its slope/intercept form gives

$$y = \frac{-c_1}{c_2} x + \frac{\pi}{c_2}$$ [13.1]

↑   ↖

slope of   intercept of isoprofit
isoprofit line   line on the y axis

If we require the slope of the isoprofit line to be less than or equal to $-3/2$, then this means

Multiplying both sides of an inequality by -1 changes the sign of the inequality, e.g. $-3 < -2$ but $3 > 2$

$$\frac{-c_1}{c_2} \le \frac{-3}{2} \quad \text{or} \quad \frac{c_1}{c_2} \ge \frac{3}{2}$$

We now keep each of the coefficients fixed, in turn, to find the required range for the other coefficient. In Worked Example 13.3, our isoprofit line was $12x + 4y = \pi$, so $c_1 = 12$ and $c_2 = 4$. Keeping c_1 fixed at 12 gives

$$\frac{12}{c_2} \ge \frac{3}{2},$$

i.e. $c_2 \le 8$. Keeping c_2 fixed at 4 gives

$$\frac{c_1}{4} \ge \frac{3}{2},$$

i.e. $c_1 \ge 6$. Our solution point will remain unchanged provided that, while the coefficient of y remains at 4, the coefficient of x is greater than or equal to 6, and, as long as the coefficient of x remains at 12, the coefficient of y is less than or equal to 8. As the coefficients of x and y are currently 12 and 4 respectively, it would appear that there would have to be large changes in the profit per unit for either deluxe or standard before the solution point would change. The manufacturer could therefore feel confident about producing models according to the optimal production schedule of 50 deluxe and 25 standard.

If our example had not involved a vertical line, we would have two inequalities to solve instead of one.

Worked example

13.6   A maximization linear programming problem has been formulated as follows.

Figure 13.10. Feasible region and isoprofit line $x + y = 24$ for Worked Example 13.6

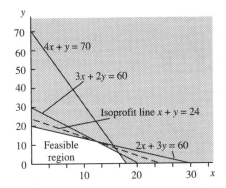

Maximize $\pi = x + y$
subject to $2x + 3y \leq 60$ constraint A
                  $3x + 2y \leq 60$ constraint B
                  $4x + \ y \leq 70$ constraint C
                  $x \geq 0 \quad y \geq 0$

(a) Show that the maximum value of the objective function is 24 when $x = 12$ and $y = 12$. Also show that all the constraints are satisfied at this solution point.
(b) Keeping the objective coefficients fixed in turn, determine the range within which the other coefficient can move in order for the solution point to remain the same.

Solution   (a) Figure 13.10 shows the feasible region, together with the isoprofit line $x + y = 24$. The solution point is given by the intersection of the lines

$$2x + 3y = 60$$

and

$$3x + 2y = 60$$

Solving these equations simultaneously gives the solution point $x = 12$, $y = 12$. The value of the objective function at this solution point is $12 + 12 = 24$. Substituting the solution into each of the constraints in turn gives

$60 \leq 60$ constraint A
$60 \leq 60$ constraint B
$60 \leq 70$ constraint C

Hence all constraints are satisfied.
(b) In this example the objective function is $\pi = x + y$. Thus the coefficients of the objective function are $c_1 = 1$ and $c_2 = 1$. We will look at the range of values for c_2 while c_1 is fixed at 1 and the range of values for c_1 while c_2 is fixed at 1. The solution point is given by the intersection of the lines

$$2x + 3y = 60 \qquad \text{line A}$$

and

$$3x + 2y = 60 \qquad \text{line B}$$

Writing these two equations in their slope/intercept form gives

$$y = \frac{-2x}{3} + 20 \qquad \text{for line A}$$

$$y = \frac{-3x}{2} + 30 \qquad \text{for line B}$$

For the solution point to remain unchanged, we use [13.1] to give

$$\frac{-3}{2} \le \frac{-c_1}{c_2} \le \frac{-2}{3}$$

We treat the two parts of the inequality separately.

(i) Considering

$$\frac{-3}{2} \le \frac{-c_1}{c_2}$$

Multiply both sides by -1 to give

$$\frac{3}{2} \ge \frac{c_1}{c_2}$$

If we keep $c_1 = 1$ then $3/2 \ge 1/c_2$ and so $c_2 \ge 2/3$. If we keep $c_2 = 1$ then $3/2 \ge c_1/1$ and so $c_1 \le 3/2$.

(ii) Considering

$$\frac{-c_1}{c_2} \le \frac{-2}{3}$$

Multiply both sides by -1 to give

$$\frac{c_1}{c_2} \ge \frac{2}{3}$$

If we keep $c_1 = 1$ then $1/c_2 \ge 2/3$ and so $c_2 \le 3/2$. If we keep $c_2 = 1$ then $c_1/1 \ge 2/3$ and so $c_1 \ge 2/3$.

In order for the solution point to remain the same: if the coefficient of x remains at 1, the coefficient of y must remain between 2/3 and 3/2; if the coefficient of y remains at 1, the coefficient of x must remain between 2/3 and 3/2.

Changes in the resource availability

The solution point of our profit maximization problem (Worked Example 13.3) was found to be at the intersection of the machining constraint $3x + 2y \le 200$ and the exclusivity constraint $x \le 50$. Increasing the value

The constraint would be parallel to the original constraint but drawn further from the origin

on the right-hand side of either of these constraints would expand the feasible region and give us a slightly different solution point. If the number of machining hours available increased from 200 to 210, the new solution would be found by solving, simultaneously, the two equations

$$3x + 2y = 210$$

and

$$x = 50$$

to give $x = 50$ and $y = 30$. The maximum profit that could be achieved would now be

$$(12 \times 50) + (4 \times 30) = £720$$

This compares with the original profit of £700 and represents an increase in profit of £20. This increase has been achieved through the additional ten machining hours. The profit has therefore increased by £2 for each additional machining hour available. The increase in the objective function for every unit increase in resource availability is generally called the **shadow price** of that resource. It represents the economic value of an additional unit of that resource. A decrease in availability would lead to the value of the objective function falling by the shadow price. If, in Worked Example 13.3, the exclusivity constraint was changed to $x \leq 60$, the solution point would be given by $x = 60$, $y = 10$. The maximum profit would now be

$$(12 \times 60) + (4 \times 10) = £760$$

The solution point would still be at the intersection of the other two constraints

The solution point would no longer be at the same vertex

Relaxing the exclusivity constraint by 10 units has led to an increase in profit of £60. The shadow price for the exclusivity constraint is therefore £6. Because the other two constraints are not fully utilized, a small change in the resource availability of either of them would have no effect on the solution point. The shadow price for both material and labour is therefore zero.

Shadow prices will generally only be valid for small changes in the availability of the resources. A large increase in any one resource will usually mean that some other resource becomes fully utilized and the solution point is restricted because of this. This increased resource will no longer form part of the boundary for the feasible region.

Worked example

13.7 For the problem defined in Worked Example 13.6, allow the right-hand sides of constraints A and B to increase by 4 units in turn, while the other constraints remain unchanged. Determine the increase in the value of the objective function in each case and use this to calculate the shadow price for constraints A and B. Comment on the shadow price for constraint C.

Solution   First increase the right-hand side of constraint A by 4 units. The problem can now be stated as follows.

Maximize $\pi = x + y$
subject to $2x + 3y \le 64$ constraint A
                    $3x + 2y \le 60$ constraint B
                    $4x + y \le 70$ constraint C
                    $x \ge 0 \quad y \ge 0$

This could be solved graphically to show that the solution point is still given by the intersection of constraints A and B. The new solution point is found by solving the following two equations simultaneously:

$$2x + 3y = 64$$

and

$$3x + 2y = 60$$

The new solution point is $x = 10.4$, and $y = 14.4$ with the new value of the objective function being 24.8, an increase of 0.8. Because the solution point is still found at the intersection of constraints A and B, all 4 units added to the constraint have contributed to this increase of 0.8 in the objective function. The increase per unit, and hence the shadow price for constraint A, is therefore 0.2. If the solution point had changed and now involved a constraint other than A or B, this would suggest that we have increased the right-hand side of constraint A by too many units. We would have to consider a smaller increase in A to try to calculate the shadow price.

Now consider increasing the right-hand side of constraint B by 4 units. The problem can now be stated as follows.

Maximize $\pi = x + y$
subject to $2x + 3y \le 60$ constraint A
                    $3x + 2y \le 64$ constraint B
                    $4x + y \le 70$ constraint C
                    $x \ge 0 \quad y \ge 0$

This could also be solved graphically, and would again show that the solution point is still at the intersection of constraints A and B. The new solution is found by solving the following equations simultaneously:

$$2x + 3y = 60$$

and

$$3x + 2y = 64$$

The new solution is $x = 14.4$, $y = 10.4$ with the new value of the objective function being 24.8, an increase of 0.8. Again the solution point is still at the intersection of constraints A and B and so the shadow price for constraint B is $0.8/4 = 0.2$.

Constraint C is not fully utilized at its present capacity and so increasing the amount of that resource available will have no effect on the optimal solution. The shadow price for constraint C is therefore zero.

The above example refers to a problem where all the constraints are of the form '$\leq$'.

If we *increase* the right-hand side of a '$\geq$' constraint, this will have the effect of *reducing* the feasible region. If the solution point lies on this constraint, this will also have the effect of *reducing* the value of the objective function. Conversely, *reducing* the value on the right-hand side of a '$\geq$' constraint will lead to the feasible region being *increased* in size, and hence to an *increase* in the value of the objective function. The shadow prices of the resources are found in just the same way as before.

Self-assessment questions 13.3

1. What is sensitivity analysis concerned with?
2. Why might the solution point change if the objective coefficients are changed?
3. Why are shadow prices generally only valid for small changes in resource availability?
4. What does the shadow price represent?

Exercise 13.3

Consider the problem which was solved in Exercises 13.2, Question 1.

(a) Determine the range of values within which each objective coefficient can move, assuming the other coefficient remains fixed, in order for the solution point to remain unchanged. Note: only one limit will need to be used.
(b) Calculate the shadow price for each of the resources of labour, component, packaging.
(c) Explain the meaning of your answer to (b).

Test exercises

1. A company produces two products, A and B, which both undergo two production processes; machining and assembly. To produce 1 unit of product A requires one hour of machining time and three hours of assembly time, and produces a profit of £20. To produce 1 unit of product B requires one hour of machining time and two hours of assembly time, and produces a profit of £10. During the next week

there are 600 hours of machining time and 1500 hours of assembly time available. The company can sell all it produces of both products but has an order for 300 units of product A which must be satisfied during the next week.

(a) If the company wishes to maximize its profit, formulate the above as a linear programming problem in order to determine the number of each product that should be produced during the next week.
(b) Plot a graph of the constraints and clearly indicate the feasible region.
(c) Determine the optimum number of each product that should be produced, and calculate the associated profit for the week.
(d) Does the optimal solution point leave any available machining or assembly time remaining unused?

2. If, in Test Exercises Question 1, the number of either product produced may not be more than twice the number of the other product,
(a) what additional constraints will be imposed on the linear programming problem?
(b) determine the difference this would make to the number of each product produced, the associated profit and the quantity of each resource that will be unused.

3. A company wants to optimize its production schedule to produce two products X and Y. It has already formulated a linear programming problem, which is defined as

Maximize profit $\quad \pi = 5X + 4Y$
subject to
$$3X + 4Y \leq 80 \qquad \text{machining constraint}$$
$$4X + 2Y \leq 90 \qquad \text{painting constraint}$$
$$X + 3Y \leq 45 \qquad \text{packaging constraint}$$
$$X \geq 0, \quad Y \geq 0$$

(a) Determine the optimum number of each product that should be produced.
(b) The company is not certain that it has calculated the profit for either product correctly. Leave each profit figure fixed in turn, and calculate the range within which the other profit figure can move, if the production mix is to remain optimal.
(c) Assuming that the profits defined in the problem for each product are correct, calculate the shadow price for each of the resources.
(d) Comment on the meaning of each of these shadow prices.

14 Financial mathematics

Objectives	When you have read this chapter you should be able to

When you have read this chapter you should be able to

- find the sum of an arithmetic progression
- find the sum of a geometric progression
- calculate simple and compound interest
- determine an effective rate of interest
- calculate an annual percentage rate
- discount to a present value a single term and a series of terms
- calculate the value of an annuity
- calculate an internal rate of return

Many decisions in business are based upon the financial implications involved. It is essential to have a sound understanding of the basic terms used and to be able to perform standard calculations. Many of these calculations are founded on simple series, so this chapter begins with an introduction to the two main types of series used.

14.1   Arithmetic progressions

An arithmetic progression (AP) is a sequence, the terms of which increase or decrease by a constant amount. The constant amount is usually called the **common difference**, and is denoted by d.

An AP is of the form

$$a, a + d, a + 2d, \cdots, a + (n - 1)d$$

A sequence is a set of numbers arranged in order. A series is a set of numbers that are arranged in order and summed

where a is the first term, d is the common difference and n is the number of terms.

Worked example

14.1 Find the value of a, d and n for the following AP:

2, 5, 8, 11, 14

Solution There are five terms, the first term is 2 and the common difference is 3, so $n = 5$, $a = 2$ and $d = 3$.

Sum of an arithmetic progression

We could calculate the sum of an AP by adding each individual term together. This, however, can be a lengthy, tedious process and so the following equation can be used instead.

The sum S_n of the first n terms of an AP is given by

KEY POINT

See Appendix G for proof

$$S_n = \frac{n}{2}\{2a + (n - 1)d\} \qquad [14.1]$$

where a is the first term, d is the common difference and n is the number of terms.

Worked example

14.2 Find the sum of the first five terms of the AP given in Worked Example 14.1.

Solution $n = 5$, $a = 2$ and $d = 3$.

$$S_5 = \frac{5}{2} \times \{(2 \times 2) + (5 - 1) \times 3\} = 40$$

Check: $2 + 5 + 8 + 11 + 14 = 40$.

14.2 Geometric progressions

A geometric progression (GP) is a sequence, the terms of which increase or decrease by a constant ratio. This constant ratio is usually called the **common ratio**, and is denoted by r. Any new term in a GP can be found by multiplying the previous term by r.

A GP is of the form

KEY POINT

$$a, \ ar, \ ar^2, \ \cdots, \ ar^{n-1}$$

Worked example

14.3 Find the value of a, r and n for the following GP:

8, 4, 2, 1, $\frac{1}{2}$

Solution This GP has five terms. Its first term is 8 and its common ratio is $\frac{1}{2}$, i.e. multiplying any term by $\frac{1}{2}$ will give the next term in the sequence. Thus, $n = 5$, $a = 8$ and $r = \frac{1}{2}$.

Sum of a geometric progression

The sum of a GP could be found by summing individual terms, or alternatively using the following equation.

The sum S_n of the first n terms of a GP is given by

KEY POINT

See Appendix H for proof

$$S_n = \frac{a(1 - r^n)}{1 - r}$$ [14.2]

where a is the first term, r is the common ratio and n is the number of terms.

Worked example

14.4 Find the sum of the first five terms of the GP given in Worked Example 14.3.

Solution From Worked Example 14.3, $a = 8$, $r = \frac{1}{2}$ and $n = 5$. Using [14.2],

$$S_5 = \frac{8\{1 - (\frac{1}{2})^5\}}{1 - \frac{1}{2}} = 15\frac{1}{2}$$

Check: $8 + 4 + 2 + 1 + \frac{1}{2} = 15\frac{1}{2}$.

Sum to infinity of a geometric progression

The value that S_n approaches when n is very large is known as the sum to infinity, and is denoted by S_∞. If $|r| \geq 1$ then as n gets large

S_∞ becomes infinite   [14.3a]

If $|r| < 1$ then as n gets large

KEY POINT

$$S_\infty = \frac{a}{1 - r}$$ [14.3b]

See Appendix A for the
definition of modulus
where a is the first term, r is the common ratio and $|r|$ is the modulus of r.

Worked example

14.5   Find the sum to infinity of the GP given by

$$8, 4, 2, 1, \tfrac{1}{2}, \ldots$$

Solution   Here $a = 8$ and $r = \tfrac{1}{2}$. Since $|r| < 1$, [14.3b] is used to find the sum to infinity, S_∞:

$$S_\infty = \frac{8}{1 - \tfrac{1}{2}} = 16$$

This means that the more values we include in the GP, the closer to 16 the actual sum would be.

Self-assessment questions 14.2

1. Give an example of an AP and a GP.
2. How can any value of a GP be found using the previous value in the sequence?
3. What does the sum to infinity of a GP tell you?

Exercises 14.2

1. For the following numbers

    $$\ldots, 117, 121, 125, 129, \ldots$$

    (a) establish whether the numbers form part of an AP or GP,
    (b) if the first number of the complete series is 1, what is the sum of the fifteenth to twenty-fifth terms inclusive?
2. Consider the following geometric progression

    $$81, 27, 9, 3, 1, 1/3, \ldots$$

    (a) Find the sum of the first eight terms.
    (b) Find the sum to infinity.
    (c) How would you find the sum of all terms after the eighth term?

14.3   Simple interest

If a sum of money is invested, and earns interest, or a loan is taken out and interest is paid, the amount being invested or borrowed is called the **principal**. Where interest only accrues on the principal, i.e. no interest is re-invested, this is known as **simple interest**. The amount of interest I is given by

KEY POINT

$$I = Prt \qquad [14.4]$$

where P is the principal, r is the interest rate (expressed as a decimal) and t is the period of time.

Worked example

14.6   If £1000 is invested at the rate of 10% per annum, simple interest, how much interest is earned in one year?

Solution   Principal $P = £1000$, rate of interest $r = 0.1$, time period, $t = 1$. Using [14.4],

$$\text{Interest } I = 1000 \times 0.1 \times 1 = £100$$

14.4   Compound interest

Of far more practical use is the concept of compound interest, whereby any interest that is earned on an investment, or loan, is re-invested, and will itself begin to earn interest. This is known as **compound interest**. For example, suppose a single investment of £1000 is made, and this earns compound interest at the rate of 10% per annum. The interest earned on the investment in the first year will be 10% of £1000, i.e. £100. The value of the investment at the end of one year will therefore be £1000 + £100 = £1100.

During the second year, interest will be earned both by the original investment of £1000 and also by the interest that was earned during the first year.

The total interest earned during the second year will be

10% of £1100 = £110

The value of the investment at the end of two years will be £1210, which is the value of the investment at the end of one year plus the interest earned during the second year.

In general, the value of the investment at the end of the nth year is given by

$$S = P(1 + r)^n \qquad [14.5]$$

where S is the value of the investment at the end of the nth year, P is the principal, r is the interest rate, expressed as a decimal, and n represents the number of years. In this example, suppose we want to find the final value S of the investment at the end of five years. $P = £1000$ and $r = 10/100 = 0.1$, so, using [14.5], the value is

$$S = 1000 \times (1.1)^5 = £1610.51$$

Worked example

14.7 A man takes out a loan of £5000. Interest is to be paid at the rate of 8% per annum. If the man does not have to start paying back the loan for two years, what will be the total amount owing when the repayments begin?

Solution The repayments will begin at the end of two years. The total amount owing by then is calculated using [14.5]:

$$S = 5000(1.08)^2 = £5832$$

14.5 Effective rate of interest

Interest rates are typically quoted as annual percentages. However, if interest is compounded more frequently than annually, the effective interest rate will be larger than the quoted annual rate. However, even though interest rates are quoted as percentages, they are more commonly used as decimals. If the quoted annual rate of interest is r (in decimal form), and there are x compounding periods in the year, the interest rate for each period will be given by r/x. (For example, if the interest is added every six months, then there would be two compounding periods in one year.) If we begin with the principal P, the value at the end of the first compounding period will be

We effectively divide the annual interest into interest per period

$$P\left(1 + \frac{r}{x}\right)$$

As there are x compounding periods in the year, the value at the end of the year will be

$$P\left(1 + \frac{r}{x}\right)^x$$

This is equivalent to $P(1 + i)$, where i represents the **effective rate of interest**, i.e.

Both sides of the equation represent the value at the end of one year

$$P(1 + i) = P\left(1 + \frac{r}{x}\right)^x$$

so

KEY POINT

$$i = \left(1 + \frac{r}{x}\right)^x - 1 \qquad [14.6]$$

where i is the effective rate of interest, expressed as a decimal, P is the principal, r is the annual rate of interest, expressed as a decimal, and x is the number of compounding periods in a year.

Worked example

14.8 Find the effective rate of interest if the quoted annual rate of interest is 8%, and compounding is done (a) monthly, (b) quarterly.

Solution (a) $r = 8/100 = 0.08$. $x = 12$ since there are 12 compounding periods per year. Using [14.6], the effective rate of interest is:

$$i = \left(1 + \frac{0.08}{12}\right)^{12} - 1 = 0.083,$$

i.e. 8.3%.

(b) $r = 8/100 = 0.08$. $x = 4$ since there are four compounding periods per year. Using [14.6], the effective rate of interest is:

$$i = \left(1 + \frac{0.08}{4}\right)^{4} - 1 = 0.082,$$

i.e. 8.2%.

Note that for a given quoted annual rate of interest, the greater the value of x, the greater the effective rate of interest.

14.6   Annual percentage rate

The **annual percentage rate** (APR) is a measure of the real rate of interest that is paid on any type of loan. By law the APR must be quoted as part of any advertisement giving details of a loan, and is the figure upon which any comparisons are usually based. If two loans are available for the same duration, the one with the lower APR will be cheaper. This is not necessarily true for quoted rates of interest, where frequency of compounding, payment dates and various other factors can make a big difference to the actual amount of interest paid. The APR also takes account of various incidental charges which are incurred as a result of taking out the loan. In the case of a mortgage, this will involve various charges such as arrangement fees, solicitor's mortgage charges and valuation charges. The interest to be paid during any year is actually based on the outstanding balance at the end of the previous year. This is the case even for repayment mortgages where the outstanding balance decreases after each payment. Because the outstanding balance is less than the balance on which the actual amount of interest being paid is based, this leads the APR to be larger than the quoted interest rate.

Worked example

14.9   A woman borrows £5000 at a quoted interest rate of 10%. £2500 of the original sum is to be repaid after six months, with the balance being repaid at the end of one year. What is the APR?

Solution   The interest to be paid is 10% of £5000 = £500. The actual amount borrowed will be £5000 for six months plus £2500 for six months. Borrowing £5000 for six months is equivalent to borrowing £2500 for one year. Similarly, borrowing £2500 for six months is equivalent to borrowing £1250 for one year. So the equivalent amount borrowed for one year is £3750. If we write [14.4] in terms of r, we have

$$r = \frac{I}{Pt}$$

so

$$r = \frac{500}{3750 \times 1} = 0.1333$$

The APR is therefore 13.3% and not 10%.

Self-assessment questions 14.6

1. How does compound interest differ from simple interest?
2. If the number of times interest is calculated in a year increases, what happens to the amount of interest earned?
3. What two factors determine the effective rate of interest?
4. Why is the APR usually greater than the quoted interest rate?

Exercises 14.6

1. A girl inherits £10000 when a rich relative dies. The money is to be invested in a trust fund for 12 years until the girl is 18 and gains access to the fund. If the money is invested at the rate of 9% per annum compound interest, what will be the value of the fund when the girl is 18?

2. A company wants to initiate a savings plan to help pay for some machinery which will be required in two years time. It can either invest in scheme A, which offers interest at the rate of 10% per annum, compounded quarterly, or it can invest in scheme B which offers interest at the rate of 11% per annum, compounded half yearly. By calculating the effective rates of interest of schemes A and B, decide which scheme the company should choose.

3. A finance company is offering a loan of £6000 to fund the purchase of a new car. It quotes an interest rate of 8%. If the £6000 is to be repaid in four quarterly payments, beginning in three months time, what is the APR?

14.7   Present value

The formula for calculating compound interest allows us to find the value of an investment at any time in the future. However, on many occasions we know the future value and need to calculate the value in present-day terms. This can be especially useful if we are trying to make comparisons between different investments. Calculating the **present value** of the investments gives us a common base for comparison. We can re-arrange equation [14.5] to give an equation in terms of the present value P:

KEY POINT

$$P = \frac{S}{(1+i)^n} \qquad [14.7]$$

where P is the present value, S is the final value, i is the interest rate expressed as a decimal and n is the number of years.

Worked example

14.10   What is the present value of an investment which will be worth £1210 in two years time if the interest rate for those two years is 10%?

Solution $S = £1210$, $i = 10/100 = 0.10$, $n = 2$. Using [14.7], the present value is:

$$P = \frac{1210}{(1+0.1)^2} = £1000$$

Note: this is what we would expect from the example given in Section 14.4.

It is more usual when finding present values to call the prevailing interest rate the **discount rate**, since we are discounting some future value back to a present value.

Worked example

14.11   A man has a choice of paying off a loan by making a single payment of £750 in two years time or by making a single payment of £800 in three years time. If the discount rate is 8%, which option should he choose?

Solution   Using [14.7], we can calculate the present values. The payment of £750 in two years time has a present value of

$$\frac{750}{(1+0.08)^2} = £643.00$$

The payment of £800 in three years time has a present value of

$$\frac{800}{(1+0.08)^3} = £635.07$$

As these two values are both in present-day terms, a direct comparison can be made, and we can see that the payment of £800 in three years time represents the cheaper option.

14.8   Discounting a series of investments

Many problems are not concerned with discounting just a single value, but involve discounting a series of values. If the amounts being discounted vary, this involves discounting each value individually and then summing.

Worked example

14.12   What is the present value of receiving £1000 in one years time, £1500 in two years time and £2000 in three years time if the discount rate is 8%?

Solution   We need to apply the discounting formula given in [14.7] to each value individually (since the amounts differ).

£1000 in one years time $P = \dfrac{1000}{(1+0.08)^1} = £925.93$

£1500 in two years time $P = \dfrac{1500}{(1+0.08)^2} = £1286.01$

£2000 in three years time $\qquad P = \dfrac{2000}{(1 + 0.08)^3} = £1587.66$

The present value of the whole series of payments is

$\qquad £925.93 + £1286.01 + £1587.66 = £3799.60$

14.9   Annuities

If the series of payments being discounted is constant for all years, the series is known as an **annuity**. To find the present value of the series of payments we could discount each item individually and then sum. However, this ignores the fact that the actual amounts are constant, and is a rather cumbersome way of making the calculation. Instead we can use [14.8]. If we let R be the constant annual cash flow, and assume that the cash flow begins in one years time, then the net present value A of the series of cash flows is given by:

$$A = \frac{R}{1 + i} + \frac{R}{(1 + i)^2} + \frac{R}{(1 + i)^3} + \cdots + \frac{R}{(1 + i)^n}$$

So the payment in one years time is discounted by one year, the payment in two years time is discounted by two years, and the payment in n years is discounted by n years. This is a GP, with first term

$$a = \frac{R}{1 + i}$$

and common ratio

$$r = \frac{1}{1 + i},$$

i.e. multiplying any term by $1/(1 + i)$ will give the next term in the series. We can therefore use [14.2] to find the sum of the first n terms in the series.

$$A = \frac{\left\{\frac{R}{1+i}\right\}\left\{1 - \frac{1}{(1+i)^n}\right\}}{1 - \left(\frac{1}{1+i}\right)}$$

$$A = \frac{\left\{\frac{R}{1+i}\right\}\left\{1 - \frac{1}{(1+i)^n}\right\}}{(1 + i - 1)/(1 + i)}$$

KEY POINT

$$A = \frac{R}{i}\left\{1 - \frac{1}{(1 + i)^n}\right\} \qquad\qquad [14.8]$$

where R is the constant annual cash flow, i is the discount rate expressed as a decimal, n is the number of years and A is the net present value of the series of cash flows.

Worked example

14.13   First prize in a competition is to receive an immediate payment of £4000 or a payment of £1000 a year for each of the next five years, the first payment being made in one years time. If the discount rate is 8%, which option has the higher value?

Solution

Amount received each year is constant at £1000, even though the value of each payment is different

The present value of the series of annual payments can be found by using [14.8], where $R = £1000$, $i = 0.08$ and $n = 5$.

$$A = \frac{1000}{0.08}\left[1 - \frac{1}{1.08^5}\right] = £3992.71$$

As this is less than the £4000 being offered immediately, the single payment of £4000 represents the better option.

14.10   Annuity due

If the series of constant cash flows begins immediately, rather than in one years time, the series is known as an **annuity due**. The present value of the series of cash flows is given by

$$A = R + \frac{R}{1+i} + \frac{R}{(1+i)^2} + \cdots + \frac{R}{(1+i)^{n-1}}$$

This is a GP with first term R and common ratio $1/(1+i)$. The sum of the series can be found using [14.2] and is given by

KEY POINT

See Appendix I for proof

$$A = \frac{R}{i}(1+i)\left\{1 - \frac{1}{(1+i)^n}\right\}$$ [14.9]

Note that there are n terms in the series even though the final term is only raised to the power $n - 1$.

Worked example

14.14   If, in Worked Example 14.13, the annual cash payments of £1000 were to begin immediately, would the decision reached be altered?

Solution   Using [14.9], for the five annual payments,

$$A = \frac{1000}{0.08}(1.08)\left[1 - \frac{1}{1.08^5}\right] = £4312.13$$

This compares to a present value of £4000 and means that the series of annual payments now represents the better option, so yes, the decision has changed.

14.11   Internal rate of return

The **internal rate of return** (IRR) is the discount rate which, when applied to the cash flows, equates the cash outlays with the cash inflows. The total cash flows, when discounted according to the IRR, will have a net value of zero. To establish the IRR, the net cash flow is calculated for any discount rate chosen at random. If the net cash flow is positive, the discount rate is increased and the calculation is repeated. If the net cash flow is negative, the discount rate is reduced and the calculation is repeated. Once discount rates have been found which lead to both positive and negative net cash flows, the IRR can be approximated by a process known as linear interpolation (Appendix J).

If a discount rate of i_1 gives a positive cash flow of N_1 and a discount rate of i_2 gives a negative cash flow of N_2, then the IRR is given by

KEY POINT

$$IRR = i_1 + \frac{N_1}{N_1 - N_2}(i_2 - i_1) \qquad [14.10]$$

$-N_2$ will be positive

Worked example

14.15   An investment outlay of £5000 will bring a return of £2000 at the end of the year for each of the next three years. What is the IRR for this investment?

Solution   The present value of the cash inflow, for any discount rate, can be found using [14.8]. The present value of the cash outflow is £5000.

For a discount rate of 8%, using [14.8],

$$A = \frac{2000}{0.08}\left[1 - \frac{1}{1.08^3}\right] = £5154.20$$

So the net cash flow is £5154.20 − £5000 = £154.20. For a discount rate of 10%, using [14.8],

$$A = \frac{2000}{0.1}\left[1 - \frac{1}{1.1^3}\right] = £4973.70$$

So the net cash flow is £4973.70 − £5000 = −£26.30. Using [14.10],

$$\text{IRR} = 8 + \frac{154.20}{154.20 + 26.30} \times 2 = 9.7\%$$

This tells us that the investment has a value to the investor of 9.7% per annum. If he is able to invest the money elsewhere and obtain a rate greater than 9.7%, or if he needs to borrow money at a rate greater than 9.7%, then he should not undertake the investment. If we were to calculate the net cash flow for a discount rate of 9.7%, the figure should be approximately zero.

Self-assessment questions 14.11

1. Why are present values so useful?
2. What is an annuity?
3. How does an annuity due differ from an annuity?
4. What does the IRR measure?

Exercises 14.11

1. The managing director of a manufacturing company thinks that if he buys a machine now, in 1993, for £35000, the company will generate additional cash flows for the following years as given below:

Year	1994	1995	1996	1997
Additional cash flow (£)	5000	12 000	15 000	15 000

At the end of the four-year period, the machine would have no value. If the expected discount rate is 8% for the whole four-year period, what is the expected profit in terms of the present value?
2. Comment on the answer obtained in Question 1 if it is expected that the discount rate will rise during the four-year period.
3. What is the present value of an annuity of £2000 a year for 20 years if payments are received at the end of each year and the discount rate remains at 8% per annum?
4. How does the present value found in Question 3 change if payments are made at the beginning of each year?
5. Calculate the IRR for the cash flows in Question 1 if the discount rate remains fixed for the next four years. Comment on the meaning of the IRR in this case.

Test exercises

1. (a) State the first six terms of the GP which has a first term of 6 and a common ratio of 0.9.
   (b) Find the sum to infinity of the GP found in (a) and the sum of the first 20 terms.

2. (a) A deposit of £1000 is made into a fund which pays a quoted interest rate of 12%. If the interest is compounded monthly, what will be the value of the fund in two years time.
   (b) What effective rate of interest does the fund in (a) operate at?

3. A company is about to purchase a new machine and is undecided about how to pay for it. It is considering three methods which have been offered to them. The cash flows for the three methods are summarized below:

Method	Cash payments at the end of year					
	0	1	2	3	4	5
A	10 000	5000	5000	5000	10 000	–
B	–	7000	7000	7000	7000	7000
C	6000	6000	6000	6000	6000	5000

   Note that cash payments at the end of year 0 represent a payment now. Decide which method represents the best option and which represents the worst option if the company's discount rate is 10%.

4. An investor has been offered a share in a property deal. For an initial investment of £20000, he has been guaranteed returns of £5000 at the ends of years 1 and 2 and £10000 at the ends of years 3 and 4. Calculate the IRR for this investment and comment on its meaning to the investor.

Appendix A
Mathematical notation

A basic knowledge of algebra is assumed throughout the book. This appendix considers some of the terms and notation used. Many of the quantities can be determined using calculators (see calculator manuals for details).

Throughout the text numbers are usually rounded to four or less decimal places, i.e. four or less numbers after the decimal point. Numbers are always rounded to the closest number, i.e. if the next number is 5 or higher round up, if it is 4 or below round down. For example, 2.3468970 will be rounded up to four decimal places, i.e. 2.3469, and 267.385291 will be rounded down to three decimal places, i.e. 267.385.

A data set containing a variable X with n items is represented by

$$x_1, x_2, x_3, \ldots, x_n$$

or is summarized by

$$x_i \text{ for } i = 1, 2, 3, \ldots, n$$

A data set containing n pairs of values for two variables X and Y is represented by

$$(x_1, y_1), (x_2, y_2), \ldots, (x_n, y_n)$$

or is summarized by

$$(x_i, y_i) \text{ for } i = 1, 2, \ldots, n$$

Other notation used is as follows.

$\times$ is multiply
/ is divide
$\pm$ means both add and subtract the quantities either side
$x \times y = xy$
$\sqrt{\ }$ is the square root
$\pi = 3.14159$
$e = \exp = 2.71828$, is the exponential constant
∞ is infinity
$-\infty$ is negative infinity

$x^0 = 1$

$x^1 = x$

$\Sigma x = x_1 + x_2 + x_3 + \cdots + x_n$ (see Appendix B)

$>$ is greater than

$<$ is less than

$\geq$ is greater than or equal to

$\leq$ is less than or equal to

$n! = n \times (n-1) \times (n-2) \times (n-3) \times \cdots \times 3 \times 2 \times 1$

e.g. $4! = 4 \times 3 \times 2 \times 1 = 24$

Note that $0! = 1$ and $1! = 1$

$|x|$ means take the modulus of x, i.e. ignore the sign,

e.g. $|-2| = 2$ and $|2| = 2$

A **vertex** is a junction of two or more constraint lines on a graph When a graph is divided into four parts, each is known as a **quadrant**. The first quadrant is the shaded area shown in Figure A1 where $x \geq 0$ and $y \geq 0$.

Figure A1. The first quadrant of a graph

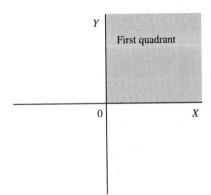

Appendix B
Subscripts and summation notation

The values of n items are represented by

$$x_1, x_2, x_3, \ldots, x_n$$

In general, the value of the ith item is denoted by x_i, where $i = 1, 2, 3, \ldots, n$.

If a pair of values are recorded for the same item, then the ith pair is represented by (x_i, y_i) where $i = 1, 2, 3, \ldots, n$.

Example

1 For the following data, what are the values of the first, third and last items?

$$1.1 \quad 1.3 \quad 1.5 \quad 1.2 \quad 1.6$$

Solution The value of the first item is 1.1, i.e. $x_1 = 1.1$. The value of the third item is 1.5, i.e. $x_3 = 1.5$. The last item is the fifth item. The value of the last item is 1.6, i.e. $x_5 = 1.6$.

Example

2 For the following data, what is the value of the first pair?

| X | 1.1 | 1.3 | 1.5 | 1.2 | 1.6 |
| Y | 3.2 | 4.8 | 3.9 | 3.0 | 4.2 |

Solution The value of the first pair is (1.1, 3.2), i.e. $x_1 = 1.1$ and $y_1 = 3.2$.

The sigma notation for Σx_i

The Greek letter Σ (sigma) is used to denote 'the sum of'. The sum of x_1 and x_2 and x_3 and so on up to and including x_n is denoted by

$$\sum_{i=1}^{n} x_i$$

i.e.

$$\sum_{i=1}^{n} x_i = x_1 + x_2 + x_3 + \cdots + x_n$$

In this book it is assumed that the summation will be performed for all possible values of x, i.e. for $i = 1, 2, 3, \ldots, n$. The following abbreviation is used for the summation:

Your scientific calculator may be able to calculate Σx_i

$$\sum_{i=1}^{n} x_i \qquad \text{is abbreviated to} \quad \Sigma x_i$$

Example

3 Calculate Σx_i for the data given in Example 1.

Solution $\Sigma x_i = x_1 + x_2 + x_3 + \cdots + x_n$

$= 1.1 + 1.3 + 1.5 + 1.2 + 1.6$

$= 6.7$

Your scientific calculator may be able to calculate Σx_i^2

The sigma notation for Σx_i^2

$$\Sigma x_i^2 = x_1^2 + x_2^2 + x_3^2 + \cdots + x_n^2$$

Note that $\Sigma x_i^2 \neq (\Sigma x_i)^2$.

Example

4 Calculate Σx_i^2 for the data given in Example 1.

Solution $\Sigma x_i^2 = x_1^2 + x_2^2 + x_3^2 + \cdots + x_n^2$

$= 1.1^2 + 1.3^2 + 1.5^2 + 1.2^2 + 1.6^2$

$= 1.21 + 1.69 + 2.25 + 1.44 + 2.56$

$= 9.15$

Note that $(\Sigma x_i)^2 = (6.7)^2 = 44.89 \neq \Sigma x_i^2$.

The sigma notation for $\Sigma x_i y_i$

Your scientific
calculator may be able
to calculate $\Sigma x_i y_i$

$$\Sigma x_i y_i = (x_1 y_1) + (x_2 y_2) + (x_3 y_3) + \cdots + (x_n y_n)$$

Note that $\Sigma x_i y_i \neq (\Sigma x_i) \times (\Sigma y_i)$.

Example

5   Calculate $\Sigma x_i y_i$ for the data given in Example 2.

Solution

$$\Sigma x_i y_i = (1.1 \times 3.2) + (1.3 \times 4.8) + (1.5 \times 3.9) + (1.2 \times 3.0)$$
$$+ (1.6 \times 3.9)$$

$$= 3.52 + 6.24 + 5.85 + 3.60 + 6.72$$

$$= 25.93$$

Note that $(\Sigma x_i) \times (\Sigma y_i) = 6.7 \times 19.1 = 127.97 \neq \Sigma x_i y_i$.

Appendix C
Normal probability table

Z	0.00	0.01	0.02	0.03	0.04	0.05	0.06	0.07	0.08	0.09
0.0	0.5000	0.5040	0.5080	0.5120	0.5180	0.5199	0.5239	0.5279	0.5319	0.5359
0.1	0.5398	0.5438	0.5478	0.5517	0.5557	0.5596	0.5636	0.5675	0.5714	0.5753
0.2	0.5793	0.5832	0.5871	0.5910	0.5948	0.5987	0.6026	0.6064	0.6103	0.6141
0.3	0.6179	0.6217	0.6255	0.6293	0.6331	0.6368	0.6406	0.6443	0.6480	0.6517
0.4	0.6554	0.6591	0.6628	0.6664	0.6700	0.6736	0.6772	0.6808	0.6844	0.6879
0.5	0.6915	0.6950	0.6985	0.7019	0.7054	0.7088	0.7123	0.7157	0.7190	0.7224
0.6	0.7257	0.7291	0.7324	0.7357	0.7389	0.7422	0.7454	0.7486	0.7517	0.7549
0.7	0.7580	0.7611	0.7642	0.7673	0.7704	0.7734	0.7764	0.7794	0.7823	0.7852
0.8	0.7881	0.7910	0.7939	0.7967	0.7995	0.8023	0.8051	0.8078	0.8106	0.8133
0.9	0.8159	0.8186	0.8212	0.8238	0.8264	0.8289	0.8315	0.8340	0.8365	0.8389
1.0	0.8413	0.8438	0.8461	0.8485	0.8508	0.8531	0.8554	0.8577	0.8599	0.8621
1.1	0.8643	0.8665	0.8686	0.8708	0.8729	0.8749	0.8770	0.8790	0.8810	0.8830
1.2	0.8849	0.8869	0.8888	0.8907	0.8925	0.8944	0.8962	0.8980	0.8997	0.9015
1.3	0.9032	0.9049	0.9066	0.9082	0.9099	0.9115	0.9131	0.9147	0.9162	0.9177
1.4	0.9192	0.9207	0.9222	0.9236	0.9251	0.9265	0.9279	0.9292	0.9306	0.9319
1.5	0.9332	0.9345	0.9357	0.9370	0.9382	0.9394	0.9406	0.9418	0.9429	0.9441
1.6	0.9452	0.9463	0.9474	0.9484	0.9495	0.9505	0.9515	0.9525	0.9535	0.9545
1.7	0.9554	0.9564	0.9573	0.9582	0.9591	0.9599	0.9608	0.9616	0.9625	0.9633
1.8	0.9641	0.9649	0.9656	0.9664	0.9671	0.9678	0.9686	0.9693	0.9699	0.9706
1.9	0.9713	0.9719	0.9726	0.9732	0.9738	0.9744	0.9750	0.9756	0.9761	0.9767
2.0	0.9772	0.9778	0.9783	0.9788	0.9793	0.9798	0.9803	0.9808	0.9812	0.9817
2.1	0.9821	0.9826	0.9830	0.9834	0.9838	0.9842	0.9846	0.9850	0.9854	0.9857
2.2	0.9861	0.9864	0.9868	0.9871	0.9875	0.9878	0.9881	0.9884	0.9887	0.9890
2.3	0.9893	0.9896	0.9898	0.99010	0.99036	0.99061	0.99086	0.99111	0.99134	0.99158
2.4	0.99180	0.99202	0.99224	0.99245	0.99266	0.99286	0.99305	0.99324	0.99343	0.99361
2.5	0.99379	0.99396	0.99413	0.99430	0.99446	0.99461	0.99477	0.99492	0.99506	0.99520
2.6	0.99534	0.99547	0.99560	0.99573	0.99585	0.99598	0.99609	0.99621	0.99632	0.99643
2.7	0.99653	0.99664	0.99674	0.99683	0.99693	0.99702	0.99711	0.99720	0.99728	0.99736
2.8	0.99744	0.99752	0.99760	0.99767	0.99774	0.99781	0.99788	0.99795	0.99801	0.99807
2.9	0.99813	0.99819	0.99825	0.99831	0.99836	0.99841	0.99846	0.99851	0.99856	0.99861

Z	3.0	3.1	3.2	3.3	3.4	3.5	3.6	3.7	3.8	3.9
P	0.99865	0.99903	0.99931	0.99952	0.99966	0.99977	0.99984	0.99989	0.99993	0.99995

Appendix D
Table of random numbers

65 23 68 00	77 82 58 14	10 85 11 85	57 11 73 74	45 25 60 46
06 56 76 51	04 73 94 30	16 74 69 59	04 38 83 98	30 20 87 85
55 99 98 60	01 33 06 93	85 13 23 17	25 51 92 04	52 31 38 70
72 82 45 44	09 53 04 83	03 83 98 41	67 41 01 38	66 83 11 99
04 21 28 72	73 25 02 74	35 81 78 49	52 67 61 40	60 50 47 50
87 01 80 59	89 36 41 59	60 27 64 89	47 45 18 21	69 84 76 06
31 62 46 53	84 40 56 31	74 96 52 23	72 95 96 06	56 83 85 22
29 81 57 94	35 91 90 70	94 24 19 35	50 22 23 72	87 34 83 15
39 98 74 22	77 19 12 81	29 42 04 50	62 34 36 81	43 07 97 92
56 14 80 10	76 52 38 54	84 13 99 90	22 55 41 04	72 37 89 33
29 56 62 74	12 67 09 35	89 33 04 28	44 75 01 57	87 45 52 21
93 32 57 38	39 36 87 42	72 55 73 97	98 36 57 41	76 09 11 68
95 69 51 54	43 19 20 49	57 25 90 55	26 20 70 98	43 73 56 45
65 71 32 43	64 67 22 55	65 65 48 86	10 88 20 12	40 18 49 25
90 27 33 43	97 84 20 57	49 91 41 20	17 64 29 60	66 87 55 97
95 29 42 45	61 34 30 13	30 39 21 52	59 28 64 98	08 76 09 27
99 74 06 29	20 55 72 70	11 43 95 82	75 37 90 24	77 43 63 21
87 87 56 91	16 97 51 50	61 36 96 47	76 68 49 11	50 56 51 06
46 24 17 74	97 37 39 03	54 83 34 00	74 61 77 51	43 63 15 67
66 79 81 43	40 92 84 72	88 32 83 24	67 01 41 34	70 19 26 93
36 42 94 58	83 30 92 39	18 40 03 00	12 90 32 27	91 65 48 15
07 66 25 08	99 27 69 48	85 32 16 46	19 31 85 02	86 36 22 96
93 10 05 72	18 26 36 67	68 48 31 69	68 58 93 49	45 86 99 29
49 50 63 99	26 71 47 94	32 71 72 91	34 18 74 06	32 14 40 80
20 75 58 89	39 04 42 73	37 93 11 07	28 77 91 36	60 47 82 62
02 40 62 09	00 71 09 37	80 44 50 37	32 70 20 38	71 86 75 34
59 87 21 38	29 78 72 67	42 83 65 21	54 79 66 42	47 86 31 15
48 08 99 66	43 38 28 13	50 25 47 93	11 15 07 84	28 30 19 07
54 26 86 75	44 15 20 39	20 03 58 54	80 29 62 53	06 97 71 51
35 35 58 45	23 58 63 66	09 62 80 92	14 55 81 41	21 48 87 34
73 84 90 49	01 21 90 29	57 06 68 73	51 10 51 95	63 08 57 99
34 64 78 00	92 59 67 74	58 48 92 09	42 20 40 37	63 80 58 93
68 56 87 47	63 06 24 71	41 98 79 06	07 18 58 29	16 49 67 37
72 47 05 42	88 07 27 55	58 74 82 08	42 28 26 48	25 32 00 31
44 44 96 75	89 57 12 60	42 38 77 36	45 69 21 68	32 70 04 96

continues

28 11 57 47	61 57 89 88	62 18 93 67	57 32 96 72	21 17 13 54
87 22 38 88	91 99 16 08	17 76 27 47	52 14 98 86	35 68 23 85
44 93 14 59	67 40 24 10	11 63 40 47	07 56 14 22	62 74 93 39
81 84 37 25	90 43 56 62	94 58 49 03	84 22 57 22	47 98 86 37
09 75 35 21	04 47 54 08	98 44 08 16	44 86 69 71	20 52 64 94
77 65 05 04	22 18 20 10	81 87 05 69	43 70 96 76	42 05 21 10
19 06 51 61	34 03 61 55	98 58 83 50	01 48 99 85	08 67 15 91
52 91 87 07	19 62 32 28	04 91 42 48	65 24 86 09	87 68 55 51
52 47 25 14	93 91 75 51	49 26 49 41	20 83 30 30	43 22 69 08
52 67 87 40	63 41 91 86	10 47 80 70	56 87 25 86	89 94 21 42
65 25 71 73	78 60 50 62	91 04 95 97	64 16 71 31	32 80 19 61
29 97 56 42	56 90 16 75	74 95 99 26	01 63 25 16	54 18 54 46
15 25 03 68	92 45 53 00	06 29 46 43	46 66 27 12	85 05 22 44
82 08 65 67	64 13 51 14	38 28 24 30	39 62 20 35	23 90 57 36
81 35 03 25	87 24 83 59	04 67 51 52	26 21 69 75	87 28 61 50

Note: Each digit in this table is an independent sample from a population where each of the digits 0–9 has a probability of occurrence of 0.1. It should be noted that these digits have been computer generated and are therefore 'pseudo' random numbers.

Appendix E

Estimates of the mean cost prices calculated from 600 simple random samples of 30 items in a made to order department of a shoe machinery manufacturer. For use with Example 7.2.

614.62	494.45	814.76	691.72	576.87	679.55	828.57
741.12	599.89	604.10	604.89	626.77	579.38	529.07
766.10	678.80	926.82	685.52	421.25	290.04	808.22
249.08	656.92	1077.50	793.16	1040.90	750.07	942.93
497.13	926.79	542.72	637.91	1022.60	347.27	471.87
337.95	269.44	889.17	510.26	347.96	796.66	782.51
474.48	444.90	498.32	1115.80	278.01	516.94	421.41
969.10	820.99	961.63	562.73	674.29	1024.50	821.26
987.87	602.37	383.15	521.73	762.49	455.06	609.55
317.70	570.33	781.37	698.03	740.29	521.24	401.76
546.92	648.75	827.02	715.32	916.61	468.20	567.56
640.95	669.18	377.85	937.28	961.91	757.26	762.46
474.29	727.05	493.89	806.70	567.25	506.17	924.11
770.14	435.24	767.39	885.49	502.33	489.83	786.85
816.08	710.27	457.68	607.93	811.01	638.52	784.01
415.36	301.40	628.25	440.20	489.14	792.98	509.64
979.28	673.66	575.10	1057.60	812.00	1054.60	1173.60
719.95	418.22	973.82	1037.10	359.11	1159.50	1062.90
847.75	610.76	367.42	872.07	767.22	311.42	460.10
688.61	404.66	540.18	555.60	588.68	557.00	273.91
678.51	385.79	764.31	479.74	726.58	434.04	468.17
671.03	809.24	864.25	1015.30	474.00	619.24	566.66
380.95	605.24	641.33	424.34	880.25	917.52	745.91
1109.60	797.43	557.06	577.70	640.71	786.27	620.22
685.48	697.34	507.27	892.57	763.18	873.67	396.17
526.24	840.46	849.76	614.97	884.00	707.17	717.12

continues

420.24	898.87	285.27	665.75	542.25	908.13	697.56
748.97	1088.70	310.28	573.42	1056.80	795.75	659.24
556.17	650.50	1089.30	742.03	604.69	400.86	571.99
727.02	625.61	661.25	505.56	551.89	818.77	490.65
316.94	740.33	414.78	1025.50	596.25	655.58	471.16
1103.80	880.41	884.63	848.41	545.54	650.26	514.10
748.70	378.62	1033.90	864.35	677.48	861.12	855.30
532.15	784.27	844.13	928.80	424.32	897.42	974.70
790.53	728.63	716.45	660.11	351.35	270.41	852.62
852.16	801.37	590.63	478.46	591.74	555.74	531.74
479.38	506.21	578.78	685.46	381.18	583.61	444.04
679.29	766.72	895.44	348.17	671.90	323.11	794.31
394.16	749.70	670.57	511.00	498.98	429.37	517.96
803.15	669.13	589.90	815.61	875.37	503.41	675.90
603.68	673.69	724.87	891.00	575.48	655.11	999.33
762.55	1102.00	799.64	773.27	619.18	660.99	623.04
413.90	526.17	527.13	239.92	543.97	1039.40	799.41
888.12	757.54	1300.90	612.66	939.71	397.58	491.22
781.97	897.16	542.55	877.61	681.24	939.03	897.32
516.43	869.48	360.66	971.49	915.34	290.78	536.21
405.26	1102.60	759.19	626.01	413.26	735.18	778.59
812.21	604.24	757.67	829.99	904.75	902.00	793.00
547.23	357.67	649.16	563.81	603.25	937.64	385.44
895.76	826.36	690.20	580.86	609.83	679.15	577.79
627.52	873.81	654.97	380.51	573.71	845.52	555.21
345.69	759.43	444.76	275.80	1308.30	518.53	611.72
325.68	653.36	891.06	825.61	671.82	601.58	387.03
689.47	391.91	1060.00	583.64	335.75	770.60	411.42
548.40	487.06	496.59	608.88	741.47	810.97	447.87
551.65	659.91	329.71	671.29	438.94	511.34	708.54
739.03	842.98	982.33	496.03	1081.20	682.34	1055.80
636.58	499.83	793.51	741.97	690.91	586.92	579.76
991.18	547.21	717.44	956.62	768.69	255.07	759.70
464.33	765.41	696.70	460.06	494.54	552.64	298.84
751.80	763.73	849.69	788.30	911.38	648.73	577.09
787.38	455.65	608.63	686.93	458.92	1150.40	647.73
628.58	849.09	701.66	595.65	860.94	1012.60	479.99
1273.90	354.19	671.90	603.11	231.92	730.30	1025.30
738.40	796.92	1012.20	440.85	667.98	436.25	673.67
611.33	577.37	271.93	1045.80	488.36	575.43	498.65
799.53	750.31	422.80	1058.70	673.05	450.24	612.09
606.37	605.17	914.61	572.11	623.68	631.14	643.79
642.79	621.80	658.26	665.51	698.75	630.20	646.53
655.09	606.39	620.42	672.26	668.93	612.95	705.22
640.07	623.54	714.98	672.62	707.72	671.05	700.53
716.01	619.91	653.81	318.29	987.72	474.29	477.52
911.95	535.23	993.59	784.21	341.74	883.61	807.95
682.51	1174.50	830.80	597.08	951.26	554.06	758.77
581.97	552.91	885.83	680.59	450.43	1047.60	905.43
549.66	511.60	721.86	719.95	539.05	664.26	426.70
849.09	274.45	570.59	342.05	285.88	457.93	760.57
654.20	1027.90	615.11	753.73	426.35	649.78	410.28
500.83	686.52	644.28	604.85	534.69	535.70	739.99
880.05	526.18	636.64	501.68	504.73	321.41	667.88
889.30	689.93	765.15	461.16	578.34	609.70	860.87
305.22	362.08	532.57	684.96	775.53	801.76	839.22

continues

540.58	708.23	1042.10	737.73	565.45	756.55	643.01
634.05	713.89	564.75	806.31	825.60	1144.80	864.13
1044.90	350.80	785.35	632.56	342.56	1236.80	829.05
529.32	422.12	731.46	454.39	803.04		

Notes: There are 600 sample means so $n = 600$; the sum of the sample means is £400473; the mean of the sample means is £667.45; the standard deviation of the sample means is £1568.21.

Appendix F
The *t* distribution

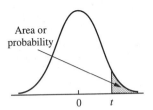

Area or probability

0   *t*

Degrees of freedom	Area in upper tail				
	0.10	0.05	0.025	0.01	0.005
1	3.078	6.314	12.706	31.821	63.657
2	1.886	2.920	4.303	6.965	9.925
3	1.638	2.353	3.182	4.541	5.841
4	1.533	2.132	2.776	3.747	4.604
5	1.476	2.015	2.571	3.365	4.032
6	1.440	1.943	2.447	3.143	3.707
7	1.415	1.895	2.365	2.998	3.499
8	1.397	1.860	2.306	2.896	3.355
9	1.383	1.833	2.262	2.821	3.250
10	1.372	1.812	2.228	2.764	3.169
11	1.363	1.796	2.201	2.718	3.106
12	1.356	1.782	2.179	2.681	3.055
13	1.350	1.771	2.160	2.650	3.012
14	1.345	1.761	2.145	2.624	2.977
15	1.341	1.753	2.131	2.602	2.947
16	1.337	1.746	2.120	2.583	2.921
17	1.333	1.740	2.110	2.567	2.898
18	1.330	1.734	2.101	2.552	2.878
19	1.328	1.729	2.093	2.539	2.861
20	1.325	1.725	2.086	2.528	2.845
21	1.323	1.721	2.080	2.518	2.831
22	1.321	1.717	2.074	2.508	2.819
23	1.319	1.714	2.069	2.500	2.807
24	1.318	1.711	2.064	2.492	2.797

continues

Degrees of freedom	Area in upper tail				
	0.10	0.05	0.025	0.01	0.005
25	1.316	1.708	2.060	2.485	2.787
26	1.315	1.706	2.056	2.479	2.779
27	1.314	1.703	2.052	2.473	2.771
28	1.313	1.701	2.048	2.467	2.763
29	1.311	1.699	2.045	2.462	2.756
30	1.310	1.697	2.042	2.457	2.750
40	1.303	1.684	2.021	2.423	2.704
60	1.296	1.671	2.000	2.390	2.660
120	1.289	1.658	1.980	2.358	2.617
∞	1.282	1.645	1.960	2.326	2.576

Note: Entries in the table give t values for an area or probability in the upper tail of the t distribution. For example, with ten degrees of freedom and a 0.05 area in the upper tail, $t_{10,0.05} = 1.812$.

Appendix G
The sum of an arithmetic progression

The sum of the first n terms of an arithmetic progression whose first term is a and whose common difference is d is given by

$$S_n = a + (a + d) + (a + 2d) + \cdots + \{a + (n-1)d\} \qquad [1]$$

The same series written in reverse is

$$S_n = \{a + (n-1)d\} + \{a + (n-2)d\} + \cdots + (a + d) + a \qquad [2]$$

Adding [1] and [2] gives

$$2S_n = \{2a + (n-1)d\} + \{2a + (n-1)d\} + \cdots + \{2a + (n-1)d\}$$

The right-hand side has n terms, each one equal to $\{2a + (n-1)d\}$, and therefore

$$2S_n = n \times \{2a + (n-1)d\}$$

so that

$$S_n = \frac{n}{2}\{2a + (n-1)d\}$$

The formula gives the sum of n terms of the arithmetic progression.

Appendix H
The sum of a geometric progression

The sum of the first n terms of a geometric progression whose first term is a and whose common ratio is r is given by

$$S_n = a + ar + ar^2 + ar^3 + \cdots + ar^{n-1} \qquad [1]$$

Multiplying both sides by r gives

$$rS_n = ar + ar^2 + ar^3 + \cdots + ar^{n-1} + ar^n \qquad [2]$$

Subtracting [2] from [1] cancels out most terms to give

$$S_n - rS_n = a - ar^n$$

$$S_n(1 - r) = a(1 - r^n)$$

and so

$$S_n = \frac{a(1 - r^n)}{1 - r}$$

This is the formula for finding the sum of n terms of a geometric progression. Multiplying both numerator and denominator of the right-hand side by -1 gives the alternative form

$$S_n = \frac{a(r^n - 1)}{r - 1}$$

Appendix I
The present value of an annuity due

To find the present value of an annuity due we must sum the series

$$A = R + \frac{R}{1+i} + \frac{R}{(1+i)^2} + \cdots + \frac{R}{(1+i)^{n-1}}$$

Using the formula for the sum of a geometric progression and taking $a = R$ and $r = 1/(1+i)$ we have

$$A = \frac{R\{1 - 1/(1+i)^n\}}{\{1 - 1/(1+i)\}}$$

$$= \frac{R\{1 - 1/(1+i)^n\}}{\{(1+i-1)/(1+i)\}}$$

$$= \frac{R\{1 - 1/(1+i)^n\}}{\{i/(1+i)\}}$$

$$= \frac{R(1+i)}{i}\left\{1 - \frac{1}{(1+i)^n}\right\}$$

Appendix J
Linear interpolation for the internal rate of return

Linear interpolation assumes that two points can be linked by a straight line. Consider Figure J1 which shows two points (i_1, N_1) and (i_2, N_2). The net cash flow is N and the discount rate is i. The equation of the line can be shown to be

$$N = \left(\frac{N_2 - N_1}{i_2 - i_1}\right)(i - i_1) + N_1$$

We seek the value of i at which $N = 0$,

$$0 = \left(\frac{N_2 - N_1}{i_2 - i_1}\right)(i - i_1) + N_1$$

from which

$$i = i_1 + \frac{N_1}{N_1 - N_2}(i_2 - i_1)$$

This is the internal rate of return.

Figure J1.

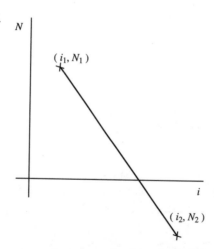

Solutions to exercises

Exercise 1.1

(a) 6   (b) 10   (c) 1495

Exercises 1.2

1 (a) Continuous quantitative.
(b) Qualitative.
(c) Discrete quantitative.
(d) Continuous quantitative.
(e) Discrete quantitative.
(f) Qualitative.

2 (a) A qualitative, B quantitative, C quantitative, D quantitative, E qualitative, F qualitative
(b) Discrete quantitative: C, D
    Continuous quantitative: B

Exercise 2.1

(a)

Level of double glazing	Number of households
Full	30
Partial	68
None	102
Total	200

(b)

Level of double glazing	Proportion of households
Full	0.15
Partial	0.34
None	0.51
Total	1.00

(c)

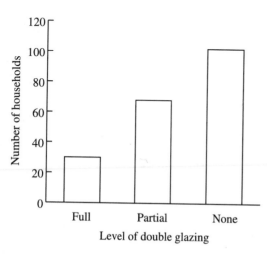

(d)

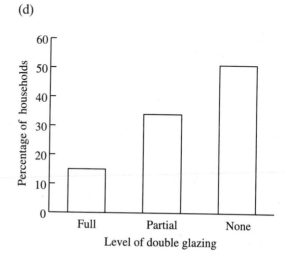

(e)

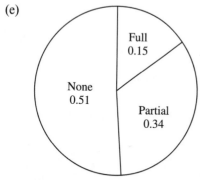

Exercises 2.2

1 (a) Frequency distribution.

Number of hours per week	Number of employees
18	10
20	17
24	8
Total	35

Relative frequency distribution.

Number of hours per week	Proportion of employees
18	0.286
20	0.486
24	0.228
	Total 1.000

(b)

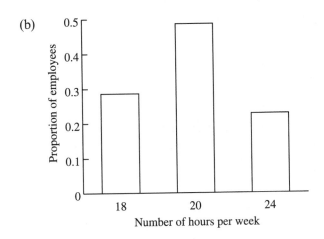

2(a)

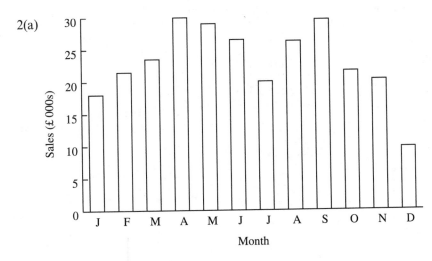

(b) (i)

Quarter	Total sales (£000s)
I	63.50
II	85.75
III	75.73
IV	51.42

(ii)

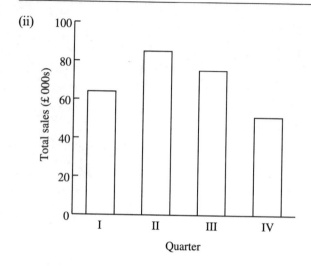

(c) Monthly trends show a double peak in sales in April and September and relatively few sales in December. Quarterly trends show a peak in the second quarter.

3 (a) Minimum = 2.124, maximum = 2.170. Choose five classes. Approximate class width = 0.0092. Round class width to 0.009.

Frequency distribution.

Breaking strength (g)	Number of samples
2.121–2.130	4
2.131–2.140	10
2.141–2.150	11
2.151–2.160	5
2.161–2.170	10
Total	40

Relative frequency distribution.

Breaking strength (g)	Proportion of samples
2.121–2.130	0.100
2.131–2.140	0.250
2.141–2.150	0.275
2.151–2.160	0.125
2.161–2.170	0.250
Total	1.000

(b)

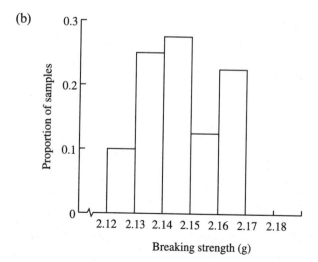

(c) Ninety per cent of these samples had a breaking strength of more than 2.13 g. These samples suggest that the actual breaking strength is more than the supposed value of 2.125 g.

4 (a) The data is discrete quantitative but many different values have occurred. The methods for continuous quantitative data are appropriate, e.g. grouped frequency distribution and histogram.

(b) Minimum $= 308$, maximum $= 763$. Choose six classes. Approximate class width $= 75.83$, rounded to 75.

Number of calls	Number of weeks
300–374	9
375–449	6
450–524	11
525–599	13
600–674	8
675–749	3
750–824	2
Total	52

(c)

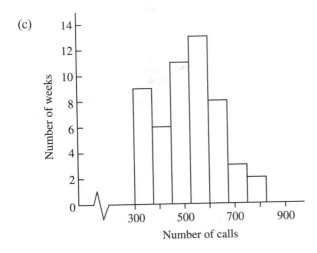

Exercises 3.1

1 (a) The mode is 'no double glazing' (none). (b) No. The data is qualitative.

2 (a) $n = 35$, $\Sigma x_i = 712$, $\bar{x} = 20.34$ hours. (b) The median is the value of the eighteenth item, i.e. 20 hours. (c) The mode is 20 hours.

3 (a) $n = 12$, $\Sigma x_i = 276.4$, $\bar{x} = 23.03$, i.e. £23,030. (b) $n = 4$, $\Sigma x_i = 276.4$, $\bar{x} = 69.1$, i.e. £69,100.

4 (a) (i) $n = 40$, $\Sigma x_i = 85.89$, $\bar{x} = 2.14725$ g.

(ii) The median is the average of the twentieth and twenty-first ranked items: twentieth ranked item has value 2.146, twenty-first ranked item has value 2.147, so the median is 2.1465 g.
(iii) The mode is 2.137 g (occurs four times).
(b) (i) $n = 40$, $\Sigma x_i = 85.89$, $\bar{x} = 2.14725$ g.
(ii) The median is the average of the twentieth and twenty-first ranked items, i.e. 2.1465 g.
(iii) The modal class is 2.141 g to 2.150 g.

Exercises 3.2

1 (a) Largest value is 24. Smallest value is 18. Range is six hours. (b) $n = 35$, $\Sigma x_i = 712$, $\Sigma x_i^2 = 14648$, $\bar{x} = 20.3429$, $s^2 = 4.8184$ hours^2. (c) $s = \sqrt{4.8184} = 2.1951$ hours.

2 (a) (i) Largest value is £30 000. Smallest value is £9640. Range = £20 360.
(ii) $n = 12$, $\Sigma x_i = 276.4$, $\Sigma x_i^2 = 6741.633$, $\bar{x} = 23.03$, $s^2 = 34.2784$, i.e. £34 278 400.
(iii) $s = \sqrt{34.2784} = 5.8548$, i.e. £5854.80.
(b) (i) Largest value is £85 750. Smallest value is £51 420. Range = £34 330.
(ii) $n = 4$, $\Sigma x_i = 276.4$, $\Sigma x_i^2 = 19764.3618$, $\bar{x} = 69.1$, $s^2 = 221.7073$, i.e. £^{2}221 707 300.
(iii) $s = \sqrt{221.7073} = 14.8898$, i.e. £14 889.80.

3 (a) (i) The range is $2.170 - 2.124 = 0.046$ g
(ii) $n = 40$, $\Sigma x_i = 85.89$, $\Sigma x_i^2 = 184.4347$, $\bar{x} = 2.14725$, $s^2 = 0.0001897$ g^2.
(iii) $s = \sqrt{0.0001897} = 0.0138$ g.
(b) (i) $n = 40$, $\Sigma x_i f_i = 85.89$, $\Sigma x_i^2 f_i = 184.4343$, $\bar{x} = 2.14725$, $s^2 = 0.0001794$ g^2.
(ii) $s = \sqrt{0.0001794} = 0.0134$ g.

Exercises 4.1

1 (a) $S = \{$A, B, A and B, neither$\}$ (b) $S = \{0, 1, 2, \ldots, \infty\}$ (c) $S = \{$win, draw, lose$\}$
(d) $S = \{$(H, H), (H, T), (T, H), (T, T)$\}$

2

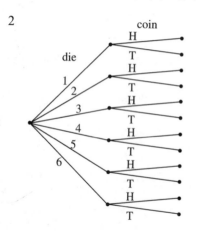

3

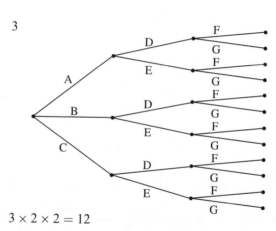

$3 \times 2 \times 2 = 12$

4 (a) {A, B, A and B} (b) {0, 1, 2, 3, 4} (c) {lose} (d) {(T, H), (H, T)}

Exercises 4.2

1 (d) and (f).

2 (a) Classical.
(b) (i) $\frac{26}{52} = \frac{1}{2}$ (ii) $\frac{13}{52} = \frac{1}{4}$
  (iii) $\frac{4}{52} = \frac{1}{13}$ (iv) $\frac{1}{52}$

3 (a) Relative frequency
(b) (i) $\frac{185}{350} = \frac{37}{70} = 0.529$ (ii) $\frac{24}{350} = \frac{12}{175} = 0.069$ (iii) $\frac{165}{350} = \frac{33}{70} = 0.471$

4 (a) $\frac{3}{52} = 0.058$ (b) $\frac{9}{52} = 0.173$ (c) $\frac{1}{52} = 0.019$ (d) $\frac{51}{52} = 0.981$

Exercises 4.3

1 (a) 0.74 (b) 0.54 (c) $P(A) + P(B) - P(A \text{ and } B) = 0.60$

2 (a) (i) $\bar{A}$ (ii) B and C (iii) A or C (iv) A or B
(b) (i) $\frac{1}{2} = 0.5$ (ii) $\frac{1}{52} = 0.019$ (iii) $\frac{4}{52} + \frac{26}{52} - \frac{2}{52} = \frac{28}{52} = 0.538$ (iv) $\frac{26}{52} + \frac{13}{52} = \frac{39}{52} = 0.75$
(c) (i), (v), (vi).

3 (a) (i) $P(A) = \frac{90}{250} = 0.36$ (ii) $P(B) = \frac{123}{250} = 0.492$
(b) (i) $P(\bar{A}) = 0.64$ (ii) $P(\bar{B}) = 0.508$
(c) $P(A \text{ and } B) = \frac{73}{250} = 0.292$
(d) $P(A \text{ or } B) = 0.36 + 0.492 - 0.292 = 0.56$

4

	A	$\bar{A}$	Total
B	42	48	90
$\bar{B}$	28	32	60
Total	70	80	150

$P(A) = 0.467$, $P(B) = 0.6$, $P(\bar{A}) = 0.533$, $P(\bar{B}) = 0.4$, $P(A \text{ and } B) = 0.28$, $P(\bar{A} \text{ and } \bar{B}) = 0.32$, $P(A \text{ or } B) = 0.787$, $P(\bar{A} \text{ or } B) = 0.813$.

5

	A	$\bar{A}$	Total
B	73	50	123
$\bar{B}$	17	110	127
Total	90	160	250

	A	Ā	Total
B	0.292	0.2	0.492
B̄	0.068	0.44	0.508
Total	0.36	0.64	1

6 (a) 0.525 (b) 0.3625 (c) 0.2125 (d) 0.15 (e) 0.625

Exercises 4.4

1 (a) $P(A \mid B) = \frac{0.17}{0.32} = 0.531$ $P(B \mid A) = \frac{0.17}{0.45} = 0.378$
(b) $P(A \mid B) = \frac{0.24}{0.3} = 0.8$ $P(B \mid A) = \frac{0.24}{0.8} = 0.3$
In (b), A and B are independent.

2(a) 0.15 (b) 0.35

3 (a) $P(A \mid B) = 0.593$ (b) $P(\bar{B} \mid \bar{A}) = 0.688$

4 (a) $\frac{17}{29} = 0.586$ (b) $\frac{21}{38} = 0.553$

5 (a) $\frac{4}{7} \times \frac{4}{7} = 0.327$ (b) $\frac{4}{7} \times \frac{3}{6} = 0.286$

6 $\frac{25}{60} \times \frac{24}{59} = 0.169$

7 $P(A) = \frac{1}{4}$ $P(B \mid A) = \frac{25}{51}$ $P(A \text{ and } B) = 0.123$

Exercises 5.1

1 (a) {0, 1, 2, ... } (c) {0, 1, 2, ... } (e) {0, 1, 2, ... 20}

2 (a) Sum to greater than 1. (c) Negative probability.

3 (a) 0.34 (b) 0.62 (c) 0.56

Exercises 5.2

1 The ten items are selected at random and should be assumed independent. There are two outcomes, defective and non-defective. The probability that any item is defective is the same for each item (0.08). The experimenter must be interested in the number of items that are defective out of the ten items.

2 (a) 0.3087 (b) 0.1681 (c) 0.0024 (d) $0.3087 + 0.3602 + 0.1681 = 0.8370$
(e) $0.0024 + 0.0284 + 0.1323 + 0.3087 = 1 - (0.3602 + 0.1681) = 0.4718$

3 (a) $0.97^{50} = 0.2181$ (b) $50 \times 0.03^1 \times 0.97^{49} = 0.3372$ (c) $0.2181 + 0.3372 = 0.5553$
(d) $1 - P(X < 2) = 0.4447$

4. $n = 10$, $p = 0.08$.
(a) 0.4344 (b) 0.3777 (c) $0.4344 + 0.3777 + 0.1478 = 0.9599$ (d) $1 - 0.9599 = 0.0401$
$\mu = 0.8$ $\sigma^2 = 0.736$

5. (a) 3.5, 1.05 (b) 1.5, 1.455 (c) 48.5, 1.455

6. $n = 15$, $p = 0.78$.
$0.2457 + 0.2010 + 0.1018 + 0.0241 = 0.5726$

Exercises 5.3

1 (a) 0.1490 (b) 0.1490 (c) $P(6) + P(7) + P(8) = 0.149 + 0.149 + 0.1304 = 0.4284$
(d) $P(5) + P(6) + P(7) = 0.1277 + 0.149 + 0.149 = 0.4257$
(e) $P(0) + P(1) + P(2) + P(3) + P(4) = 0.0009 + 0.0064 + 0.0223 + 0.0521 + 0.0912 = 0.1729$
(f) $1 - 0.1729 = 0.8271$

2 (a) 0.1353 (b) 0.2707 (c) $0.1353 + 0.2707 + 0.2707 = 0.6767$ (d) $0.2707 + 0.2707 + 0.1804 = 0.7218$
(e) $1 - P(X \leq 3) = 1 - 0.8571 = 0.1429$

3 $0.0844 + 0.0888 + 0.0888 + 0.0846 = 0.3466$

4 $1 - P(X = 0) = 1 - 0.3679 = 0.6321$

Exercises 5.4

1. Binomial, $0.6050 + 0.3056 = 0.9106$
Poisson, $\lambda = np = 0.5$ $0.6065 + 0.3033 = 0.9098$

2 $\lambda = 3$
(a) 0.2240 (b) 0.0498 (c) $0.0498 + 0.1494 + 0.2240 + 0.2240 = 0.6472$ (d) $1 - P(X < 2) = 0.8008$
(e) $0.2240 + 0.2240 + 0.1680 = 0.6160$

3 $n = 3000$, $p = 0.00024$, $\lambda = 0.72$.
(a) 0.4868 (b) $1 - (0.4868 + 0.3505) = 0.1627$

4 $p = 0.007$, $n = 500$, $\lambda = 3.5$.
$1 - (0.0302 + 0.1056 + 0.1850 + 0.2158) = 0.4634$

Exercise 6.2

1 (a) (i) B (ii) same (b) (i) A (ii) B

Exercises 6.3

1 (a) 0.99413 (b) 0.9641 (c) $P(Z < 0.92) = 0.8212$ (d) 0.5 (e) 0.99861 (f) 0.99989 (g) 0.99903

2 (a) $1 - 0.9699 = 0.0301$ (b) $P(Z > 0.85) = 1 - 0.8023 = 0.1977$ (c) $1 - 0.99903 = 0.00097$
(d) $1 - 0.9803 = 0.0197$ (e) $1 - 0.5 = 0.5$

3 (a) 0.8106 (b) $1 - 0.9382 = 0.0618$ (c) 0.99825 (d) $1 - 0.5279 = 0.4721$

4 (a) $0.9706 - 0.8770 = 0.0936$ (b) $0.9772 - (1 - 0.9772) = 0.9544$
(c) $(1 - 0.5239) - (1 - 0.9767) = 0.4528$

5 (a) $1 - 0.9875 = 0.0125$ (b) $0.8159 - (1 - 0.8159) = 0.6318$ (c) $1 - 0.9767 = 0.0233$ (d) 0.99865
(e) $0.8413 - 0.5 = 0.3413$

Exercises 6.4

1 (a) $P(Z < 0.625) = 0.7357$ (b) $P(Z < 3.125) = 0.99903$
(c) $P(Z > 3.125) = 0.00097$ (d) $P(Z < -1.25) = 0.1056$
(e) $P(Z > -2.5) = 0.99379$ (f) $P(-1.25 < Z < 1.25) = 0.7888$
(g) $P(-1.875 < Z < -0.625) = 0.2342$

2 (a) $P(X > 60) = P(Z > 1.43) = 0.0764$ (b) $P(X < 30) = P(Z < -2.86) = 0.00212$
(c) $P(50 < X < 60) = P(0 < Z < 1.43) = 0.4236$

3. $P(X < 1) = P(Z < -2.4) = 0.0082$

Exercises 6.5

1 (a) Not appropriate as $np < 5$. (b) Appropriate.

2 (a) $P(X < 16.5) = P(Z < 0.33) = 0.6293$ (b) $P(X > 22.5) = P(Z > 2.52) = 0.00587$
(c) $P(9.5 < X < 20.5) = P(-2.23 < Z < 1.79) = 0.9504$

3 $p = 0.45$, $n = 200$,
$P(X < 99.5) = P(Z < 1.35) = 0.9115$.

Exercise 7.1

14.70	321.21	194.23	45.79	3.45
203.96	65.13	1898.43	2654.65	659.57
15.98	10.56	684.35	100.21	5.46
235.46	208.64	35.18	65.87	54.86
576.34	654.32	1239.50	56.12	57.52
74.31	678.99	1210.23	84.50	41.98

Exercise 7.2

$n = 30$, $\Sigma x_i = 12151.5$, $\Sigma x_i^2 = 16104864.3$.

(a) $\bar{x} = £405.05$ (b) $s^2 = £^2 385\,617.2147$ (c) $s = £620.9808$

Exercises 7.5

1 $\sigma = 126.94$, $n = 25$, $\sigma_{\bar{X}} = 25.388$.

2 $n = 40$, $s = 374.64$, $s_{\bar{X}} = 59.2358$.

Exercises 7.6

1 (a) 6.314 (b) 9.925 (c) 2.624 (d) 1.321 (e) $t_{30,0.025} = 2.042$, $t_{40,0.025} = 2.021$, so $t_{35,0.025} = 2.0315$.

2 $x = 1.328$

3 $x = -3.355$

Exercises 7.7

1 (a) $\bar{x} = 92.6$ (b) $\sigma_{\bar{x}} = 7.9057$ (c) Normal.

2 (a) $\bar{x} = 168.3$ (b) $s_{\bar{x}} = 14.2853$ (c) t distribution.

3 (a) $\bar{x} = 171.5$ (b) $s_{\bar{x}} = 11.1631$ (c) Normal.

Exercise 7.8

(a) $\bar{x} = £80.61$ (b) $s_{\bar{X}} = £4.91$ (c) Normal (d) $P(70.61 < \bar{X} < 90.61) = P(-2.0367 < Z < 2.0367)$
$$= 0.9793 - (1 - 0.9793)$$
$$= 0.9586$$

Exercises 8.2

1 (a) $\sigma_{\bar{X}} = 18.5613$ (b) $23.04 \pm 1.64 \times 18.5613 = -7.4005$ to 53.4805; 90% confident that the population mean falls within the range -7.4005 to 53.4805. (c) $23.04 \pm 1.96 \times 18.5613 = -13.3401$ to 59.4201; 95% confident that the population mean falls within the range -13.3401 to 59.4201. (d) $23.04 \pm 2.58 \times 18.5613 = -24.8482$ to 70.9282; 99% confident that the population mean falls within the range -24.8482 to 70.9282.

2 (a) $\sigma^2 = 400$ so $\sigma = 20$. $\sigma_{\bar{X}} = 4$. (b) $59.048 \pm 1.64 \times 4 = 52.488$ to 65.608; 90% confident that the population mean falls within the range 52.488 to 65.608. (c) $59.048 \pm 1.96 \times 4 = 51.208$ to 66.888; 95% confident that the population mean falls within the range 51.208 to 66.888. (d) $59.048 \pm 2.58 \times 4 = 48.728$ to 69.368; 99% confident that the population mean falls within the range 48.728 to 69.368.

3 (a) $\sigma_{\bar{X}} = £2.1229$ (b) $127.62 \pm 1.64 \times 2.1229 = £124.1384$ to $£131.1016$
(c) $127.62 \pm 1.96 \times 2.1229 = £123.4591$ to $£131.7809$
(d) $127.62 \pm 2.58 \times 2.1229 = £122.14291$ to $£133.0971$
(e) We are 99% confident that the average quarterly bills of all customers in this town are between £122.14 and £133.10. The mean is estimated quite accurately since the standard error of the means is small.

Exercises 8.3

1 (a) (i) $\bar{x} = 5.55$ (ii) $s = 2.6966$ (iii) $s_{\bar{X}} = 0.3814$
(b) $5.55 \pm 1.64 \times 0.3814 = 4.9245$–$6.1755$
(c) $5.55 \pm 1.96 \times 0.3814 = 4.8025$–$6.2975$
(d) $5.55 \pm 2.58 \times 0.3814 = 4.5660$–$6.5340$

2 (a) (i) $\bar{x} = 27.675$ (ii) $s = 11.3146$ (iii) $s_{\bar{X}} = 1.7890$
(b) $27.675 \pm 1.64 \times 1.7890 = 24.7410$–$30.6090$
(c) $27.675 \pm 1.96 \times 1.7890 = 24.1686$–$31.1814$
(d) $27.675 \pm 2.58 \times 1.7890 = 23.0594$–$32.2906$
(e) For example, based on this sample we are 95% confident that the average time spent by households per week watching television is between 24.17 hours and 31.18 hours.

Exercises 8.4

1 (a) (i) $\bar{x} = 114.325$ (ii) $s = 90.1763$ (iii) $s_{\bar{x}} = 22.5441$
(b) $114.325 \pm 1.753 \times 22.5441 = 74.8052\text{--}153.8448$
(c) $114.325 \pm 2.131 \times 22.5441 = 66.2835\text{--}162.3665$
(d) $114.325 \pm 2.947 \times 22.5441 = 47.8875\text{--}180.7625$

2 (a) (i) $\bar{x} = 2076.8032$ (ii) $s = 759.4460$ (iii) $s_{\bar{x}} = 151.8892$
(b) $2076.8032 \pm 1.711 \times 151.8892 = 1816.9208$ to 2336.6856
(c) $2076.8032 \pm 2.064 \times 151.8892 = 1763.3039$ to 2390.3025
(d) $2076.8032 \pm 2.797 \times 151.8892 = 1651.9691$ to 2501.6373
(e) For example, based on this sample we are 95% confident that the average yield of potatoes using this new pesticide lies between 1763.30 tonnes and 2390.30 tonnes.
(f) We would need to know the average potato yield when the standard pesticide is used to control the blight.

Exercises 9.1

1 Let μ represent the mean time spent by households watching television each week.

$H_0 : \mu = 35$ hours
$H_1 : \mu < 35$ hours

2 Let μ represent the mean quarterly bills of all domestic consumers in the town.

$H_0 : \mu = £135$
$H_1 : \mu \neq £135$

3 Let μ represent the mean yield of potatoes when sprayed with the new pesticide.

$H_0 : \mu = 1750$ tonnes
$H_1 : \mu > 1750$ tonnes

Exercises 9.2

1 (a) The mean time spent per week watching television could be 35 hours.
(b) The mean time spent per week watching television is less than 35 hours. This sample suggests that, on average, households spent 26.93 hours per week watching television.

2 (a) The mean quarterly bills of domestic consumers in this town could be £135.
(b) The mean quarterly bills of domestic consumers in this town is not £135. This sample suggests that the mean quarterly bill is £120.05.

3 (a) The mean yield of potatoes when sprayed using the new pesticide could be 1750 tonnes.

(b) The mean yield of potatoes when sprayed using the new pesticide is more than 1750 tonnes. This sample suggests that the average yield is 2100 tonnes.

Exercises 9.5

1 (a) (i) $Z = \dfrac{|23.04 - 25|}{76.53/\sqrt{17}} = 0.1056 < 1.96$

Do not reject H_0, i.e. the population mean could be 25.

(ii) $Z = \dfrac{23.04 - 50}{76.53/\sqrt{17}} = -1.4525 > -1.64$

Do not reject H_0, i.e. the population mean could be 50.

(iii) $Z = \dfrac{23.04 - 0}{76.53/\sqrt{17}} = 1.2413 < 1.64$

Do not reject H_0, i.e. the population mean could be 0.

(b) There is a very wide range of possible values for μ. This is because the standard error of the sample means is quite large.

2 $Z = \dfrac{|127.62 - 135|}{52/\sqrt{600}} = 3.4764 > 2.58$

Reject H_0 at the 1% level of significance, i.e. there is strong evidence to reject H_0. This sample suggests that the mean quarterly bills of all domestic consumers in this town is less than £135 and is estimated to be £127.62.

Exercises 9.6

1 (a) (i) $Z = \dfrac{|5.55 - 4|}{2.6966/\sqrt{50}} = 4.0644 > 2.58$

Reject H_0 at the 1% significance level, i.e. there is strong evidence to reject H_0. Population mean is not 4. This sample suggests that the population mean is greater than 4 and is estimated to be 5.55.

(ii) $Z = \dfrac{5.55 - 3}{2.6966/\sqrt{50}} = 6.6867 > 2.33$

Reject H_0 at the 1% significance level, i.e. there is strong evidence to reject H_0. Population mean is greater than 3. This sample suggests that the population mean is 5.55.

(iii) $Z = \dfrac{5.55 - 6}{2.6966/\sqrt{50}} = -1.1799 > -1.64$

No evidence to reject H_0, i.e. the population mean could be 6.

(b) The range of possible values of the population mean is around 6 (more than 3 and not significantly different from 6).

2 $Z = \dfrac{27.675 - 35}{11.3146/\sqrt{40}} = -4.0945 < -2.33$

Reject H_0 at the 1% significance level, i.e. there is strong evidence to reject H_0 which means the population mean is less than 35 hours. This sample suggests that households spend, on average, 27.68 hours watching television every week.

Exercises 9.7

1 (a) Assume the population has a normal probability distribution.

(b) (i) $T = \dfrac{|114.325 - 80|}{90.1763/\sqrt{16}} = 1.5226$

$t_{15,0.025} = 2.131$
$T < 2.131$ so no evidence to reject H_0, i.e. the population mean could be 80.

(ii) $T = \dfrac{114.325 - 150}{90.1763/\sqrt{16}} = -1.5825$

$t_{15,0.05} = 1.753$
$T < 1.753$ so no evidence to reject H_0, i.e. the population mean could be 150.

(iii) $T = \dfrac{114.325 - 170}{90.1763/\sqrt{16}} = -2.4696$

$-t_{15,0.05} = -1.753$ and $-t_{15,0.01} = -2.602$
$T < -1.753$, $T > -2.602$ so reject H_0 at the 5% significance level but not at the 1% significance level, i.e. the population mean is less than 170. This sample suggests that the population mean is 114.325.
(c) The population mean can be a wide range of values. The tests suggest that the population mean could be around 80 or around 150 but is less than 170.

2. Assume that the population of potato yields is normally distributed.

$T = \dfrac{2076.8032 - 1750}{759.4460/\sqrt{25}} = 2.1516$

$t_{24,0.05} = 1.711$ and $t_{24,0.01} = 2.492$
$T > 1.711$, $T < 2.492$ so reject H_0 at the 5% significance level but not at the 1% significance level, i.e. the population mean is more than 1750 tonnes. This sample suggests that the average yield of potatoes is more than 1750 tonnes and is estimated to be 2076.8 tonnes.

Exercise 10.1

1 Age would be the independent variable and salary the dependent variable.

Exercises 10.2

1 (a) Strong linear relationship. (b) No relationship. (c) Linear relationship.
(d) Non-linear relationship. (e) Non-linear relationship.

2
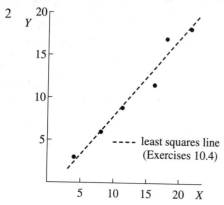
Approximate linear relationship.

3
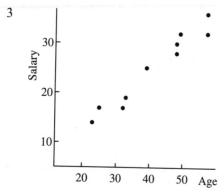
Strong linear relationship.

4
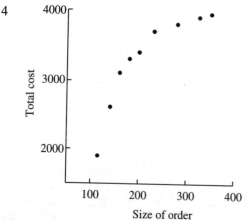
Non-linear relationship.

5

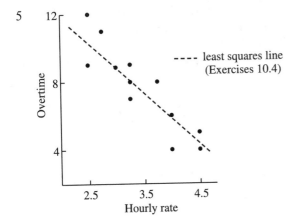

Approximate linear relationship.

6

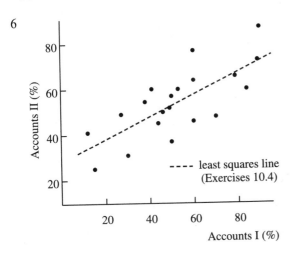

Approximate linear relationship

Exercises 10.3

1 (a) Very strong positive linear relationship.
(b) Virtually no linear relationship.
(c) Fairly strong positive linear relationship.
(d) No linear relationship, non-linear.
(e) Very strong correlation but the scatter diagram shows a non-linear relationship.

2. $n = 6$, $\Sigma x = 78$, $\Sigma x^2 = 1222$, $\Sigma y = 67$, $\Sigma y^2 = 955$, $\Sigma xy = 1074$, $r = 0.9787$. Very strong positive linear relationship.

3 $n = 10$, $\Sigma x = 411$, $\Sigma x^2 = 18\,295$, $\Sigma y = 250$, $\Sigma y^2 = 6788$, $\Sigma xy = 11\,121$, $r = 0.9738$. Very strong positive linear relationship.

4. $n = 9$, $\Sigma x = 1980$, $\Sigma x^2 = 490\,250$, $\Sigma y = 29\,650$, $\Sigma y^2 = 101\,372\,500$, $\Sigma xy = 6\,917\,500$, $r = 0.8782$. Strong positive correlation but scatter diagram shows a non-linear relationship.

5 $n = 12$, $\Sigma x = 41.25$, $\Sigma x^2 = 147.3125$, $\Sigma y = 92$, $\Sigma y^2 = 778$, $\Sigma xy = 298.25$, $r = -0.8991$. Strong negative linear relationship.

6 $n = 20$, $\Sigma x = 1048$, $\Sigma x^2 = 64\,524$, $\Sigma y = 1082$, $\Sigma y^2 = 62\,930$, $\Sigma xy = 61\,578$, $r = 0.7512$. Fairly strong positive linear relationship.

Exercises 10.4

1 $y = -1.5208 + 0.9760x$
(see scatter diagram for Exercises 10.2, Question 2).

2 Salary $= 0.2152 + 0.6030 \times$ age
Age 30, salary $=$ £18\,305.
Age 65 is outside range of data.

3 We would be finding a linear relationship for what is actually a non-linear relationship.

4 Overtime $= 18.885 - 3.2635 \times$ hourly rate
(see scatter diagram for Exercises 10.2, Question 5).

5 Accounts II(%) $= 27.4812 + 0.5080 \times$ Accounts I(%)
(see scatter diagram for Exercises 10.2, Question 6).
Accounts I $= 55\%$, Accounts II $= 55.42\%$.

Exercises 11.1

1

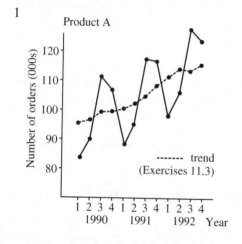

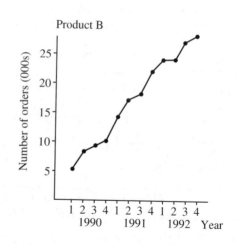

Product C

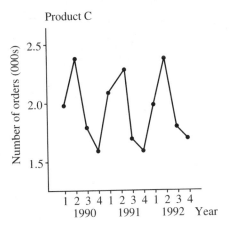

Product D

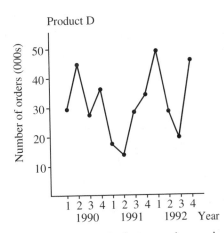

Product A shows seasonal and increasing trend components: product B shows an increasing trend component but no seasonal component; product C shows a seasonal component but no trend; product D shows no seasonal or trend components.

2

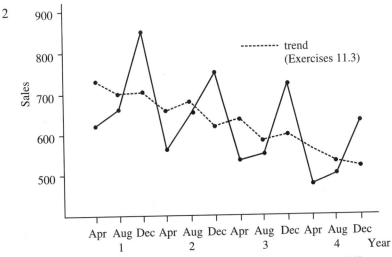

There appears to be a decreasing overall trend and seasonal differences. The sales data collected for December are much higher than for April and August.

3

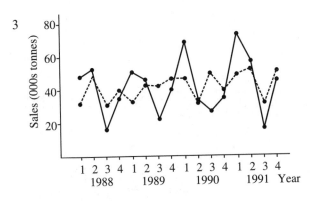

There is a slightly increasing trend. Quarter 1 has high sales, whereas quarter 3 always has the lowest sales.

4

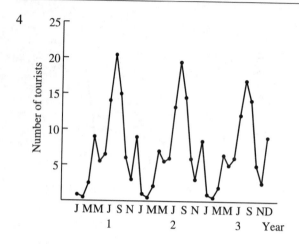

There is a strong seasonal component, July, August and September have much higher numbers of tourists, whereas January, February and March have very low numbers. There is possibly a slightly decreasing overall trend.

Exercises 11.3

1 (a)

Year	Quarter	Orders	Four-point moving averages	Centred moving averages	Seasonal components	Deseasonalized orders
1990	1	84				95.90
	2	90				96.93
			98.25			
	3	112		98.75	1.1342	99.56
			99.25			
	4	107		99.875	1.0713	99.93
			100.5			
1991	1	88		101.25	0.8691	100.47
			102			
	2	95		103.125	0.9212	102.32
			104.25			
	3	118		105.5	1.1185	104.90
			106.75			
	4	116		108.125	1.0728	108.34
			109.5			
1992	1	98		110.75	0.8849	111.88
			112			
	2	106		113	0.9381	114.16
			114			
	3	128				113.79
	4	124				115.81

1 (b)

Quarter	Seasonal component	Adjusted
1	0.8770	0.8759
2	0.9297	0.9285
3	1.1264	1.1249
4	1.0721	1.0707
Total	4.0052	

(c) For plot see solution for Exercises 11.1, Question 1. There is an approximately linear trend.
(d) $n = 12$, $\Sigma x = 78$, $\Sigma x^2 = 650$, $\Sigma y = 1263.99$, $\Sigma xy = 8495.38$, TR $= 92.63 + 1.9542t$.

2

Year	Month	Sales	Moving average	Seasonal components	Deseasonalized sales
1	April	620			730.01
	August	660	710	0.9296	702.35
	December	850	690	1.2319	701.86
2	April	560	683.33	0.8195	659.37
	August	640	650	0.9846	681.07
	December	750	643.33	1.1658	619.29
3	April	540	613.33	0.8804	635.82
	August	550	603.33	0.9116	585.29
	December	720	583.33	1.2343	594.52
4	April	480	566.67	0.8471	565.17
	August	500	536.67	0.9317	532.08
	December	630			520.20

(a) No
(b)

Month	Seasonal component	Adjusted
April	0.8490	0.8493
August	0.9394	0.9397
December	1.2107	1.2111
Total	2.9991	

(c) For plot see solution for Exercises 11.1, Question 2. Approximately linear trend with a negative slope.
(d) $n = 12$, $\Sigma x = 78$, $\Sigma x^2 = 650$, $\Sigma y = 7527.03$, $\Sigma xy = 46229.58$.

3

Year	Quarter	Sales	Four-point moving averages	Centred moving averages	Seasonal components	Deseasonalized sales
1988	1	48				31.64
	2	52				48.46
	3	16	37.75	38	0.421	30.48
	4	35	38.25	37.5	0.933	39.55
1989	1	50	36.75	37.5	1.333	32.96
	2	46	38.25	38.875	1.183	42.87
	3	22	39.5	41.75	0.527	41.90
	4	40	44	42.5	0.941	45.20
1990	1	68	41	41.5	1.638	44.83
	2	34	42	41.375	0.822	31.69
	3	26	40.75	41.375	0.628	49.52
	4	35	42	44.75	0.782	39.55
1991	1	73	47.5	46.25	1.578	48.12
	2	56	45	46.25	1.211	52.19
	3	16	47.5			30.48
	4	45				50.85

Quarter	Seasonal component	Adjusted
1	1.516	1.517
2	1.072	1.073
3	0.525	0.525
4	0.885	0.885

There is very little trend (plot given in solution for Exercises 11.2, Question 3). $n = 16$, $\Sigma x = 136$, $\Sigma x^2 = 1496$, $\Sigma y = 660.29$, $\Sigma xy = 5821.83$, TR $= 36.034 + 0.6158t$.

4 12. Four months have seasonal components greater than 1, July, August, September and December, indicating an above average number of tourists. January, February and March have very low seasonal components indicating low numbers of tourists.

Exercises 11.4

1

Quarter	Trend seasonal forecast
1	$118.03 \times 0.8759 = 103.38$
2	$119.99 \times 0.9285 = 111.41$
3	$121.94 \times 1.1249 = 137.17$
4	$123.90 \times 1.0707 = 132.66$

2 $485.85 \times 0.9397 = 456.55$

3

Quarter	Trend seasonal forecast
1	$46.50 \times 1.517 = 70.54$
2	$47.12 \times 1.073 = 50.56$
3	$47.73 \times 0.525 = 25.06$
4	$48.35 \times 0.885 = 42.79$

Exercises 11.5

1

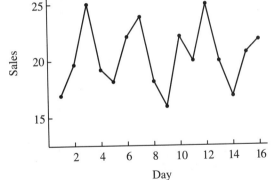

Day	1	2	3	4	5	6	7	8	9	10	11	12
Smoothed values	17	20	23	20.6	19.04	20.82	22.73	19.89	17.56	20.22	20.09	23.04

Day	13	14	15	16
Smoothed values	21.21	18.69	20.07	21.23

2

Week	1	2	3	4	5	6	7	8	9	10	11	12
$c = 0.2$	117	117.8	118.04	119.03	118.83	118.26	118.61	118.49	119.19	119.35	118.48	119.18
$c = 0.3$	117	118.2	118.44	119.81	119.27	118.29	118.80	118.56	119.59	119.71	118.30	119.41

$c = 0.2$ gives the best results, week 13 forecast is 119.18.

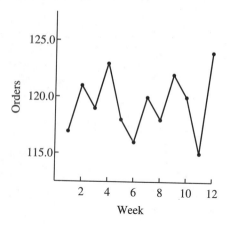

Exercises 12.3

1 Increase in RPI from January 1989 to January 1992 is

$$\frac{135.6 - 111.0}{111.0} \times 100 = 22.16\%$$

An increase of 22.16% in original investment would give a value of £1221.60. As her savings had increased to £1250, the investment had performed better than the RPI.

2 As January 1993 is the base period, January 1993 = 100. Index numbers are given by

Month	J	F	M	A	M	J	J	A	S	O	N	D
Index number	100	110.8	116.5	119.3	112.2	105.1	102.3	102.3	108.0	109.4	112.2	125.0

3 Alcoholic drink index will increase by 10% of 151.0 = 15.1. Tobacco index will increase by 20% of 150 = 30.0. Motoring expenditure index will increase by 15% of 137.9 = 20.7. The total increase in the RPI will be

$$\frac{78 \times 15.1}{1000} + \frac{35 \times 30.0}{1000} + \frac{136 \times 20.7}{1000} = 5 \text{ units}$$

i.e. the RPI would increase from 137.9 to 142.9, representing an increase of 3.6%.

Exercise 12.6

(a) $\Sigma q_0 p_0 = 12 \times 10\,000 + 31 \times 19\,500 + 8 \times 9500 = 800\,500$
$\Sigma q_0 p_1 = 12 \times 10\,400 + 31 \times 21\,000 + 8 \times 9950 = 855\,400$
$\Sigma q_0 p_2 = 12 \times 10\,650 + 31 \times 22\,750 + 8 \times 10\,200 = 914\,650$

Laspeyre price index for 1992 based on 1991 is

$$L_p = \frac{\Sigma q_0 p_1}{\Sigma q_0 p_0} \times 100 = \frac{855\,400}{800\,500} \times 100 = 106.9$$

Laspeyre price index for 1993 based on 1991 is

$$L_p = \frac{\Sigma q_0 p_2}{\Sigma q_0 p_0} \times 100 = \frac{914\,650}{800\,500} \times 100 = 114.3$$

(b) $\Sigma p_1 q_1 = 14 \times 10\,400 + 32 \times 21\,000 + 8 \times 9950 = 897\,200$
$\Sigma p_1 q_0 = 12 \times 10\,400 + 31 \times 21\,000 + 8 \times 9950 = 855\,400$
$\Sigma p_2 q_2 = 14 \times 10\,650 + 36 \times 22\,750 + 6 \times 10\,200 = 1\,029\,300$
$\Sigma p_2 q_0 = 12 \times 10\,650 + 31 \times 22\,750 + 8 \times 10\,200 = 914\,650$

Paasche quantity index for 1992 based on 1991 is

$$P_q = \frac{\Sigma p_1 q_1}{\Sigma p_1 q_0} \times 100 = \frac{897\,200}{855\,400} \times 100 = 104.9$$

Paasche quantity index for 1993 based on 1991 is

$$P_q = \frac{\Sigma p_2 q_2}{\Sigma p_2 q_0} \times 100 = \frac{1\,029\,300}{914\,650} \times 100 = 112.5$$

(c) In parts (a) and (b) we have already calculated

$\Sigma p_0 q_0 = 800\,500$
$\Sigma p_1 q_1 = 897\,200$
$\Sigma p_2 q_2 = 1\,029\,300$

Value index for 1992 based on 1991 is

$$V = \frac{\Sigma p_1 q_1}{\Sigma p_0 q_0} \times 100 = \frac{897\,200}{800\,500} \times 100 = 112.1$$

Value index for 1993 based on 1991 is

$$V = \frac{\Sigma p_2 q_2}{\Sigma p_0 q_0} \times 100 = \frac{1\,029\,300}{800\,500} \times 100 = 128.6$$

(d) The value indices tell us the increase in the salary bills for the three departments: from 1991 to 1992 the increase is 12.1% and from 1991 to 1993 the increase is 28.6%.

Exercises 13.1

1 Let x be the number of product A produced and y be the number of product B produced. The linear programming problem is as follows.

Maximize	$400x + 300y$	profit in £s
subject to	$5x + 5y \le 40$	labour constraint
	$6x + 10y \le 60$	component constraint
	$3x + 8y \le 40$	packaging constraint

2 Let x be the number of type X shelves purchased and y be the number of type Y shelves purchased. The linear programming problem is as follows.

Minimize $x + y$ total number of shelves
subject to $4x + 3y \leq 2400$ constraint on available cash
            $4x + 2y \geq 1800$ shelving requirement
            $y \geq x$ requirement caused by shape of area to be shelved

Exercises 13.2

1 (a)–(b)

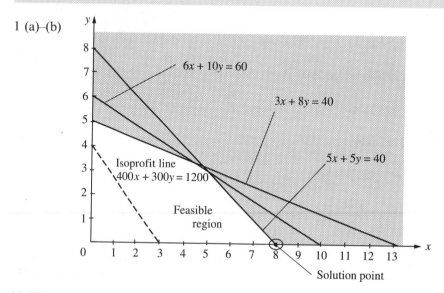

(c) The solution is given by the intersection of the line $5x + 5y = 40$ with $y = 0$. The solution is therefore $x = 8$, $y = 0$. Profit is given by $\pi = 400 \times 8 + 300 \times 0 = £3200$. Substituting $x = 8$, $y = 0$ into each constraint in turn gives

$5 \times 8 + 5 \times 0 = 40$ therefore all labour time is used
$6 \times 8 + 10 \times 0 = 48$ therefore 12 components remain unused
$3 \times 8 + 8 \times 0 = 24$ therefore 16 hours of packaging time remains unused

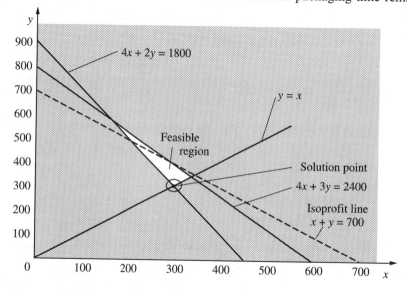

2 (a) The solution point is the intersection of the lines $4x + 2y = 1800$ and $y = x$ (remember that in this case we are minimizing and so we move the isoprofit line towards the origin). The solution is $x = 300$, $y = 300$, i.e. purchase 300 of each type of shelf.
(b) Total cost to the company will be £4 × 300 + £3 × 300 = £2100

Exercise 13.3

(a) The solution point is at the intersection of the line $5x + 5y = 40$ and the x axis.
    If the coefficients in the objective function are positive, the only slope that concerns us is the line $5x + 5y = 40$. Writing this line in its slope/intercept form gives $y = -x + 8$. Therefore,

$$\frac{-c_1}{c_2} \leq -1 \quad \text{and} \quad \frac{c_1}{c_2} \geq 1$$

If c_1 is fixed at 400,

$$\frac{400}{c_2} \geq 1 \quad \text{and} \quad c_2 \leq 400$$

If c_2 is fixed at 300,

$$\frac{c_1}{300} \geq 1 \quad \text{and} \quad c_1 \geq 300$$

The solution point remains unchanged provided that the coefficient of y is no greater than 400 while the coefficient of x remains at 400 and the coefficient of x is at least 300 while the coefficient of y remains at 300.
(b) If the labour availability increases from 40 to 45 hours, the solution point remains at the intersection of the labour constraint and the x axis. The new solution is $x = 9$, $y = 0$ and the value of the objective function is now given by $\pi = 400 \times 9 + 300 \times 0 = £3600$. This increase of £400 is due to the extra five hours labour time available and so the shadow price for labour is £400 ÷5 = £80. The components and packaging resources are not fully utilized and so both have shadow prices of zero.
(c) Our answer to part (b) tells us that any additional hour of labour time will increase our profit by £80, and one fewer hour of labour time will reduce our profit by £80. One unit more, or less, of either components or packaging will have no effect on the optimal solution. Remember that the shadow prices usually only apply for small changes in resource availability

Exercises 14.2

1 (a) The difference between successive numbers is 4. The numbers therefore form an AP with common difference $d = 4$.
(b) With $a = 1$, $d = 4$ and using [14.1]

$$S_{14} = \frac{14}{2}(2 \times 1 + 13 \times 4) = 378$$

$$S_{25} = \frac{25}{2}(2 \times 1 + 24 \times 4) = 1225$$

The sum of the fifteenth to twenty-fifth terms inclusive is $S_{25} - S_{14} = 1225 - 378 = 847$.

2 $a = 81$, $r = \frac{1}{3}$.
(a) Since $|r| < 1$, we use (14.2) to find

$$S_8 = \frac{81(1 - (\frac{1}{3})^8)}{1 - \frac{1}{3}} = 121.48$$

(b) Using (14.3b)

$$S_\infty = \frac{81}{1 - \frac{1}{3}} = 121.5$$

(c) The sum of all terms after the eighth term would be given by $S_\infty - S_8$, i.e. $121.5 - 121.48 = 0.02$.

Exercises 14.6

1 Using [14.5] the value of the fund in 12 years time will be given by $S = 10\,000(1.09)^{12} = £28\,126.65$

2 Using [14.6], for scheme A, $r = 0.10$ and $x = 4$ and so the effective interest rate is given by

$$i = \left(1 + \frac{0.10}{4}\right)^4 - 1 = 0.1038 = 10.38\%$$

For scheme B, $r = 0.11$ and $x = 2$ and so the effective interest rate is given by

$$i = \left(1 + \frac{0.11}{2}\right)^2 - 1 = 0.1130 = 11.30\%$$

3 Interest to be paid is 8% of £6000 =£480. The actual amount borrowed will be

£6000 for three months $= £1500$
£4500 for three months $= £1125$
£3000 for three months $= £750$
£1500 for three months $= £375$

and so the equivalent amount borrowed for one year is £3750. Using [14.4]

$$r = \frac{480}{3750.1} = 0.128$$

and so the APR is 12.8%.

Exercises 14.11

1 Using [14.7] repeatedly, the present value of the cash inflows is given by

$$P = \frac{5000}{1.08} + \frac{12\,000}{1.08^2} + \frac{15\,000}{1.08^3} + \frac{15\,000}{1.08^4}$$

$$P = \pounds 4629.63 + \pounds 10\,288.07 + \pounds 11\,907.48 + \pounds 11\,025.45 = \pounds 37\,850.63$$

$$\text{Expected profit} = \pounds 37\,850.63 - \pounds 35\,000.00 = \pounds 2850.63$$

In terms of present value, the extra profit generated by the purchase of the machine will be £2850.63.

2 If interest rates rise the present value of the cash inflows will decrease, as interest rate only appears in the denominator. It is possible that the project could then make a loss, and it may be better not to purchase the machine.

3 Using [14.8], the present value

$$A = \frac{2000}{0.08}\left[1 - \frac{1}{(1.08)^{20}}\right] = \pounds 19\,636.30$$

4 Annuity becomes an annuity due so the present value is found using [14.9],

$$A = \frac{2000}{0.08}(1.08)\left[1 - \frac{1}{(1.08)^{20}}\right] = \pounds 21\,207.20$$

(This solution could be found by multiplying the solution to Question 3 by 1.08.)

5 For any interest rate, the present value of the cash inflows can be bound by using [14.7] repeatedly. For an interest rate of 8%, the cash inflow is

$$\frac{5000}{1.08} + \frac{12\,000}{1.08^2} + \frac{15\,000}{1.08^3} + \frac{15\,000}{1.08^4} = \pounds 37\,850.63$$

the net cash flow is therefore £37 850.63 − £35 000 = £2850.63. For an interest rate of 15%, the cash inflow is

$$\frac{5000}{1.15} + \frac{12\,000}{1.15^2} + \frac{15\,000}{1.15^3} + \frac{15\,000}{1.15^4} = \pounds 31\,860.59$$

the net cash flow is therefore £31 860.59 − £35 000 = − £3139.41.

$$\text{IRR is } 8 + \frac{2850.63}{2850.63 + 3139.41} \times 7 = 11.3\%$$

This is the breakeven rate of interest for the company. If money is costing them less than 11.3% they will make a profit. If it is costing them more than 11.3% they will incur a loss.

Index